Women, Writing and the Iraqi Ba'thist State

Edinburgh Studies in Modern Arabic Literature
Series Editor: Rasheed El-Enany

Writing Beirut: Mappings of the City in the Modern Arabic Novel
Samira Aghacy

Women, Writing and the Iraqi Ba'thist State: Contending Discourses of Resistance and Collaboration, 1968–2003
Hawraa Al-Hassan

Autobiographical Identities in Contemporary Arab Literature
Valerie Anishchenkova

The Iraqi Novel: Key Writers, Key Texts
Fabio Caiani and Catherine Cobham

Sufism in the Contemporary Arabic Novel
Ziad Elmarsafy

Gender, Nation, and the Arabic Novel: Egypt 1892–2008
Hoda Elsadda

The Unmaking of the Arab Intellectual: Prophecy, Exile and the Nation
Zeina G. Halabi

Egypt 1919: The Revolution in Literature and Film
Dina Heshmat

Post-War Anglophone Lebanese Fiction: Home Matters in the Diaspora
Syrine Hout

Prophetic Translation: The Making of Modern Egyptian Literature
Maya I. Kesrouany

Nasser in the Egyptian Imaginary
Omar Khalifah

Conspiracy in Modern Egyptian Literature
Benjamin Koerber

War and Occupation in Iraqi Fiction
Ikram Masmoudi

Literary Autobiography and Arab National Struggles
Tahia Abdel Nasser

The Libyan Novel: Humans, Animals and the Poetics of Vulnerability
Charis Olszok

The Arab Nahḍah*: The Making of the Intellectual and Humanist Movement*
Abdulrazzak Patel

Blogging from Egypt: Digital Literature, 2005–2016
Teresa Pepe

Religion in the Egyptian Novel
Christina Phillips

Space in Modern Egyptian Fiction
Yasmine Ramadan

Occidentalism: Literary Representations of the Maghrebi Experience of the East–West Encounter
Zahia Smail Salhi

Sonallah Ibrahim: Rebel with a Pen
Paul Starkey

Minorities in the Contemporary Egyptian Novel
Mary Youssef

www.edinburghuniversitypress.com/series/ssmall

Women, Writing and the Iraqi Ba‘thist State

Contending Discourses of Resistance and Collaboration, 1968–2003

Hawraa Al-Hassan

EDINBURGH
University Press

Edinburgh University Press is one of the leading university presses in the UK. We publish academic books and journals in our selected subject areas across the humanities and social sciences, combining cutting-edge scholarship with high editorial and production values to produce academic works of lasting importance. For more information visit our website: edinburghuniversitypress.com

Edinburgh University Press Ltd
The Tun – Holyrood Road
12(2f) Jackson's Entry
Edinburgh EH8 8PJ

First published in hardback by Edinburgh University Press 2022

Typeset in 11/15 Adobe Garamond by
Servis Filmsetting Ltd, Stockport, Cheshire,

A CIP record for this book is available from the British Library

ISBN 978 1 4744 4175 9 (hardback)
ISBN 978 1 4744 4176 6 (paperback)
ISBN 978 1 4744 4177 3 (webready PDF)
ISBN 978 1 4744 4178 0 (epub)

Contents

List of Figures vii
Acknowledgements viii
Series Editor's Foreword x
Note on Translation and Transliteration xiii

Introduction: Women, Wars and Weapons: Mapping the Cultural Battlefield of Ba'thist Iraq 1

Part 1

1 History Writing and Canon-making: the Place of Women in Narratives of the Iran–Iraq War 25
2 The Infamous Iraqi *Majidat*: Chastity, Chivalry and Collective Identity in the Novels of Saddam Hussein 64

Part 2

3 Fighting Fire with Fire: the Islamic Novel in Iraq and the Battle for Hearts and Minds 107
4 The National Gets Personal: Autobiographical Writings by Iraqi Women 151

Conclusion: Binaries, Bonds and Moving beyond the Ba'th 201

Figures

All located in the Appendix

1 Taken without permission from Canadian artist Jonathon Earl Bowser, the cover of Saddam's first novel *Zabiba and the King* (2001)
2 The cover of *Get Out, Damned One!* for the post-fall of Saddam edition
3 The original cover of *Get Out, Damned One!* (2002 or 2003) produced in a similar style to *The Fortified Castle*
4 The cover of the only edition of *The Fortified Castle* (2001)
5 Saddam's quasi-autobiography *Men and a City* (2002)
6 *A Travel Ticket* (1999) by 'Alyā' al-Anṣārī
7 *When a Man Thinks* (1993) by Khawla al-Qazwīnī
8 *And Darkness Dissipated* (1993) by May al-Ḥusaynī
9 *Memoirs of a Student Abroad* (1995) by Khawla al-Qazwīnī
10 *The Seeker of Truth* (1980) by Bint al-Hudā
11 *Virtue Prevails* (1980) by Bint al-Hudā
12 *I Wish I Had Known* (1981) by Bint al-Hudā

Acknowledgements

It is difficult to express gratitude for all the events and individuals that have culminated in the publication of my first book. So perhaps it is fitting to begin by expressing thanks to the force that has brought everything together, to the almighty who has given me strength and sustained me and my family in difficult times. I also owe a debt of gratitude to the community of scholars who have supported me and believed in the value of my research: the Edinburgh Studies in Modern Arabic Literature Series Editor Professor Rasheed El-Enany; the team at Edinburgh University Press; my doctorate supervisor Professor Yasir Suleiman and Dr Paul Anderson at the Centre of Islamic Studies, Cambridge; and the readers who recommended publication, especially Dr Dina Matar.

In a book about women, it seems appropriate to dedicate the book to the network of women that have supported me during the course of its writing, editing and completion: to my aunt, my second mother, Khala Um Wael for helping to care for my children: thank you for being the selfless woman you are and finding joy in facilitating the success and fulfilment of others. To my daughter Neba (Nibs) who 'just wants me to be happy', and to friends who have come from unexpected places and have grown in unexpected ways in my heart. To Fahima and Zahra Al-Sinan for their help in finding most of the books in Chapter 3 and to my aunt and inspiration Naseema and her son Mousa for providing me with resources and a space to discuss my ideas.

To my students who give me more recognition than I deserve and to the kindness of strangers thrown into my way by fate, and especially to Dawn Booth and Tanya McCalmon whose encouragement has been a catalyst leading to the birth of this book. To my husband, Alawi, for his undying love and friendship; and to his family and mine for their love, appreciation and the simple moments of joy that have flooded my life with wisdom and gratitude. Finally, and most importantly, for the first seeds of knowledge and love sown in the land of childhood: to you mama and baba I dedicate this and all future endeavours.

Series Editor's Foreword

Edinburgh Studies in Modern Arabic Literature is a unique series that aims to fill a glaring gap in scholarship in the field of modern Arabic literature. Its dedication to Arabic literature in the modern period (that is, from the nineteenth century onwards) is what makes it unique among series undertaken by academic publishers in the English-speaking world. Individual books on modern Arabic literature in general or aspects of it have been and continue to be published sporadically. Series on Islamic studies and Arab/Islamic thought and civilisation are not in short supply either in the academic world, but these are far removed from the study of Arabic literature qua literature, that is, imaginative, creative literature as we understand the term when, for instance, we speak of English literature or French literature. Even series labelled 'Arabic/Middle Eastern Literature' make no period distinction, extending their purview from the sixth century to the present, and often including non-Arabic literatures of the region. This series aims to redress the situation by focusing on the Arabic literature and criticism of today, stretching its interest to the earliest beginnings of Arab modernity in the nineteenth century.

The need for such a dedicated series, and generally for the redoubling of scholarly endeavour in researching and introducing modern Arabic literature to the Western reader, has never been stronger. Among activities and events heightening public, let alone academic, interest in all things Arab, and not least Arabic literature, are the significant growth in the last decades of the translation of contemporary Arab authors from all genres, especially fiction, into English; the higher profile of Arabic literature internationally since the award of the Nobel Prize in Literature to Naguib Mahfouz in 1988; the growing number of Arab authors living in the Western diaspora and writing both in English and Arabic; the adoption of such authors and others by mainstream, high-circulation publishers, as opposed to the academic publishers of the past; and the establishment of prestigious prizes, such as the International Prize for Arabic Fiction, popularly referred to in the Arab world as the Arabic Booker, run by the Man Booker Foundation, which brings huge publicity to the shortlist and winner every year, as well as translation contracts into English and other languages. It is therefore part of the ambition of this series that it will increasingly address a wider reading public beyond its natural territory of students and researchers in Arabic and world literature. Nor indeed is the academic readership of the series expected to be confined to specialists in literature in the light of the growing trend for interdisciplinarity, which increasingly sees scholars crossing field boundaries in their research tools and coming up with findings that equally cross discipline borders in their appeal.

Within the tide of studies (mostly non-literary) of Saddam Hussein's and the Baʿath Party's Iraq, particularly since the fall of the regime in 2003, this monograph represents an original contribution in an area little attempted. This is not a traditional study of the literary canon of a particular period, but an interdisciplinary approach that will not limit itself to high art, but include propagandistic, state-sponsored literature, including novels written by Saddam Hussein himself as part of the state's effort at national indoctrination. It is also a gendered study focusing on the role of women as conceived by the Baʿath Party in forming the national imaginary, whether as writers contributing to propagandised literature or as characters in such fiction written by themselves or by male authors, as in the case of Saddam Hussein. What adds to the originality of the approach is the author's extension of her investigations beyond the literary text as such to what French theorist, Gérard Genette, calls the 'paratext', that is, the entire production process, including the choice of cover, publicity, marketing, distribution, pricing, managed reception, state prizes for literature seen to serve its ideology regardless of 'literary' quality etc. She combines political communication theory with Genette's work on paratexts to give us a comprehensive view of 'mediatised literature' and cultural production under one of the most ideologically driven regimes in the history of the Middle East.

Professor Rasheed El-Enany, Series Editor,
Emeritus Professor of Modern Arabic Literature,
University of Exeter

Note on Translation and Transliteration

The book follows the IJMES transliteration system for Arabic. I have chosen to transliterate in full names of authors writing in Arabic in order to distinguish them from writers writing in English. For ease of reading, I have marked the ʿayn and alif only for titles of texts in Arabic and other Arabic words and quotations. I also have used the accepted English spellings for prominent political figures such as Saddam Hussein and Ayatollah Mohammed Baqir Al-Sadr. I have provided full transliteration of titles and authors in the notes and bibliography. The vast majority of texts studied in this book have not been translated into English, and so all the literary translations are my own. I have endeavoured to be as accurate and consistent as possible in the translation and transliteration elements of this book, but at any errors found in it are entirely my own.

Introduction: Women, Wars and Weapons: Mapping the Cultural Battlefield of Ba'thist Iraq

When Saddam Hussein infamously proclaimed that the word and the bullet came from the same barrel, he created an embattled cultural space which would persist because of, and in spite of, his dominance of Iraqi politics for almost twenty-five years. This book is not an analysis of the status of women in Iraq under Saddam Hussein; nor is it exclusively about Iraqi women writers inside or outside the country, or about constructions of gender and gender identity. Instead the focus of the book is, to use the words of Abir Hamdar, on the 'ongoing struggle for symbolic power in the Arab world'.[1]

It addresses what has been termed the 'burden of representation' on women as symbolic signifiers of national difference[2] through the analysis of state-sponsored literary narratives under the Ba'th and the resistive discourses they provoked. In many ways the book is also about the forgotten history of the Iraqi novel, where a voluntary amnesia has occurred in the attempt to purge Iraqi literary history from the taint of totalitarianism and propaganda. Unsurprisingly, then, most of the novels examined in this book do not fall within the Arab literary canon, as I have chosen to focus on political and/or explicitly ideological texts that have been marginalised and often completely excluded from the scope of critical enquiry. In order to reach a better understanding of the relationship between writing, the state and the 'Woman Question', the book considers the state's large-scale dissemination and prioritisation of ideological novels starting with and during the Iran–Iraq War, as an extension and expansion of the first Ba'th's budding interest in culture and book production. It also examines Saddam Hussein's surprising recourse to culture in the build up to the United States' impending invasion of Iraq in 2003, when he decided to author four novels himself. These two moments have shaped the contours of Iraq's literary history under the absolute rule of the Baʿth, and in many ways, responses and challenges to the state as well.

There are two narratives that underpin the argument in this book: the first is the story of women under the Baʿth and the contradictory state views with which they had to contend due to the proxification of discourses on women to express state views on other issues such as racial difference and religion and morality. The privileging of symbolic depictions of women in public discourse as markers of national unity replaced equitable and real legislative, economic and social advancements for Iraqi women. In this sense, Iraq was not exceptional, as nationalist rhetoric towards women and social policy are very often inconsistent.[3] The Baʿth's emphasis on getting women into work had little to do with progressive views on women and women's empowerment, as much as it responded to state needs: first, during the country's so-called 'golden years', when a boom in oil production led to severe labour shortages, and thus, according to Nadje Sadig Al-Ali, the ideal of the working mother was not only widely accepted but encouraged by the state and society at large[4]; and, second, in order to gain the upper hand economically against Iran during the war, thereby requiring women to take the jobs vacated by men on military conscription. Towards the end of the war, and with the impending return of Iraqi men from the frontline, the human and economic costs of the war had to be recalculated. As such, public discourse began to change, and women were now encouraged to return to the home and bear children in order to close the demographic gap between Iraq and Iran and to make way for the return of military-aged men from the frontline.

The Baʿth's almost complete eradication of illiteracy amongst women may have earned the recognition of the United Nations in 1982, but it seems to have been part of a calculated long-term plan to ideologically 'invest' in Iraqi women as associated with children and the familial and collective future.[5] In her book *Creating Consent in Baʿthist Syria: Women and Welfare in a Totalitarian State*, Esther Meininghaus describes how state hegemony is maintained through mass organisations in Syria which provide welfare services in return for consent.[6] Likewise, the Iraqi Baʿthist state's provision of various services in the education and cultural sectors, including its support for publications specifically directed at women, represented an investment in the conditions necessary for female consent, particularly when coupled with an intense and effective programme to eradicate illiteracy. Achim Rohde describes the state's increasing involvement in the affairs of women as aimed at mobilising and controlling women in the service of the state, rather than empowering them,[7] meaning that any advances made on women's issues such as increased participation in the workforce, support with childcare and free transportation to and from work were short-lived, as these were dictated by temporary economic, rather than strictly ideological needs. According to Abbas Kadhim: 'Saddam's regime carefully manipulated women, making a show of them as symbols of the nation's solidarity – then conveniently dispensing with them once the state's objectives had been achieved.'[8] Likewise, Dina Rizk Khoury asserts that the state did not reward the sacrifices of the female arm of the Ba'th Party: the General Federation of Iraqi Women (GFIW), which had called for a radical amendment to the personal status law, but had instead been directed to move from 'a social/developmental agenda' to being 'intimately bound to the managing of the [Iran–Iraq] war's social and political repercussions'.[9] Ultimately, though, far from being merely a state-strengthening activity, the Ba'th was aware of the value-laden significance and symbolic power of the 'Women Question' as a marker of enlightenment and progress.

The second narrative that lies at the heart of this book is the turbulent trajectory of the modern Iraqi novel and its relationship with state patronage. By the most modest estimates, critics have counted over seventy-five state-approved novels and short collections published only during the Iran–Iraq War, many as part of the infamous *Qadisiyat Saddam* novel or short story series.[10] In its efforts to instrumentalise the arts during the Iran–Iraq War (an endeavour that was unprecedented in the modern Arab world), the Ba'th did not allow the novel to grow organically out of Iraq's cultural and economic conditions; in fact, the frenzied mass-production of novels and short stories during the war represented a violent caesarean birth from the womb of Iraqi literary history. Iraq had been following the natural trajectory of a traditional poetry-based cultural production, which was gradually developing the material conditions necessary for modern narrative production. In his seminal work, Benedict Anderson famously argued that both the novel and the newspaper emerged as a result of the rise in print capitalism in Europe, which contributed to a new conception of time as simultaneous, allowing different members of the nation access the same written materials at the same time, thereby forming a shared national consciousness. This in turn facilitated a spatial and geographical imagining of the borders of the nation and 'fellow citizens' within it.[11] In its efforts to synthetically 'create' a new national identity, the Baʿth also forcefully 'created' a modern propagandistic Iraqi novel at the peak of nationalist mobilisation and economic prosperity. The national identity that this 'new' Iraqi novel propagated was, perhaps inevitably, racially exclusive and prioritised Arab men by validating certain parochial tribal values.

Charles Tripp has explained that the aim of artistic production, especially nationalist works, is the fostering of solidarities through a shared vocabulary and experience. According to Tripp, this process overrides individual experiences by homogenising them into one experience:

> In the act of reading, interpreting and commenting, the very encounter with art can foster such solidarities . . . can thus form a part of collective memory and imagination, displacing or overriding thousands of individual memories to stand as the epitome or summation of historical experience. Established power has always used this technique . . . to create a common, mutually reinforcing imagery that will shape the present and the future, convincing people that this 'was the way it was'.[12]

According to Anderson, nationalism is designed to 'smooth over contradictions' through the selective representation of history, particularly ignoring civil strife.[13] In Iraq, the novel has been envisioned as an ideal cultural space for the expression of nationalism, potentially providing imaginary solutions to real social and political problems; hence, the prevalence of utopian discourses in the official novel. The penchant towards processes of homogenising highlights the function of totalitarianism as 'a universal monologic voice, diffused throughout social space; it is extending the political into non-political spheres'.[14] Resistance, then, for my purposes is taken to mean the creation of a counter discourse or narrative which challenges the homogeneity of the utopian narrative projected by the state. Resistance texts in this book fall into two categories: resistance through similitude, whereby the didacticism of pro-state texts is met with equally ideological texts; and through direct opposition, where structure and content form a unified whole designed to challenge totalitarianism at the level of perception. The use of aesthetics and generic and structural ingenuity will be examined in the final chapter, which contains the only texts in the book which do not fall under propaganda.

The state has been described as a 'system of power, rooted in discursive practices, in other words, culture'.[15] For the purposes of this book, I take culture to mean either an intellectual activity practised by litterateurs and cultural practitioners, or I refer to 'culture' in the symbolic sense as a marker of progress and holder of soft power. It seems that an expansion of the term 'culture' is necessary to include popular culture and cultural products as legitimate objects of study. The book asserts that canonical/artistic texts and those relegated to the peripheries of literary scholarship, namely, didactic or propagandistic texts, can and should be studied together as part of a framework of transtextuality, where, in the words of Gérard Genette, texts 'speak to each other'. According to Moore and Hamdar 'culture has been problematically conflated with particular creative forms, as "high culture", seen as refinement away from popular or mass structures of feeling that are often religious'.[16] The inclusion of religious novels by Shia women in the 'resistance' part of the book explores the potential of what is often deemed as the ultimate 'anti-discourse' to nationalism: religion, to threaten the Ba'th's 'modernisation' project vis-à-vis women using popular modes of cultural production wrested from the state.

Nira Yuval-Davis points to a shift in the social sciences towards 'the culturalisation of political language', rather than, interestingly, the opposite: the politicisation of culture. Shifting the paradigm from the political instrumentalisation of culture to the encroachment of culture into politics has several implications. On the one hand, it allows for those traditionally excluded from political discourses to be included, though not necessarily on their own terms. Yuval-Davis notes that in culturised discourse 'gendered bodies and sexuality play pivotal roles as territories, markers and reproducers of the narratives of the nation and other collectivities'.[17] This configuration places women outside the realm of politics traditionally and implies that the political and cultural are mutually exclusive categories. Significantly, however, the 'intrusion' of culture into the political realm potentially paves the way for resistance, as traditionally 'non-political' elements could find a space to express counter-hegemonic voices. Gill Bottomley asserts that culture generates 'conscious and unconscious forms of resistance-to homogenisation, to devaluation, to marginalizing by those who fear difference'.[18] In Iraq, the Baʿthist state's large-scale adoption and production of propaganda narratives made even the most subtle negotiations, or what Deniz Kandiyoti calls 'bargaining', difficult, as sheer bulk was used as a censorship mechanism to swamp voices of alterity. Dina Matar notes that certain paradigms in social theory which are based on binaries such as 'free' and 'restricted', 'state' and 'society' consolidate views of the state as 'an entity to be resisted without paying attention to how it, too, is preoccupied with culture, thereby undermining the role of the state through resistance and contestations'.[19] The contested relationship between power and culture ultimately leads to tension between 'the tendency for stabilization and continuity and perpetual change and resistance', that is, attempts by the state to create a shared culture and heterogeneous responses.

As education was perceived as a vehicle for indoctrination by the state, and written materials as the epicentre of the war for the hearts and minds of Iraq's masses, the entertainment value of written texts was downplayed, and cultural products were dragged into 'serious' wider debates about morality, national identity and gender roles. The desire to inculcate certain values and foster bonds that would be conducive to state dominance and hegemony explains the didactic and instructional quality of state-sponsored texts. Taken in this context, the instructional quality of the works of religious women potentially interfered with the state's educational ideological apparatus deemed crucial for the establishment of new nationalist socialist bonds that cemented loyalty to the state. As texts written by religious women ventured into the realm of education, instruction and prolestysing, they began to pose a threat to the state's ideology, and, subsequently, most authors left Iraq or published their novels in Beirut. By appealing to a wider Shia audience for purposes beyond education, religious novels by women contributed to the formation of a prescriptive pan-Shia female identity which challenged the premise of the state in its privileging of nationalist bonds.

In essence, I would argue that the story of the Iraqi novel mirrors that of women in Iraq under the Baʿth. Used during times of economic plenty and expended with when its use-value had been exhausted and state funding for cultural products was scarce, the Iraqi novel was adopted, discarded and then re-adopted according to state propaganda needs and economic scarcity. Likewise, women and women's issues underwent similar processes of appropriation and marginalisation: used at first as a signifier of the Baʿth's liberal nationalist agenda, and benefiting from Iraq's economic boom and an expansion of employment opportunities in the 1960s and 1970s, the status of women subsequently shifted to a purely symbolic function during the Iran–Iraq War and sanctions period. The book considers the place of culture and cultural products in the discursive battle between those that would stress the enlightened aspect of the Baʿth and those that would stress its repressiveness. A lot has been said about the state-strengthening aspects of culture under Saddam Hussein and the Baʿth's process of 'manufacturing consent' to use the now ubiquitous Chomskian term. There remains, however, a lack of nuanced understandings of the place of culture in the Iraqi Baʿth's state system beyond a simplistic structuralist Marxist interpretation of complete reliance of the ideological state apparatus on the material base. The oversimplification in Iraq's case is often essentially political, particularly those analyses that preceded the invasion of Iraq in 2003 and aimed at demonising the regime in a way that would support calls to topple it. The extent to which culture was key in maintaining hegemony and containing dissent is not a major concern of the book, but rather the state's perception of the potential amenability of certain cultural forms to ideological appropriation, particularly narrative forms. State views of culture as a nation-building tool was part and parcel of the Arabising endeavour of the Baʿth, which aimed at fostering loyalty through the establishment of social bonds and the shaping of a national consciousness. Ironically, the emphasis on culture and certain cultural forms created a new space for the state's opponents to respond in ways they had not done before, for example, the use of the novel by Islamic authors to create a publicly formed concept of piety that went against the secular values of the state.

The development of the publishing sector was one manifestation of the processes of modernisation in Iraq's years of plenty, which encompassed other areas including the development of a new education system and the expansion of the press, journalism and translation activities – all of which led to 'the emergence of a new reading public and a change in literary sensibility;

and the genesis of the various genres of narrative discourse in Arabic'.[20] An analysis of book production under the Ba'th provides a clear indication of the shifts in state policy on the arts generally and literature specifically. Hiyām Nā'il al-Dawāf's book (1975–94), originally a PhD thesis, divides the period under study into four equal divisions of five years: 1975–9, 1980–4, 1985–9 and 1990–4. The author notes that 1990 was the highest producing year out of the entire period (1,865 books published in Iraq and none abroad) followed by 1985 (1,557 books published inside Iraq and 70 abroad). In third place is 1980 (a total 1,293 books with a record 248 published outside Iraq), which is still higher than the number produced in 1979: the highest producing year in the first (1970s) period. The lowest producing years during the Iran–Iraq War are 1982 (973 books, including 191 produced outside Iraq) and 1987 (1,335 with only 6 published outside Iraq). In fact, fluctuations in book production are impossible to miss, and seem to mirror the regime's frantic 'war of words' dictated by ideological necessity. Saddam Hussein himself was referred to as the 'leader of necessity' or *al-qa'id al-durura* in Ba'thist political discourse, which was reflected in the state's production of what Salām 'Abbūd, an opponent of the Ba'th calls *adab al- durura* ('literature of necessity').[21] The inconsistency that comes hand in hand with this utilitarian approach to cultural production is attributed by al-Dawāf to the different conditions in Iraq at various stages in the war. The author explains that the years 1981–3 were the lowest in the second period of her study (1980–4) due to compulsory military conscription and 'the comprehensive national mobilization of all economic, social and political factors to defend the homeland'.[22] However, this analysis fails to explain why after Iraq had supposedly entered the 'austerity' phase, it then began publishing large numbers of books in the years 1984 and 1985. According to the author, the rise in book numbers in the middle years of the war was due to the fact that 'publishing trends followed subjects about the Iran–Iraq War', and notes that the years 1985–9 were the most productive years as a whole. Al-Dawāf concludes that 'the most productive years were those of the Iran–Iraq War, as the war did not negatively affect publishing trends. In fact, by and large publishing flourished as there were no restrictions on publishing requirements'.[23]

In terms of content, Ba'thist cultural production pre-Saddam favoured the social sciences (23.2 per cent of books produced 1975–9), and history and geography (19 per cent). Literature comes in seventh place with only 7.9 per cent of books produced falling in the adab category. By contrast, in the second period (1980–4) literature rises dramatically to second place and more than doubles its percentage of books published (18.4 per cent), also bearing in mind that the total number of books produced was much higher than in the first stage. In the most productive stage of book production (1985–9), literature tops the list for the first time (24 per cent), closely followed by the social sciences (21.3 per cent). The reasons why literature tops the tables in three out of the four periods of al-Dawāf's study are made explicit in the author's discussion of the most active publishing house during the war: Dar al-Shu'un al- Thaqafiya al-'Amma, established in the 1980s. According to al-Dawāf, this publishing house implemented what it called *mabda' al-taklif* (the 'principle of responsibility'), and attempted to dissuade writers from 'writing according to their own moods and plans'. The study also claims that litterateurs were constantly putting pressure on the publishing house and that it was always required 'to encourage literary production when there was a need for it (war poetry, war narratives, etc.) or because there were new generations of authors who ought to be given the rightful opportunities they deserve'. The focus on the production of literature not only as a propaganda tool, but also as a marker of culture and civilisation supported Ba'thist claims that the war had in fact revitalised Iraq's cultural life. Moreover, the privileging of literature as a marker of Iraq's identity provides some explanation as to why women were not given the opportunity to write much literature during the war. As the novel expressed Iraq's collective identity, it had to be expressed through the prism of masculinity as an ultimate manifestation of pride and strength.

According to al-Dawāf, government printing presses imposed low prices 'to help authors and promote creativity for cultural, rather than commercial purposes'.[24] Although there are no accurate numbers as to how many copies of state-sponsored pro-war works were sold or circulated, or the extent to which they were integrated in school curricula under Saddam's rule,[25] what is certain is that most of these literary works never went beyond the first edition of publication, despite their very low prices. This has less to do with lack of demand or audience for these works (the state paid little heed to financial considerations when it came to anti-Iranian propaganda, and the literary market was inundated with these works regardless of their popularity), but rather because they had reached their expiration date, and had fulfilled their temporary, but necessary duty. Nicholas O'Shaughnessy notes that the life span of propaganda is notoriously short, especially war propaganda which flares up and dies down with the renewal or cessation of hostilities.[26] Ultimately, however, an analysis of Iraqi publishing trends highlights the fact that the Iran–Iraq War was first and foremost an ideological war, as there is a notable lack of research and publication in the sciences, for example, in order to boost Iraq's military advantage on the ground. The use of literature and the arts to 'score points' against the enemy as part of both its propaganda war and its nation-building efforts, meant that the issue of 'women's liberation', central to the Baʿth's progressive ideology in the 1970s, was brushed aside in favour of achieving short-term political goals.

As well as being produced instantaneously as the war was unfolding, the novels of the Iran–Iraq War are characterised by both their excessive number and length. Works are generally long, especially at the beginning of the war; something which is taken to an almost parodic extreme with Saddam's excessively lengthy literary works at the beginning of the new millennia. By the end of the war, however, texts are generally less dense physically and discursively, as extreme depictions of Iraqi nationalism become redundant. The discursive 'excess' which characterised literary production during the war testifies to the Baʿth's awareness of the power of the word *as a weapon* to be resorted to at times of crisis, and the fact that the state was constantly 'on the offensive' discursively, meant that it was not achieving the clear militarily victories it had promised. In 1982, for example, when Iraqi forces were forced to retreat back into their own territory (the first major turning point of the war), thirteen novels were produced in the following year alone (less than five 'proper' novels had been produced to that point compared with tens of short stories). In his twenty-month study of the 'war short story', state literary critic 'Umar Ṭālib claims that the 'dip' in literary production in January and February 1981 was because the 'heroic victories' of the Iraqi army had overwhelmed writers so much that they could not write about them.[27] In fact, Iraqi losses were pushing writers towards more incitement (*tahrid*), whereas authors could 'rest on their laurels', as it were, when Iraq was doing well, as propaganda mobilisation would not have been urgently required. Elie Podeh uses the term 'fullness' to describe a similar process in the formation of a state calendar in modern Iraq whereby a 'full' calendar (in terms of the designation of new holidays and celebrations to overwrite previous ones) indicated a kind of state crisis, often a crisis of legitimation.[28]

Despite all the artistic shortcomings of state-sponsored literary production during the war, the state embarked on a massive campaign to market its novels as 'high art' reflections of a noble cause: notable Arab intellectual figures and literary giants were invited to lavish literary festivals such as the *Mirbad*, high-profile state literary prizes were created (such as the Saddam's *Qadisiya* Prize for the Novel), and laudatory reviews were publicised in newspapers and attached as appendages to 'award-winning' novels and short stories. As such, the Ba'th managed to support its claims that the war with Iran had somehow 'invigorated' Iraqi literature and culture, and endowed the Iraqi novel with an unrivalled canonical status. The exclusion of women from so large a cultural endeavour, both as producers and overseers has not been previously discussed and warrants more scholarly attention as an indicator of the discursive, social and legal shifts in state practices regarding women, which would become more apparent in the 1990s.

Nawar Al-Hassan Golley argues that how texts are received is more important than aesthetic considerations.[29] Indeed, scholars of cultural history have noted that it is often more important that books exist than that they are read.[30] On the other hand, traditional studies of literary production have often dismissed, or referred only in passing to popular or not sufficiently 'artistic' literary works. According to the prominent Arabist Roger Allen, for example, 'some (nationalist) works will almost certainly prove to be of purely ephemeral merit, but there are clearly many others which are destined to endure'.[31] The distinction drawn here between works of fleeting value and those that can acquire an eternal status in the canon is essentially one of high and low culture. Texts are material, as well as ideological or discursive products, packaged and presented in certain ways in order to be received accordingly, and circulating in textual environments as manifestations of social and political discourses. The book argues for the inclusion of both canonical and non-canonical texts together as valuable objects of study in order to arrive at a better understanding of Iraq's cultural history. French literary theorist Gérard Genette's seminal work *Paratexts: Thresholds of Interpretation* moves beyond both reader-centred analyses of texts and deterministic structuralist views of literary works as reliant on the 'base' or 'infrastructure' to use Althusserian terminology. The paratexts approach focuses on seemingly superfluous textual and visual data surrounding the main text – such as book covers, titles, authors' names, prefaces and blurbs – all of which are in fact, according to Genette, key to its reception. This extra data is what in fact allows a text to enter the world of discourse in a controlled manner and to be interpreted in desirable ways according to the aims of the state.

Paratexts are defined by Genette as 'thresholds'; the 'para' prefix signifies both proximity and distance; an 'in between' space which opens up possibilities for the text to engage with the 'real' world, linking the textual with the socio-political. To what has broadly been termed 'context' in literary studies, Genette ascribes different typologies, for instance, any prior information on the part of the reader about the text or its author Genette terms 'épitext', whereas the historical moment of the text's production is labelled its 'temporal situation'.[32] Moreover, Genette seems to conceive of the various types of context and textual data targeting reader reception as similar, perhaps even equal, categories conflating processes of reception with those of production. The choice of paratexts by producers of texts is determined by political and economic factors inherent in state–culture interactions, as well as the efforts of stakeholders who, although taking their cues from the state in the first instance, often went beyond Baʿthist guidelines at times of ambiguity in order to guarantee compliance with state imperatives. State-sponsored literary criticism is thus a valuable paratext in this regard, not only as a means of better interpreting the literary texts in question, but also for the socio-historical information it provides about the war as experienced by Iraq's literate public and the intelligentsia. Textual analyses in the forthcoming chapters will focus on the most prominent paratexts that affect interpretations of the texts in question. In the case of Saddam Hussein's novels, for example, analysis of the visual data on covers combined with the 'épitext' surrounding the narratives is of utmost importance, whereas titles are emphasised in the novels of the Iran–Iraq War. Acknowledgements and the publisher's péritext, where there is an explicit intervention on the part of the publisher (in the form of forewords, for example) to define reader expectations, are analysed in the novels of Islamic and secular resistance authors, respectively.

Paratexts also implicate more people as 'ideology brokers',[33] whilst emphasising the reciprocal nature of propaganda, rather than a straightforward 'top-down effect'. According to Suleiman, titles, covers, blurbs and illustrations engage more people than the texts themselves, and readers may even rush past them without being fully aware of the ideological load they carry.[34] By examining non-canonical works which fall into the gaps between disciplines, and by focusing on paratexts, the book ultimately aims to 'ideologise' the mundane, or that which is considered superfluous. In the words of Hayden White:

> since every text, grand or humble, is seen to be equally representative, equally interpretive of its proper milieu, the very notion of a text that might serve as an especially privileged interpretive model is set aside. And if the classic text is problematized, so, too, is the distinction . . . between reliably transparent texts or documents and 'ideologically' distorted, unreliable or opaque texts . . . Considered as historical evidence, all texts are regarded as being equally shot through with ideological elements . . .[35]

The book's approach emphasises the socio-historical value of literary texts in what is now termed as 'interdisciplinary' research. In their book *After Poststructuralism: Interdisciplinarity and Literary Theory*, Easterlin and Riebling challenge post-structuralist theories and methodologies which have now become the 'establishment' in academia, asserting that 'models drawn from both the hard and the social sciences can guide literary studies in a promising direction, offering alternatives to constructivist theorizing and critical practices constrained by "free play"'.[36] They add that theory should always be held accountable to a 'real world', be it political, social or natural, and insist that, for example, 'Foucauldian models of power make significant political action impossible'.[37] Although I agree with the authors' arguments for interdisciplinarity and the potential limits of post-structuralism, I would not advocate the complete abandonment of post-structuralism, especially given the way in which it has opened literary studies to disciplines such as philosophy, history and psychoanalysis in the first place. Furthermore, the largely negative views the authors hold of post-structuralism seem to stem at times from oversimplifying, homogenising and even misunderstanding some of the key post-structuralist ideas alluded to in the Foucault quotation above. By highlighting the impossibility of resistance from a Foucauldian approach to power, Easterlin and Riebling claim that individual participants in oppressive regimes can be absolved from responsibility and blame. However, seemingly contradictory readings can be derived from Foucault's configuration of power, as the idea that 'power comes from everywhere' can in fact be empowering by its opening up the possibility of multiple resistances.

In the introduction to his work *The Political Unconscious*, Fredric Jameson famously argues for 'the priority of the political interpretation of literary texts . . . as the absolute horizon of all reading and all interpretations'.[38] He asserts that 'ideology is not something which informs or invests symbolic production; rather the aesthetic act is itself ideological, and the production of aesthetic or narrative form is to be seen as an ideological act in its own right . . .'[39] By opening the text up to four levels of interpretation (anagogical, moral, allegorical and literal), whilst maintaining the framework of historicism in a way that limits the text's interpretive possibilities, Jameson stresses the semi-autonomy and 'parallelism' of levels (the economic, the political, the juridical, ideology and culture), which is in contrast to the traditional approach in Marxian thought where the superstructure relies solely on the base. However, he also remains fervently against post-structuralist readings of texts, such as Barthes' symbolic 'Death of the Author', as for him excluding the author necessarily relegates to the margins an essential aspect of the text's historical background. The decentring of the author as the locus of 'true' meaning and the opening of literary works to a myriad of, often contradictory, interpretations according to the shifting and unstable identities of the reader are hallmarks of post-structuralist approaches to literary texts, and can be useful when contemplating the possibility of resistance. In the case of literary propaganda in Iraq, where fictional narratives function as a proxy of ideology, the post-structuralist world of infinite destabilised textual meaning can have a remedial effect, should we be tempted to adopt a strict deterministic view of official literature in this period. For example, if it is assumed that the 'authorless' novels of Saddam Hussein (where the author's identity remains implicit) were in fact the product of a joint effort by a 'panel' or written by a ghost writer/writers, as was claimed by some sources in the media, there would be a potential freeing up of interpretations through the omission of a crucial paratextual element in the analysis. However, the propaganda messages in the texts are so explicit that even if we did apply Roland Barthes'

'Death of the Author' approach, we would be hard pressed to offer an original alternative reading. Genette's *Paratexts* approach allows for different levels of historicisation of texts, from the rigidly determinist to the open and flexible, which makes it adaptable for both canonical and non-canonical texts.

The instability of genre, where 'the truly vital meanings of a text are often contained not in any specific generic category into which the text may be placed, but rather in the play of differences between its genres'[40] is a particularly pertinent consideration when approaching the novels in this book that blur distinctions between the nationalist novel as 'realist fiction', autobiography as 'non-fiction', and didactic political or religious tract. Generic categories have been viewed as processes of interpretation[41] which correspond to a collective cultural consciousness. According to Tzvetan Todorov, 'a society chooses and codifies the acts that most closely correspond to its ideology; this is why the existence of certain genres in a society and their absence in another reveal a central ideology, and enable us to establish it with considerable certainty'.[42] Yasir Suleiman contends that 'the literary form is as important as nationalist content in promoting the cause of the nation'.[43] In the novel genre, as opposed to poetry, for example, individual protagonists are firmly rooted in a social milieu and merely represent 'one of many'[44] voices in the nation. Ba'thist state literature does not celebrate the multiplicity of voices in the nation as 'normal' nationalist literature does; in fact, what it does is to 'impose coherence on multiple memories "standing in" for half remembered and sometimes chaotic lived experiences'. For Tripp, this is precisely 'the resource on which many try to draw, whether defending or attacking established power'.[45] The unease with which propaganda novels deal with women and ethnic and religious minorities, and the way in which they profess admiration for a single Iraqi identity based on the most powerful social group (Sunni Arab men) leads to the bleaching out of local colour and customs, and the imposition of a homogeneous 'ideal' citizen.

The literary processes of both resistive and collaborative works reveal a preoccupation with the making and breaking of bonds. Bonds engender loyalty and affiliation and can potentially develop into networks of dissent. The Ba'th Party attempted to subsume bonds of ethnicity, tradition and religion into homogeneous nationalist bonds, using the novel as both vehicle and symbol in this process. However, the type of nationalism posited by the state underwent an evolution according to the ideological emphases of the state which veered towards a spectrum of liberal and conservative discourses. During the Iran–Iraq War, the state focused this process on consolidating a narrower understanding of nationalist bonds by privileging male camaraderie as representative of the national unity of Iraq and creating new 'othering' mechanisms to symbolically purge undesirables. These shifts are evident in the most clichéd and overused nationalist trope: marriage, which epitomises the kind of bonds idealised by the state. For example, whereas in Saddam Hussein's 2000 novel *Zabiba and the King* marriage represented the ideal nationalist bond between the ruler and the ruled, in his 2002 semi-autobiographical novel *Men and a City* it embodied the insular and inward-looking ideology espoused by the Baʿth in the late 1990s, as signified by the centrality of the concept of 'the companionate marriage' expressed in terms of racial, tribal and familial compatibility. On the other hand, in texts that reflected Islamic revivalism in Iraq, marriage as a religious duty was emphasised as it represented a way for the faithful to cement religious, and often transnational, bonds in the face of a government that was increasingly perceived as 'godless'. Contrarily, secular resistive discourses posit a cosmopolitan humanism as an alternative bond to both marriage and ideological affiliation. This is because Western military involvement in Iraq transformed the meaning of resistance: from being purely directed to the Baʿthist state to encompass the forces of global imperialism as well.

In the organisation of the book into resistance and collaboration sections, it is not my intention to deliberately pit hegemonic male discourses against resistive female discourses. The nature of political power has meant that pro-state discourses were by default produced by men, meaning that there is often an assumption that Arab women's texts are by default subversive, or that the act of writing by an Arab woman is by definition subversive. There were women who, of course, partook in the state's narrative on Baʿthism's liberation of women, particularly in the context of the activities of the GFIW. In his scathing indictment of the complicity of writers in the Baʿthist cultural project, Salām ʿAbbūd mentions isolated instances of women who wrote panegyric poetry glorifying the war, and laments that female writing was just as propagandistic as men's: 'one would have hoped women would write differently about a war as ugly and unjust as this one'.[46] The expectation that women's writing should be inherently more sensitive to the suffering caused by war and violence essentialises female responses and extracts them from their context to form an entity that is unaffected by socio-historical or political factors. However, political positions, particularly pro- or anti-state views were determined by the historical moment and the ascendancy of different, often contradictory, discourses. Towards the end of the war there were texts by women that indirectly served the state's agenda by depicting the acute hardships inflicted on the civilian population. The emphasis on civilian (read 'feminine' responses as 'passive' rather than 'active' citizens) was crucial discursive preparation for the state's push for peace after eight long years of a calamitous war.

Chapter 1 'History Writing and Canon-making: the Place of Women in Narratives of the Iran–Iraq War' details the under-representation of women in the majority of cultural activities pertaining to the Iran–Iraq War as symptomatic of state tendencies towards consolidating the public and the private as distinct spheres, and its publicising and encouragement of more traditional gender roles in Iraqi society in the media and in literary production. Because the value of canonicity is challenged as the ideal means of understanding Iraqi cultural history, I have also chosen to analyse the novels of Saddam Hussein as the ultimate representative of the state in Chapter 2. Torn between supposedly progressive Ba'thist discourses and practices regarding women, and political and economic changes which led to more conservative approaches to the 'Woman Question', the novels of Saddam Hussein exemplified the mixed messages on women perpetuated by the Ba'th. Chapter 2 argues that there is a dilemma inherent in depicting the feminine ideal in the novels, in which 'woman as symbol' contradicts 'woman as real individual' or believable literary character. This dilemma is on one level an artistic question regarding weaknesses in plot, allegory and characterisation, but the novels more importantly shed light on extra-literary debates, as contradictions in depicting women in Saddam's novels translate into anxiety regarding Iraq's national identity, where the focus on female chastity translates into an obsession with the purity of rural origins and a utopian Iraqi past.

Chapter 3 examines the subversive religious novels of four Iraqi Shia women writers: Āmina al-Ṣadr, May al-Ḥusaynī, 'Alyā' al-Anṣārī and the Kuwaiti author of Iraqi origin Khawla al-Qazwīnī. These novels provide interesting examples of how the representation of female piety and the female body are made into symbolic sites of contention, where secular and Islamic discourses struggle for ascendency, and where we find a discursive struggle between various utopias symbolised by woman. An important consideration will be whether the body, as Fedwa Malti-Douglas asserts, will necessarily always be the most privileged category of analysis in Arab women writers' work.[47] The chapter contends that religious female novelists use a conservative Islamic discourse as a means of delegitimising the state and its cultural discourses and appendages, such as secular women's magazines which focused on the uncovered female body as a site of liberation. It also considers whether or not a conservative female discourse can still be considered revolutionary or resistive in the context of a secular authoritarian state despite its seemingly reactionary elements.

Chapter 4 explores the convergence of the personal and political in Iraqi women's life writing. It does not subscribe to the view that all writing by Arab or Iraqi women is necessarily political, but in the case of Haifa Zangana, Dunya Mikhail and Nuha al-Radi writing fiction is a conscious individual choice with public repercussions. Moreover, the choice to write to an English-speaking audience is significant as 'original' texts acquired renewed significance in the light of their publication (sometimes even re-publication) after the United States' invasion of Iraq in 2003. This chapter also considers how and when gender discourses are seen as non-threatening by the state, and when they are deemed as an unacceptable challenge to state hegemony and practices. Narrativising female experiences as autobiography rather than as fiction challenges the dichotomy of private–public spheres as gendered spaces. It also allows for resistance through personalisation in the face of the homogenising narrative of the state, whilst utilising aesthetic tools to reflect on moral and philosophical issues. The chapter ultimately represents a culmination of competing state and resistive discourses, which highlights the practical applications of Genette's concept of 'transtextuality'.

According to Zahra Ali, material development in Iraq was often a façade and surface manifestation of social change.[48] For the Baʿth, the materiality of book production was an embodiment of its progressive project regarding culture, regardless of the quality of content of texts produced. In the process of the establishment of this new cultural battlefield, resistance opportunities were created in spite of the state's use of sheer bulk and other forms of coercion and censorship which effectively pushed dissenting voices to the margins and then beyond the borders of Iraq. As made clear by the interpretivist epistemologies borrowed from post-structuralist thinkers such as Michel Foucault, the seeds of resistance are embedded in even the most hegemonic structures, and there remain multiple possibilities for resistance. Although it is not possible to talk of a world of 'free play' in the context of Iraqi Ba'thist cultural production, discussions of resistance are possible if the significance of economic determinants, gendered power struggles and the political contexts of cultural contestations are not underestimated.

Notes

1. Abir Hamdar and Lindsey Moore (eds), *Islamism and Cultural Expression in the Arab World* (London: Routledge, 2015), p. 2.
2. Nira Yuval-Davis and Ruth Helm, *Gender and Nation* (London: Sage, 2008), p. 47.
3. Beth Baron, *Egypt as a Woman: Nationalism, Gender, and Politics* (London: University of California Press, 2005), p. 5.
4. Nadje Sadig Al-Ali, *Iraqi Women: Untold Stories from 1948 to the Present* (London: Zed Books, 2007), p. 133.
5. Cynthia Enloe, 'Womenandchildren: Making Feminist Sense of the Persian Gulf Crisis', *The Village Voice*, 25 September 1990.
6. Esther Meininghaus, *Creating Consent in Ba'thist Syria: Women and Welfare in a Totalitarian State* (London: I. B. Tauris, 2016).
7. Achim Rohde, *State–Society Relations in Ba'thist Iraq: Facing Dictatorship* (London: Routledge, 2014), p. 13.
8. Abbas Kadhim, 'Widows' Doomsday: Women and War in the Poetry of Hassan Nassar', in Faegheh Shirazi (ed.), *Muslim Women in War and Crisis: Representation and Reality* (Austin, TX: University of Texas Press, 2010), p. 144.
9. Dina Rizk Khoury, *Iraq in Wartime: Soldiering, Martyrdom and Remembrance* (Cambridge: Cambridge University Press, 2013), p. 56.
10. The battle of Qadisiya of 636 was a decisive battle in the early period of the Muslim conquests between the Arab Muslim army under the leadership of Sa'd Ibn Abi al-Waqqas and Rustum, the commander of the Persian army. The Muslim victory at al-Qadisiya (in modern-day Iraq) ultimately led to the collapse of the Sassanid Empire and remained a symbol of the strength and divine vindication throughout Arab Muslim history. Saddam's appropriation

of al-Qadisiya during the Iran–Iraq War was aimed at evoking an immemorial conflict between Arabs and Persians, as well as situating himself as the heir of Arab military glory.

11. Benedict Anderson, *Imagined Communities: Reflections on the Origins and Spread of Nationalism* (London: Verso, 1991), pp. 24–5.
12. Charles Tripp, *The Power and the People: Paths of Resistance in the Middle East* (New York: Cambridge University Press, 2013), p. 307.
13. Anderson, *Imagined Communities*, pp. 7 and 203.
14. Tripp, *The Power and the People*, p. 307.
15. Ibid., p.133.
16. Hamdar and Moore, *Islamism and Cultural Expression in the Arab World*, p. 2.
17. Yuval-Davis and Helm, *Gender and Nation*, p. 39.
18. Gill Bottomley, 'Post-multiculturalism? The Theory and Practice of Heterogeneity', paper presented at the conference *Post-colonial Formations: Nations, Culture, Policy*, Griffith University, Brisbane, Queensland, July 1993.
19. Dina Matar, 'Rethinking the Arab State and Culture: Preliminary Thoughts', in Tarik Sabry (ed.), *Arab Cultural Studies: Mapping the Field* (London: I. B. Tauris, 2012), p. 125.
20. Sabry Hafez, 'Islam in Arabic Literature: the Struggle for Symbolic Power', in Abir Hamdar and Lindsey Moore (eds), *Islamism and Cultural Expression in the Arab World* (London: Routledge, 2015), p. 38.
21. Salām ʿAbbūd, *Thaqāfat al-ʿunf fi al-ʿIrāq* (kulūniya: Manshūrat al-Jamal, 2002), p. 20.
22. Hiyām Nā'il al-Dawāf, *Ḥarakat nashr al-kutub al-ʿirāqīyya: dirāsa maydānīyya li-al-kutub al-manshūra wa al-nāshirīn li-al-fatra 1975–1994* (Baghdād: Wizārat al-Thaqāfa wa-al-Iʿlām, Dār al-Shu'ūn al- Thaqāfīya al-ʿĀmma ʿĀfāq ʿArabīya', 2000), p. 79.
23. Ibid., p. 245.
24. Ibid., p. 171.
25. According to al-Dawāf, 46.9 per cent of books produced in 1985–9 were school curricula, and her analysis of printing presses shows that this same period witnessed the highest percentage of government publications. Ibid., p. 101.
26. Nicholas Jackson O'Shaughnessy, *Politics and Propaganda: Weapons of Mass Seduction* (Manchester: Manchester University Press, 2004), p. 111.
27. ʿUmar Ṭālib, *al-Ḥarb fi al-qiṣṣa al-ʿirāqīya* (Baghdād: Wizārat al-Thaqāfa wa-al-Iʿlām, Dā'irat al-Shu'ūn al-Thaqāfīya wa-al-Nashr, 1983), p. 73.

28. Elie Podeh, 'From Indifference to Obsession: the Role of National State Celebrations in Iraq: 1921–2003', *British Journal of Middle Eastern Studies* 37 (2010): 179–206.
29. Nawar Al-Hassan Golley, *Reading Arab Women's Autobiographies: Shahrazad Tells Her Story* (Austin, TX: University of Texas Press, 2003), p. xiv.
30. Bertrand Taithe and Tim Thornton (eds), *Propaganda: Political Rhetoric and Identity 1300–2000*, Themes in History (Stroud: Sutton, 1999).
31. Roger Allen, *The Modern Arabic Novel: An Historical and Critical Introduction*, 2nd edn (Syracuse, NY: Syracuse University Press: 1995), p. 69.
32. Gérard Genette, *Paratexts: Thresholds of Interpretation* (Cambridge: Cambridge University Press, 1997), p. 35.
33. Yasir Suleiman, *A War of Words: Language and Conflict in the Middle East* (Edinburgh: Edinburgh University Press, 2004), p. 94.
34. Yasir Suleiman, *Arabic in the Fray* (Edinburgh: Edinburgh University Press, 2013).
35. Hayden White, *The Content of the Form: Narrative Discourse and Historical Representation* (Baltimore, MD: Johns Hopkins University Press, 1987), p. 187.
36. Nancy Easterlin and Barbara Riebling, *After Poststructuralism: Interdisciplinarity and Literary Theory* (Evanston, IL: Northwestern University Press, 1993), p. 2.
37. Ibid., p. 3.
38. Frederic Jameson, *The Political Unconscious* (Ithaca, NY: Cornell University Press, 1981), p. 28.
39. Ibid., p. 79.
40. Thomas O'Beebee, *The Ideology of Genre: a Comparative Study of Generic Instability* (University Park, PA: Pennsylvania State University Press, 1994), p. 250.
41. Ibid.
42. Tzvetan Todorov, *Genres in Discourse* (Cambridge: Cambridge University Press, 1995), p. 19.
43. Yasir Suleiman and Ibrahim Muhawi (eds), *Literature and Nation in the Middle East* (Edinburgh: Edinburgh University Press, 2006), p. 5.
44. Timothy Brennan, 'The National Longing for Form', in Homi K. Bhabha (ed.), *Nation and Narration* (New York: Routledge, 2006), p. 49.
45. Tripp, *The Power and the People*, p. 260.
46. 'Abbūd, *Thaqāfat al-'unf fi al-'Irāq*, p. 55.

47. Fedwa Malti-Douglas, *Men, Women, and Gods: Nawal El Saadawi and Arab Feminist Poetics* (London: University of California Press, 1995).
48. Zahra Al-Ali, *Women and Gender in Iraq: Between Nation-building and Fragmentation* (Cambridge: Cambridge University Press, 2018), p. 75.

PART I

1

History Writing and Canon-making: the Place of Women in Narratives of the Iran–Iraq War

The material conditions of a large-scale appropriation of culture to serve the propaganda interests of the state were ripe in Iraq by the time the war with Iran erupted 1980, both in terms of the mechanisms of production and the preparation of a literate audience. An extensive and highly successful campaign by the Ba'th Party to eradicate illiteracy began in 1978, spearheaded by Saddam Hussein himself – then vice president – which earned him an honorary award by the United Nations. According to estimates, 50 per cent of Iraqis were illiterate by the 1980s compared with 98 per cent at the turn of the twentieth century.[1]

Women particularly benefited from Ba'thist literacy campaigns and job initiatives, as women's literacy rates went up by 300 per cent.[2] Additionally, primary education was made compulsory by the state and education at all levels was free for all Iraqis, thereby creating a rapidly growing readership, and the subsequent demand for printed materials invigorated the press and publishing sectors in the country. Dozens of newspapers, specialised periodicals and dailies were produced as a result of active state encouragement,[3] including the most productive publishing house for the arts and humanities, Dar al-Shu'un al-Thaqafiya al-'Amma, established in the 1980s. By the end of the war, however, many specialised journals and magazines whose contents were not amenable to propagandistic usage were scrapped, with new ones taking their place according to the propaganda needs of the state, for example, the armed forces were allocated funds for a new newspaper in 1988. Moreover, publications directed at women, which had hitherto been expanded, were gradually limited, as the state concentrated its efforts on publications related to the war which did not prioritise women or women's issues.

Novel reading, which had previously been construed as a 'feminine' activity due to the abundance in Iraqi book markets of popular romances and foreign translations read primarily by women, was now 'elevated' through direct appropriation and sponsorship of the state to a national symbol of Iraqi masculinity. Moreover, state-sponsored novels were enforced in intellectual circles as an integral part of the Arab canon, as well as being disseminated through serialisation in newspapers as 'popular' reading for the masses. Literary production in Iraq during the Iran–Iraq War was part of the wider Baʿthist project to rewrite history, envisioned as an essential basis for ideological nation-building, as well as fulfilling important propaganda needs for total war mobilisation. Although women fulfilled a crucial symbolic function as 'the nation incarnate' in Baʿthist state discourses on politics and culture, they were minor producers of these, and did not feature prominently in state-sponsored literature during the war-ridden 1980s. As consumers, recipients and disseminators of the war story, the GFIW, with its 850,000 members, played a significant role.[4] However, despite a veritable boom in the publishing industry, bolstered by rising oil prices and Baʿthist imperative, the discursive content of cultural production during these years remained almost exclusively directed by the state and state writers; that is to say, by men. This came in spite of the involvement of women in the material practices (or *infrastructure*) of cultural production as they took on more jobs in publishing and other industries vacated by men going to war.[5] Based on the premise that material and ideological practices are interrelated, this chapter argues that a combination of material and ideological factors led to the marginalisation of the Iraqi female voice from the official war story.

According to state propaganda messages at the beginning of the war, men and women were equally responsible for the defence of the nation, with women actively taking the jobs of men sent to the frontline to address national labour shortages. By the mid-1980s, however, women were encouraged to return to the home and bear children for the sake of the homeland. As many commentators have noted, the Iran–Iraq War was responsible for a regression in progressive discourses on women and reversed the economic, legal and social gains made by them in the 1970s. Instead, a more traditional and conservative discourse on women emerged in Baʿthist Iraq, especially from 1984 onwards, accompanied by legal and legislative changes restricting women's freedom of movement and according more powers to male heads of households. The tokenistic inclusion of broader female contributions to the war effort in cultural and political discourses did not accurately reflect the erosion of Iraqi women's rights and independence during the war years. For example, the so-called 'gold donations' campaign spearheaded by the GFIW received much media attention as part of the state's efforts to highlight the mobilisation of all sectors of Iraqi society, whereas the hardships encountered by widows of soldiers killed in the war, a specifically 'female' problem, was rarely publicised. Similarly, pro-war writings by women at the beginning of the war were not specifically encouraged or validated as valuable experiences to be shared, and when they did appear, they were mostly depersonalised and tokenistic representations of Iraqi women's dedication to the war and to Saddam Hussein included in state-sponsored literary anthologies, rather than autonomous or free-standing texts. The state may not have explicitly intended to exclude women's voices in state-sponsored literature, but the way the war was conducted ensured that the values associated with a militarised masculinity, considered 'active citizenship' would overshadow female (civilian) responses to war, deemed as 'passive citizenship'.

So why was the contribution of women writers to state-sponsored Iraqi prose writing on the war so limited, and is it inevitable that war as a traditionally male undertaking would lead to the exclusion of the female perspective? This chapter argues that state literary criticism directed writers to produce realistic – almost journalistic – accounts of battles in a way that necessarily excluded those without direct experience of fighting. As such, literature would fulfil a dual purpose in line with Baʿthist ideology: to document Iraqi victories for posterity as 'history proper' rather than fiction, and to boost the morale of soldiers and civilians alike in a bid to win the war through tales of extraordinary feats on the battlefield. The civilian experiences of women would thus be rendered irrelevant in a pragmatic sense, especially at the peak of the war and mobilisation, but women remained symbolically significant, specifically as representatives of national honour that had to be safeguarded. Interestingly, even towards the end of the war, when civilian experiences which highlighted the tragedy and human toll of the war were validated in order to support the cessation of hostilities advocated by the state, the voices of women remained marginalised. Some female writers even remained fixated on the experiences of men at war, often using male protagonists in their stories. One reason for this was perhaps that the act of 'history writing', as an extension of 'history making', was ultimately designed to highlight the strength of men through military victories and prowess, rather than weakness of women in the wake of tragedy and personal loss.

This also explains why although there were up to 40,000 women in the Popular Army by 1982, no female memoir-style novel or novella emerged despite the soldier memoir sub-genre being especially popular. It seems that Saddam Hussein's assertion that the word and the bullet came from the same barrel would have its ramifications for both female writers and women in the armed forces, whose voices were equally marginalised. Although images of female militancy featured occasionally in Iraqi media, it is doubtful that the women who were trained in the Popular Army participated at all in actual combat.[6] The eagerness of the state to exploit the symbolic value of female militancy as an indication of the extent of the mobilisation and unity of Iraqi society forms a marked contrast to its failure to implement real policies of equality, despite the campaigning of the GFIW. This discrepancy between symbolic gestures of Ba'thist openness towards women, and the implementation of that rhetoric in the betterment of their lives, is symptomatic of the high ideological value of gender discourses at times of national crisis.

The Ba'th Party regarded its rule as utopian for women, as it claimed it had freed them from the shackles of ignorance and backwardness through its intensive literacy campaigns and increased job opportunities in the 1970s, which came hand in hand with more progressive discourses about women's place in Iraqi society. At the same time, women were an uncontested symbol of a primordial nationalism, representing familial and kinship bonds and the continuity of the nation through procreation, which became a crucial issue during the Iran–Iraq War where growth in numbers was both necessary and symbolically significant. In many ways, the issue of women's writing during the Iran–Iraq War is part of a wider debate about the Ba'th Party's contribution to the plight of Iraqi women, and whether Ba'thist strategies vis-à-vis women were regressive or progressive, or in the words of Noga Efrati 'productive or reproductive'.[7] On the one hand, the state advocated a total war that would involve all members of Iraqi society as an extension of the Ba'th's socialist revolution against backwardness. On the other hand, the excessive featuring of women in the public eye during wartime was by and large seen as bad for propaganda. As the traditional bearers of mourning, women are almost always the symbolic manifestations of the human toll of war, be it as bereaved mothers, grief-stricken widows or orphaned daughters. The strong presence of women in political and cultural discourses had a potentially emasculating effect that threatened the success of Saddam's propaganda campaign which centred on victory being achieved by men. As with many issues, the Ba'th did not have a clear or coherent long-term policy on women and women's rights, and this chapter attempts to understand the state's contradictory position by exploring depictions of women and femininity in propaganda literature.

The process of 'making history' and recording it for posterity during the Iran–Iraq War, was an extension of what Ba'thist historians termed the 'arabisation' of history, which involved adopting a dedicated Arabist perspective and applying it to all interpretations of history and contemporary political realities. The use of embedded journalists from the Arab world as a means of supporting the idea of Iraq as the Arab world's eastern flank to garner popular support from Arab governments and masses was unprecedented and relied on physical evidence of Iraq's cultural superiority as an extension of its military advantage. Photojournalism became a popular and economical means of conveying propaganda messages through images of male military might and prowess that could be understood by literate and illiterate Iraqis alike. Arguing in the same vein as Hiyām Nāi'l al-Dawāf, visiting Lebanese journalist Ibrāhīm Birjāwī noted in his memoirs from the frontline in 1987, that the effects of the war on the publishing industry were very positive indicating that the war was most likely to be won.[8] Physical evidence in the form of photographs and texts became even more important when the state was facing the crisis of making peace, leading it to embark on an extensive campaign to market the war as a victory, as if it had fought some other imaginary war regardless of Iraq's difficult political and economic post-war conditions. Increased unemployment, signs of demoralisation among soldiers and the steady deterioration in standards of living meant that a radical response was needed. In order to avoid the political suicide of admitting defeat, the state began building victory monuments as a way of solidifying its perceived victory against Iran in concrete terms.[9] Likewise, the power of language to shape reality is what made 1990, the first year after the end of the war, the highest producing year in terms of books in almost twenty years of Baʿthist rule. For Saddam and the Baʿth, it was not enough to give a semblance of normalcy, rather, the state also felt the need to materially prove that it had emerged from the war even stronger than before, and that it had the unanimous support of the Iraqi and Arab people.

The role and messages of news media vary over circumstances and time in any given conflict and not only across different conflicts. Strategic gains or failures during the Iran–Iraq War immediately affected choice of vocabulary, characterisation and other stylistic elements in state-sponsored novels, short stories and poems, as well as depictions of women and femininity. As the Iran–Iraq War was a particularly long one, it should not be treated as a totality. In fact, there is a marked discursive shift from pan-Arabism to Iraqi nationalism after 1982, when Iran took the war to Iraqi soil, although the Arab–Persian polemic remained as a persistent subtext.[10] Public perceptions of the war also changed on the home front as the war of the cities began in 1984 (alongside full-out chemical warfare by Iraq), which constituted a kind of litmus test for Iraqi nationalism. According to Davis, this was a test that Iraq passed as a nation-state, as it had remained intact during the war despite various ethnic and religious divisions.[11] It is at this point where more contributions by women to literary production emerge, inadvertently serving the interests of the state by highlighting the brutality and human cost of the war and justifying the government's bid for peace. However, as will become clear later, pro-war writings towards the latter years of the war remained dominated by men due to a combination of pragmatic and ideological factors.

The hurry to churn out a large number of state-sponsored texts in order to keep up with fluctuating political and military realities accounts for their lack of quality and the half-hearted nationalist sentiments which many of the texts express, despite a thin veneer of patriotism and often rampant xenophobia. Excessive production was also indicative of Baʿthist autocratic snobbery which assumed that writers would write what they were told to write, and that the people would consume whatever these writers produced, thus eliminating a potential outlet for the public to vent its frustrations. This faux-pas in the state's cultural policy contributed to growing resentment by the end of the war, which the Ba'th attempted to address by allowing depictions of suffering and deprivation in the media and literature. The chapter focuses on early and late writings by one of the Ba'th's most widely celebrated novelists during the war, Jāsim al-Raṣīf, in order to better understand the micro-shifts and contradictions in state discourses on woman and nation, owing to writers' interpretation of state-sponsored literary criticism rather than individual artistic choices or style.

The link between the development of the printed press and the emergence of the novel in Europe has, since Anderson's seminal work *Imagined Communities*, been established, although it is by no means incontestable. In Iraq, however, it has been the case that literate audiences of newspapers and dailies were encouraged to see themselves as one nation in literary narratives. For example, early nationalist narratives in Iraq tended to equate the personal journey of the hero with the journey of the nation towards reclaiming its former glories. Iraqi short stories during the war with Iran appeared almost immediately in the literary sections of Iraq's most popular daily newspapers such as *al-Jumhuriya* and the party's *al-Thawra*, and many novels like *Al-Raqs 'ala aktaf al mawt*, the war's first novel, were serialised.[12] In a 1981 interview with *al-Jumhuriya* writer Abd al-Sattar Nasir advocated a new literary philosophy in line with Ba'thist imperatives:

> The story today must address the reader in a different manner; in other words, war narratives need to be clear and simple in order to reach as many readers as possible, despite their different mentalities and levels. A soldier on the frontline needs to read, as does the employee, peasant and housewife; *they all need to read together*. The writer is responsible to all these people, as they too want to understand the meaning of this war. It is thus important for the writer to relieve ordinary people of obscure symbolism and language play, in order for his work to be more accessible.[13]

Despite denying that the creation and dissemination of new texts which all members of the Iraqi public 'can read together' would not entail any lowering of literary standards, but rather constitutes a kind of nationalist 'democratization of literature', Nasir's views represent a rallying call for the production of propaganda precisely because directness, lack of ambiguity and symbolism are all hallmarks of the genre. The Baʿth's emphasis on the 'democratization of culture' led to the implementation of what Erol Köroğlu calls 'the common minimum standard' whereby 'characteristics like theoretical depth, complexity or a literary language are not required, since the main aims are to control and to motivate certain ideas . . . Messages are communicated to their recipients in the simplest possible way.'[14] Similarly, an Iraqi state literary critic asserted in 1982 that 'the subject of war narratives is serious, even dangerously important because of the potential strategic use of literature to educate and direct public opinion'.[15]

Three major points should be made about literary production during the Iran–Iraq War which are relevant to this chapter: first, that these works were instantaneous rather than retrospective, meaning that they were all written exclusively during the war, and not one year after its end in 1988. Because they had no direct access to the war in its early stages, women began writing reflective accounts in a belated and piecemeal fashion. Works reflecting on the war written many years after its end were not endorsed or sponsored; as with the sanctions there was no longer a significant budget for literary and cultural production, and, more importantly, no ideological payoff. Iraq had also immediately embarked on another war, and for the state's immediate purposes, remembering the war with Iran was useless. The second point to be made is that literary production during the war was excessive in quantity, yet low on aesthetic or artistic quality – a point noted by critics and advocates alike. Notably, Miriam Cooke counts only three women writers among this corpus and no female winner of a state literary prize. What is more, there were very few stand-alone works by women, as short pieces were sometimes included as part of anthologies alongside texts by Kurdish and other minority writers to indicate a broad public consensus supporting the war. Besides interfering with the creative processes of writing and writers, excessive production not only led to immense pressure on experienced Iraqi male litterateurs to have a clear pro-war stance, but also marginalised established female writers who were pushed aside in favour of young and inexperienced male writers who wrote with the so-called 'realism' (*waqiʿiya*) and zeal required by the state for mass mobilisation.

Thirdly, and finally, the texts represented the literary parallel to Baʿthist political discourse, with resistance made possible only when the state permitted it, that is, towards the end of the war as it was preparing to make peace with Iran. Miriam Cooke sees elements of dissent in pro-war writings by both men and women, citing Luṭfiya al-Dulaimī's *Budhur al-nar* (*Seeds of Fire*, 1988) as 'an example of subversive writing from the pen of a woman whose earlier works were hailed as impeccably patriotic'.[16] Cooke's analysis implies a wide margin of free will on the part of Iraqi writers and assumes that female writings on war will, more often than not, be subversive. Abbas Kadhim also notes that Luṭfiya al-Dulaimī's works are the exception among ideological texts written during the war.[17] Rather than viewing war and state censorship as a totality, it seems that anti-war works were indeed written in Iraq, and under the auspices of the state itself, but these were all written in the last eighteen months to two years of the war when it had become clear that the conflict had reached a military stalemate. As such, depictions of the harsh realities of war were designed to shock and horrify readers, thereby highlighting the mercy of the state in its decision to negotiate for peace. The year 1988 stands out in Cooke's analysis of 'the stories that the women wrote' in which she applauds the 'considerable courage' shown by female writers' depictions of the brutality and horror of the war.[18]

It is no coincidence that the state permitted the publication and circulation of anti-war works in 1988, the final year of the war; works which would have been considered potentially dangerous and subversive only a few years earlier. In Wiebke Walther's review of Cooke's *Women and the War Story*, she acknowledges some of the book's findings, but adds that Cooke tends to 'project her own critical ideas onto works that are in fact simply war propaganda'.[19] Achim Rohde provides an interesting explanation as to why there was relatively more freedom accorded to secular, as opposed to religious, women's movements in Iraq, which is that they were deemed less threatening and their publications were therefore censored less.[20] Rizk Khoury provides another reason why potentially subversive texts were produced in Iraq during the war: 'only in less widely read literary accounts . . . did a more complex, critical narrative of the war experience emerge'.[21] The implication that critical views of the war (which came to be separated from criticism of the state only towards the end) were tolerated because they circulated only in intellectual circles seems to elide the fact that these narratives could not have possibly been produced at the beginning of the war or at the height of political and military mobilisation. It also credits the state with providing a clear margin of intellectual freedom when censorship was often capricious, prompting writers to err on the side of caution and avoid obscurantism as advised by state literary critics. Moreover, the idea that elite and public discourses were essentially different contradicts the Baʿth's stated position on building a national literature through the novel that, although produced from 'above', was nevertheless designed to cement bonds amongst the Iraqi public.

The instantaneous nature of the mass of state-sponsored literary works represented an attempt to rewrite history as it was being made, using sheer bulk to swamp any voices of alterity. As such, the Baʿth was able to engineer a shift in Iraqi and Arab public and elite perceptions of the war at its unfolding, which was most opportune. Rather than being a transparent reflection of the world, the full potential of language as a means of acting upon the world and shaping realities was used in Iraq during the war. By monopolising discourse whilst simultaneously producing it at a fierce rate, counter-hegemonic discourses were paralysed. Official novels during the Iran–Iraq War went beyond 're-writing history', they even sought to distort the present in preparation for it becoming history. This is what Saddam attempted to achieve with his final novel of 2003 *Get Out, Damned One!* which went a step further by proposing to anticipate the American invasion of Iraq, and their defeat at the hands of the female heroine, interpreted by many as being Saddam's daughter Raghad. This process of 'history-making' is significant because it signals the exclusion of women from the official war narrative in a bid to remember men first, not as individuals but as symbols of power and military might.

Literary Criticism and Propaganda Management

Iraqi civilians and combatants alike were constantly under fire from words during the Iran–Iraq War, which entailed the adoption of an unorthodox censorship policy by the Baʿthist state. Censorship usually implies the prospect of belatedness in the production of texts, as these are scrutinised in detail through a highly bureaucratic process before publication is permitted. In this case, however, the state removed many restrictions on publishing in the humanities, whilst simultaneously creating and imposing a new language to shape the consciousness of writers who could not but emulate it. In the words of Rizk Khoury, the state created 'a memory discourse that set the parameters within which Iraqi soldiers and intellectuals narrated their experience'.[22] Moreover, with the threat of violence constantly looming in the background, the state thus eliminated the *need* for censorship; rules regarding what was permitted and what constituted a red line are not necessarily made explicit, but instead the web of discourses perpetuated by the state ensnared the intellectual into exercising self-censorship. High-handed censorship is the exception in all totalitarian regimes, where self-censorship is the norm, and writers are often merely swept away by that tide. For the rare few, however, these literary works seemed to stem from genuine ideological conviction. However, very few novels and short stories from the war bear the unique stamp of their authors, especially those that received praise and recognition from the Iraqi state and Arab intellectuals (often included as judges in literary panels for state prizes). Instead, a monologic voice dominates almost all literary discourses, as if they were authored by the same source. 'Abd al-Laṭīf al-Ḥirz describes the war as a sea of ink in which all writers' quills were dipped.[23]

According to Erol Köroğlu's discussion of Ottoman propaganda literature, propaganda can be successful only if it strikes a delicate balance between effective state management and freedom from authoritarianism, as otherwise the state could miss an opportunity for creating potential outlets for public frustrations. In Iraq, the dominance of an authoritarian leadership ensured the artistic failure of its propaganda literature, despite allowing writers more freedom to depict the suffering resulting from the war when political negotiations for peace began. Like literary production itself, literary criticism also mirrored the short-term propaganda goals of the state: militantly praising the novels extended studies at its peak, and almost completely disappearing from book format towards the end of the war. There continued to be shorter articles of literary criticism in journals, periodicals and newspapers, including forewords and introductions to books and anthologies by notable figures in the Iraqi cultural scene, such as Muhsin Jasim Musawi, Basim Hammudi and Salim Abd al-Qadir al-Samirai. Musawi, the former editor in chief of *Afaq 'Arabiya* also wrote the prefaces to several parts of *Qisas taht lahib al-nar* (*Stories under Gunfire*), an anthology of state-endorsed war short stories. However, even established litterateurs and other major contributors to state literary criticism could not keep up critically with the sheer mass of literary works produced, and by the end of the war it was not necessary for them to do so. The canonical status which the state aspired that its war novels would reach was impossible to achieve considering the limits on freedom of expression, and despite all its efforts; from celebrity author endorsements of high-profile literary festivals and awards, to the corpus of literary criticism which came hand in hand with the texts in order to ensure a more effective performance from state writers.

ʿUmar Ṭālib's book *al-Harb fi al-qissa al-ʿiraqiya* is one of the most useful studies of narrative literary propaganda; although it covers only the first twenty months of the war, Ṭālib does provide many useful insights on notable literary publishing phenomena, providing an indication as to why women were excluded from producing literary texts during the war. Ṭālib's work is part of a large corpus of state literary criticism designed to guide and direct propaganda writings in line with state imperatives. Literary criticism of this kind was also designed to lend weight to literary propaganda works as worthy 'objects of study'. According to Ṭālib, the young Iraqi generation was responsible for over 50 per cent of literary production in the first twenty months of the war.[24] Although many new authors sank back into obscurity after the war, writing was a swift way to catapult young writers to stardom and offered tempting financial remuneration. This opportunism is evident in the large number of entries (fifty) in the inaugural year of the *Qadisiyat Saddam* prize for the novel. Moreover, writers on the frontline (like Adnan al-Sa'igh, the state's premier court poet) were often relieved of military service, which could have been another incentive for taking up writing. The swamping of the literary market with texts by new male writers not only limited opportunities for new female writers, but also necessarily excluded more established women writers who were pushed aside by those eager to curry the favour of the state by producing literary works at an astonishing rate.

Ṭālib also notes that the high number of texts written by journalists and others working in the media sector had at times weakened literary production generally due to excessive realism, documentation and literal depictions of heroism. The incorporation of a journalistic style often meant that real incidents from the battlefield were transposed onto a narrative framework without much adaptation or appreciation of the uniqueness of the literary genre as distinct from mere reportage.[25] Samah Selim describes the 'immature' stage in the Egyptian novel as being characterised by *uslub taqriri* instead of *uslub taswiri*, 'documentary' as opposed to a 'representational' style.[26] This distinction is applicable to state-sponsored works, and makes it possible to talk about a regression of sorts in the artistic novel in Iraq where journalists encroached upon the literary sphere, thereby 'mediatising' literature in a way that makes it seem like a mere extension of other sectors in the public sphere, particularly media and politics, rather than a unique space unto itself.[27] The implication for women of this blurring of boundaries between the literary and media sphere is that a 'desirable' journalistic style in literature excludes women by default, because they do not have direct access to the war front (as correspondents, for example), whilst also being under-represented in major press outlets, meaning that they were often not up to date with the latest from the battlefield.

'Umar Ṭālib also details the emergence of a distinct narrative genre during the war, which by definition excluded women: the 'war memoir' or 'memoirs from the frontline' (*mudhakarat min al-jabha*) written by writers-turned-soldiers or soldiers-turned-writers.[28] Among the most well-known of such writers were Faiṣal 'Abd al-Ḥassan, Jāsim al-Raṣīf, Wārid Badr Sālim, Ḥassan Muṭlaq (later executed by Saddam), Khuḍair 'Abd al Amīr, 'Abbās Muḥsin and 'Ali Khayūn. According to 'Abbūd, a writer named Aḥmad Khalaf even claimed to have used the actual memoirs and diaries of Iraqi soldiers to inform his work, and developed them into scenes of invincible Iraqi heroism, like American movies from the 1980s.[29] Echoing Saddam Hussein's infamous 'word as bullet'[30] simile, 'Abd al-Sattār Nāṣir conflates story-telling with warfare in the foreword to his short story collection *Martyr 1777* saying: 'this collection of armed stories enters the war side by side with planes, rockets and cannons . . . I will fight with a simple weapon . . . for I am a story writer with nothing in my pockets but the bullets of my writings.'[31] Similarly, in *al-Raqs 'ala aktaf al-mawt* (*Dancing on the Shoulders of Death*), a young Iraqi soldier-poet 'Isam is said to be just as good at 'talking with arms' as he is at 'talking with words'.[32] The soldier-poet is a staple figure in Iraqi war novels and often features in award-winning state-approved novels, such as *al-Sab' yadhak* (*The Lion Laughs*) by Aḥmad Qabbānī.[33] There was also a trend towards depicting soldiers with literary ambitions as prose authors rather than as poets, for example, in Jāsim al-Raṣīf's *al-Fasil al thalith* (*The Third Troupe*), Fa'iz the protagonist has a diary, rather than a poetry notebook.[34]

Ṭālib's study attempts to balance constructive criticism with apologia; for example, he points to the excessive zeal on the part of young writers whom he says have written passionate but rushed works due to their belief in the justness of their country's nationalist war. This explains why there are frequent grammatical and typographical errors in the works (he lists these at one point, in a discussion of one novel). Ṭālib's unwavering ideological position allows him to interpret negatives such as bad writing, lazy editing and non-rigorous publishing procedures as positives. Another Iraqi critic ʿAlī ʿAbd al-Ḥusayn Mukhīf also excuses the low quality of the mass of literary works produced as owing to hastiness and genuine zeal, and insists that the impressive quantity of war novels will eventually yield impressive quality, perhaps after the end of the war, when its impressions had been properly digested. However, no 'great novel' ever materialised, nor did any new scholarly criticism, which Mukhīf predicted would accompany novels written after the war. Ultimately, criticism of the shortcomings of the Iraqi war novel was merely to ensure an improved propaganda performance of Iraqi novelists. According to Yasir Suleiman, 'nationalist thinkers stress the importance of "quality" in nationalist literature not as an attribute for its own sake, but as a means to creating a more effective literature in mobilising terms'.[35]

In Iraq's highly charged political atmosphere, there was no place for ambiguity in literary production; writers were not only obliged to participate in the state's propaganda war, but also had to ensure that their views were made crystal clear. This may help to explain the so-called 'excessive zeal' manifest in most of the novels of this period; some writers may have indeed been eager to ingratiate themselves to the government, but perhaps others merely feared being misunderstood. Despite the fact that storylines had been exhausted by the time the study was written in 1983, one Iraqi writer is even criticised by Mukhīf for using new material that would not lead to positive interpretations of the war.[36] Ironically, however, it seems that the exaggerated display of loyalty towards the regime is interpreted as bordering on parody, arousing the suspicion of state literary critics, eager to pounce on the slightest sign of discontent. Thus, the vicious cycle is perpetuated again and again: the state obliges well-known writers to author novels and allows enthusiastic budding writers to contribute; it tells them what to write and how, and then expresses its dissatisfaction with the entire corpus of works despite the multiple literary prizes it has awarded, and the intense marketing campaign by literary critics from Iraq and the rest of the Arab world surrounding the works. By constantly expecting better from writers whilst straitjacketing their creative choices, the Baʿth guaranteed that no great war novel was ever written inside Iraq, neither by men nor by women.

ʿAlī ʿAbd al-Ḥusayn Mukhīf's study *Fī qiṣṣat al-ḥarb* is the last major critical study of Iraqi war narratives, and is in many ways the most militant, as it was written at the peak of propaganda mobilisation. Mukhīf begins by detailing the grand scale of the war and its historic implications, and justifies the current disappointing state of prose writing in Iraq by claiming that the war is too great to be depicted and has caused an understandable shock to the senses and sensibilities of Iraqi writers from which they have yet to recover.[37] Paradoxically, however, Mukhīf goes as far as to claim that the Iran–Iraq War novel surpasses in quality any other modern Arab war novel, as the war is unlike any Arab war before it. Mukhīf's study sheds light on the dilemma facing litterateurs in Iraq during the war, handicapped by the often-contradictory demands of the state: writers were required to be committed but not preachy, realistic but not pessimistic.[38] Their protagonists should be heroic and ideal, but not invincible,[39] and their writing style must be symbolic, but not obscure.[40] Mukhīf's guidelines for writers also included: first, depicting the Iraqi army as defenders not aggressors,[41] yet ensuring that the power and superiority of Iraq and its successive victories in battles are highlighted; and, secondly, steering away from press representations and stereotypes of the enemy, yet also inciting against Iran as an outlet for legitimate public frustrations and anger.[42] Writers are encouraged to produce realistic depictions of Iran and Iranians, in order to help understand 'the enemy psyche' better, rather than for literary strength: 'the truth is that our knowledge of the enemy is severely lacking, especially as most of our writers are unfamiliar with the enemy's language. For this reason, they are unable to depict the inner happenings of that country, or accurately represent its characters, relying solely on miscellaneous articles from the Arab and Iraqi presses.'[43] The preoccupation with the minutiae of documenting the war and attacking the enemy through discourse naturally excluded women, who were experiencing the war in a completely different way. Moreover, as is evident from Mukhīf's guidelines above, much of the discussion on the representation of

Iraq and Iraqis centres on traditionally masculine attributes such as strength, prowess, fortitude and stamina. By contrast, as critics have noted, Ayatollah Khomeini was depicted as weak and effeminate by Iraqi media as a means of further discrediting him and Iranian men more generally.[44]

A major handicap for writers was content; Mukhīf insists that the raw materials for war literature are uncontested and must depict Iraqi heroism and humanitarian ideals at all times, as well as propagating peace and highlighting the lofty ideals and superior morals of Iraqi soldiers. He coins a new paradoxical term: 'Iraqi objectivity', which encapsulates the Ba'thist project to 'Arabise' history whilst attempting to maintain scholarly integrity. By establishing what the content of the novels should be, Mukhīf's study essentially becomes an analysis of form and language only, in the assumption that form and content are separable. This 'granted-ness' of militant content all but explicitly excluded women from participating in literary production sponsored by the state, which did not encourage or acknowledge accounts from the home front until the very end of the war. Interestingly, after Mukhīf's critical study in 1984, there were no more critical works examining literary production during the war as a whole and retrospectively.[45] In the same way, not one pro-war novel was written about the war after 1988, and one assumes that any works awaiting publication were hastily abandoned with its abrupt end: there was simply nothing new to be said about the war, either in literature or in literary criticism, unless an attempt is made to challenge state orthodoxies, which was difficult.

The novels of the Iran–Iraq War were essentially reactive not meditative, serving the instrumental purpose of what psychologists might call 'task orientation'; mobilising the Iraqi population, both civilian and military, to serve the immediate needs of the war effort. Accordingly, the best texts would have to utilise a 'transparent' language which does not draw attention to itself, meaning that they would ideally be prose works, and not poetry. For according to Sartre, only the prose medium is capable of instrumentalising language in order to act upon the world in a committed manner. He adds that for the prose writer, words are a means to an end, whereas words are an end in themselves in poetry.[46] The main purpose for advocating explicitness in literary production under Saddam was in order to allow propagandist cultural practitioners to impose a single meaning and to strip language of its subversive potential; in other words, in order to make 'thought-crime' impossible, in the vein of Orwell's *1984*.

Women and Nation in *The Third Troupe* and *Red Line*

The war period represented a new experiment in the relationship between writers and the state in the Arab world, which has left deep and long-lasting fissures among Iraq's writers and cultural practitioners, and a resistance/collaboration polemic that is still evident in Iraqi public discourse today. In his recent novel, Jāsim al-Raṣīf (1950–), one of the most prolific writers of the Iran–Iraq War, writing from his new home in Nebraska, dedicates his 2007 novel to 'those who have refused to become nails in the shoes of invaders'.[47] The anonymous recommendation at the back of the book adds that the novel is a contribution to Arabic resistance literature, 'immortalizing the momentary gap between true citizenship for a human being in a free country, and denied citizenship in an occupied country'. Born in Mosul in the north of Iraq, al-Raṣīf worked as an editor for the state's premier newspaper *al-Jumhuriya* from 1978 to 1994, and has reprinted several of his earlier works from Beirut after breaking with the regime and leaving Iraq. On his blogspot, he publicises all his novels, noting that five won state literary prizes (without mentioning that some of these were war literature prizes, and conveniently dropping the title of the prize, *Qadisiyat Saddam*[48]). Likewise, on the website of Qatar's Katara Prize for the Arabic novel, al-Raṣīf's biography entry emphasises the literary merit of the author's essentially propagandistic literary works from the war by claiming that the texts formed part of university curricula in Iraq before they were pulled from bookshops upon his arrest in 1994.[49] In 2001, a copy of al-Raṣīf's last novel of the war, *Hijabat al-jahim* (*The Veils of Hell*), found its way to the School of Asian and African Studies' Library, personally autographed by the author: 'A gift to the University of London / with respect, Jasim al-Rasif/ 23.8.2001'. This particular novel is the most ambivalent of al-Raṣīf's works (his best in fact), which is probably why he chose not only to reprint it, but to also disseminate it in a prestigious Western academic library.

In the 1980s, al-Raṣīf epitomised the soldier/writer image popular in Iraq at the time; he participated in the war for the entire eight years, six of these were on the frontline in the north of Iraq, producing five novels during this period. For his efforts, al-Raṣīf was awarded state literary prizes in 1983, 1987 and 1988, including the then prestigious *Qadisiyat Saddam* literary prize. Al-Raṣīf's debut novel (in two parts) *al Fasil al thalith* (*The Third Troupe*) won first prize in the *Qadisiyat Saddam* competition in 1983. The events of the novel revolve around the tragic love story of an Arab soldier Fa'iz (meaning 'Victor', a significant name choice), deployed in the Kurdish areas north of Iraq, and the beautiful and daring Prishnak, a Kurdish girl from a nearby village. The menace of the Iranian enemy is easily countered by a superior army on the frontline, but the Popular Army's (*al-jaysh al-shaʿbi*) ability to 'protect' Kurdish villages from *al-mukharribin* (vandals), the word used by the author to describe Kurdish rebels allied to Iran, is often in doubt.

The couple are abruptly killed by the Iranians soon after announcing their engagement: Fa'iz in what is described as 'a suicide mission' to avenge his close friend and comrade Khalid; and Prishnak on her way up the mountains to deliver food to her fiancé and his comrades. This ending supports claims of 'realistic' storytelling and depictions of the war, as well as portraying martyrs as happy and willing human sacrifices. ʿAbbūd observes that whilst martyrs from the beginning of the war died with smiles on their faces, towards the end of the war, these smiles become deformed and twisted, signaling that these martyrs died with 'torn souls'.[50] There is always unease with endings in Iraqi propaganda literature, precisely because the wars on which Saddam embarked were ambiguous, with the end not on the horizon and the outcome unknown. There also seems to be an implicit distrust of the chameleon-like changeability of state discourse, making writers particularly wary of giving a final word on whether peace or total victory was the most desirable end to the war, and lest military realities on the ground force the regime to reconsider the ideals it had espoused. Interestingly, the novels of Saddam also end awkwardly, except (ironically) his last when the end of his rule is in sight.

As Nadje Sadig Al-Ali has noted, Iraqi Arab men were encouraged to marry Kurdish women as part of the state's Arabisation policies in the north.[51] Such marriages occur frequently in novels from the early stage of the war, no doubt to support the nationalist myth of unity perpetuated by the Baʿth. However, there are no instances where Kurdish men marry Arab women, as it is more acceptable for a Kurdish woman to 'belong' to an Arab husband through marriage, whereas Arab women are never 'given away' to

Kurds, whose nationalist credentials are always suspect. The message here seems clear: it is possible, even desirable, for the state to assimilate minorities, rather than allow them self-autonomy, or even to share the resources of the nation, which marrying Arab Iraqi women would imply. According to David Ghanim, the enemy outside is often constructed along the lines of enemies inside, whereby fear of strange men in the cult of virginity exemplifies the fear of foreigners stealing the resources of nation.[52] As such, the unfulfilled marriage of Prishnak and Fa'iz is not really a marriage of equals or representative of the Ba'th's supposed reformist rhetoric, whatever the text may claim. Indeed, the union between an Arab man and a Kurdish woman seems to have been an exhausted theme; for example, in the winning of the *Qadisiyat Saddam* prize in 1984, *al-Sab' yadhak* (*The Lion Laughs*), the protagonist Hamid is married to a whiny Kurdish woman who does not want him to participate in the war. The theme persists to the 2000s in Saddam Hussein's third novel *The Fortified Castle*, where, like *The Third Troupe*, the engagement between the Kurdish girl and an Arab man is not consummated in marriage. However, Saddam's novel is more explicitly nationalist than al-Raṣīf's, as we do not know where Fa'iz from *The Third Troupe* is from exactly, whereas Saddam describes the ethnic and geographical origins of his characters in detail. Perhaps this is due to the fact that in the midst of the Iran–Iraq War, a blatant nationalist metaphor such as marriage would have not needed further clarification. On the other hand, in 2001, a more complex political and discursive environment existed, which included overtly Islamist, tribalist and Iraqi and Arab nationalist elements. Therefore, readers of Saddam's novel, including those who were too young to have witnessed the war, had to be reminded of the marriage metaphor as nationalist trope. According to Fatima Mernissi, marriage signifies gender conflict rather than unity,[53] and this seems to be the case in the Kurdish–Arab marriage plots, as well as the extended nationalist metaphors that they signify.

Although Fa'iz and Prishnak equally die for Iraq (the latter albeit for more 'selfish' individualistic reasons), the death of a Kurdish woman in place of a Kurdish man typifies the implicit criticism against all but a few Kurds which permeates the text. For example, Prishnak's female friend turns out to be the mysterious 'masked fighter' driven by the inaction of Kurdish men to don the clothing of a male soldier at night in order to take revenge against the *al-mukharribin* (vandals) wreaking havoc in her village. When they discuss who this ghost warrior (*al-shabah*) may be, the villagers suggest it is 'the spirit of some forefather, angered by the cowardice of their descendants in facing the vandals'.[54] The girl prefers to remain anonymous for fear of being considered aggressively masculine in a very traditional, almost reactionary, Kurdish village. On the other hand, Prishnak flaunts all social conventions by openly declaring her love for Fa'iz , to the dismay of all those around her. The presence of strong Kurdish female characters also mirrors the strong and progressive Iraqi state which they represent (just like in Saddam's novels), as well as the pioneering egalitarian spirit of the modern Baʿth versus the old-fashioned and backward traditions of the Kurds. Ultimately, the masked female fighter serves to emasculate Kurdish men, and may explain why there are no depictions of Iraqi female soldiers despite their presence in the army. To symbolically allow women to take on the role of men or, even worse, to defend men, would have been unacceptable given Iraqi propaganda's emphasis on the machismo of its soldiers.

The author describes rainfall in the Kurdish winter as a process of washing the sins of the village, which reveals a persistent distrust of the national loyalties of Kurds in spite of the thinnest veneer of utopian nationalism made explicit in the Fa'iz–Prishnak match. Prishnak warns Fa'iz that her family may not allow her to marry him because he is Arab, to which he replies: 'in war, everything must change . . . there is no difference between us, we are both Iraqi'.[55] In another scene, an unarmed Kurdish fighter in the Popular Army is shot dead by a rebel for refusing to desert the army: 'why are you defending a land which is not yours, when you are a Kurd, and the country belongs to Arabs? / In these areas there are Arab soldiers, why do they not flee and say this land is not ours. It is Kurdish land.' The patriotic Kurd replies: 'These lands are for us all, there is no difference.'[56] Interestingly, Kurdish parents are rarely positive characters in war novels, for example, Rahimi's wife's family returns her to him despite knowing that he is abusing her. Also, Prishnak's mother does not want her to marry a non-Kurd and encourages her to be a stereotypically meek female. As mothers symbolise the motherland, the Kurdish people are portrayed as a weak, close-minded and suspicious race.

Those villages which have fallen to Kurdish rebel fighters or have cooperated willingly with them (out of fear) are also said to have become 'whorehouses' and centres for alcoholism and illegal smuggling activities.[57] As vicious as depictions of the enemy usually are in war novels like al-Raṣīf's,[58] the emphasis on the sexual depravity of Kurdish rebels and collaborators are deeply unsettling, not least because they are recounted again and again, drumming the message into the reader's psyche so that it remains a lasting image of the novel. The two village collaborators Rahimi and Humma Rash are too cowardly to join the ranks of 'drop-outs, deserters, criminals and unknown Iranians'[59] which supposedly form Kurdish rebel units, but are involved in other forms of collaboration, such as spying, passing secret information to the enemy and smuggling goods to cover Iran's 'enormous shortages'. Rahimi's other covert dealings with Iran include pimping his own wife to Iranian soldiers and to the drunk Humma Rash against her will until she collapses from the psychological trauma and exhaustion of repeated rape.

The rape of Iraqi women does not feature in novels on the war, as it implies that Arab men were not able to safeguard the honour of Iraqi *majidat*,[60] whereas in *The Third Troupe*, the author describes the violation of Kurdish women in shocking detail, almost as a punishment for the lack of 'manliness' on the part of Kurdish men who complain that the army is not protecting them, rather than relying on their own initiative, courage and dignity.[61] In a particularly disturbing scene, Kurdish rebels force a man to watch while his wife is raped in front of him for being the sister of a soldier in the Popular Army.[62] The woman is so distraught and ashamed at the defilement of her honour that she does not say a word to her husband, until she reaches home and commits suicide through self-immolation in front of her children.[63] The husband attempts but fails to die with his wife but suffers severe burns and loses his mind as a result of the ordeal. In his inability to either avenge his wife or die honourably (the couple have small children, so one assumes that the man was young enough to have been eligible for military service), this unnamed man typifies the emasculation of Kurdish men in the novel. Such unspeakable acts of cruelty against women by some Kurdish men as a result of the inaction and cowardice of others are etched in the reader's memory because the gruesome details are not only explicit but are also constantly repeated so as not to be forgotten. Repetition is a key propaganda technique in this novel; the prose often sounds unnatural and contrived, especially when villagers discuss the news in minute detail and keep repeating the entire story of the self-immolating rape victim. At one point, Iranian *mullah*s are blamed for causing the raped woman's husband to go insane: 'they call us kuffar (infidels), those who claim to follow Islam when their hands are stained with the blood of Muslims; those black-hearted hate-filled mullahs, but we are well and at peace with ourselves'.[64] And in case we have forgotten it, the story is retold again.[65]

Scenes from the battlefront are uninteresting due to the monotonous sequence of Iraqi victories and Iranian blunders and losses. At the beginning of the novel, the Iranians are described as 'a crazy flock of goats',[66] 'frightened rabbits',[67] 'human beasts'[68] and 'animals' who 'stupidly cook' their own fighters': 'tell the cooks to put a bit of salt and spice on them' Khalid says 'coldly and dismissively', as enemy soldiers burn alive.[69] Furthermore, the Iraqi response to the death and torture of enemies is vengeful: 'let me fill this dead body with bullets',[70] and derisive, with constant blood-chilling laughter interspersing battle scenes. The conflation of manliness with extreme violence and the performative aspect of doing battle imposes a certain genre of Hollywood-style writing which excludes those who do not have direct access to military action. On the other hand, Iraq's humane and noble treatment of Iranian prisoners of war is given special attention, as it provides a legitimate basis for Iraq's military victories, the triumph of 'good' over 'evil'. In *Dancing on the Shoulders of Death*, the protagonist, makes this explicit with the use of black and white representations of 'us' and 'them' as part of a Manichean worldview: 'Why are we winning? Because we are right (*'ala haq*); because we are defending ourselves and our principles; because at last we have a leadership that has made history and knows how to strategize, and because the hearts of all our people are with us on the battlefield'.[71]

The heightened sense of Iraqi moral superiority eventually leads to superhuman feats of bravery and successive swift victories against an enemy crumbling from within. These accomplishments are recounted in a journalistic style, another genre which by default marginalises women's voices. One soldier in the troupe named Baqi, corrects a villager by saying that 342 Iranians had been killed in the latest battle and not 242, whereas there were only nineteen Iraqi martyrs: 'our boys over there are doing unbelievable things!'[72] A villager asks Fa'iz about enemy casualties and Iraqi losses: 'our sacrifices are few, God willing?', to which Fa'iz replies 'of course! We don't let them off easily! Only 16 Iraqi martyrs and 749 Iranian dead.'[73] The logistical difficulty of providing such 'accurate' numbers go unquestioned in the novel, but on a meta-textual level, these details highlight the role of Iraqi novels as realistic and truthful history documents. Indeed, village gossip reads like a tabloid newspaper, emphasising Iran's internal crisis with gusto; a civil war is predicted, as Iranians 'are eating each other up',[74] and 'Bani Sadr admits to the existence of a political crisis in his country. Iran is prolonging the war, the villagers claim, in order to distract citizens from the abysmal situation at home, which includes rampant disease, poverty, arrests and imprisonments, executions and espionage.'[75] Baqi adds: 'God knows where Iran is headed.'[76]

On a structural and stylistic level, the rudimentary third-person narration in *The Third Troupe* (with little or no authentic stream of consciousness) serves to distance readers from the protagonists and to prevent feelings of pity or empathy towards them. The use of the third-person was extremely popular at the start of the war, whereas many novels like al-Raṣīf's later works offered a more equal juxtaposition between civilian and military life by using the first-person. The deaths of both protagonists and by extension their unconsummated love in *The Third Troupe* supports rather than challenges state propaganda messages and Baʿthist visions of Iraqi nationalism. First, protagonists in novels from the Iran–Iraq War often die, but this is always framed as a necessary exception following a multitude of Iraqi victories. Secondly, these literary deaths are hurried in the last pages of the novel, which does not allow the reader to 'mourn' them as it were, especially as they seem to *want* to die. For example, the wounded Fa'iz refuses to abandon his troupe. and Prishnak, whose political conviction is not as strong as Fa'iz's, rather naively ventures into the battle zone for a second time to see Fa'iz on the pretext of delivering food, which she knows the army does not need anyway. Interestingly, naivety and the virtue of 'hoping for the best' is exalted as a positive trait in Iraqi war novels, as it implies a reliance on the strategic wisdom and aptitude of the state, rather than the gut-instinct of the individual. This trait is often framed as innocence, leading to 'child-like' characterisations of both male and female protagonists. For example, Fa'iz hugs his rifle like a child hugs her doll.[77] and Iraqi soldiers laugh 'like children' when they shoot down an enemy plane.[78] Likewise, Fa'iz's joy is described as childlike after asking for Prishnak's hand in marriage,[79] and in return Prishnak insists that her dowry is only a symbolic one dinar (ironically, the original cost of this novel and the standard price for most others, as the government had begun to subsidise propaganda texts). In *The Lion Laughs*, readers are encouraged to laugh off the tragedy of war like the cheerful and perpetually optimistic protagonist: 'even if the war lasts tens of years, there will be no place for sadness in it'.[80] Written at the peak of the war, this novel capitalises on the innocence and jolly patience of its protagonist to prepare the public to accept a long war, if needs be.

The paratextual information provided by the title of the work *The Third Troupe*, which refers to Fa'iz's troupe and not to Fa'iz himself or his lover, for example, trivialises their individual love story in order to avoid the danger of personalising loss in the context of a wider cause or the greater good. The author, like the head of the troupe who berates soldiers for displaying grief at the loss of comrades, does not even allow the protagonists to mourn each other, as they are killed almost simultaneously; an act of authorial mercy designed to allay their fears of losing each other. Previously, the head of the troupe reprimands Khalid for his almost suicidal venture to the frontline in an attempt to bury Fa'iz's dog (a symbolic gesture of loyalty towards his friend who was missing in action). He adds that this is the first time anyone from his troupe has ever cried for a comrade. The head officer then calls Khalid into his office and asks him to stop mourning his friend, which he accepts for the sake of the homeland. As mourning seems to traditionally be a role that belongs to women during war, this rejection of mourning as unpatriotic can also be interpreted as an attack on feminine responses to the tragedies of war. The trivialisation and sentimentalisation of suffering during the war was symptomatic of the state penchant towards homogenisation of voices and experiences for the sake of the establishment of nationalist bonds.

Titles of novels from the Iran–Iraq War were predominately depersonalised, often abstract concepts and oxymorons, rather than personal names. Example titles of opposites or oxymoron include: *al-Kibar wa al-sighar* (*The Great Ones and Lowly Ones*), *al-Layl wa al-nahar* (*Night and Day*), *al-Buka' al-jamil* (*Beautiful Weeping*), *al-Kharab al-jamil* (*Beautiful Destruction*), *Nujum fi sama' al-nahar* (*Stars in the Sky of Day*), *Rabi' fi sayf sakhin* (*Spring in a Hot Summer*) and *Kathir min al-'ishq, qalil min al-ghadab* (*A lot of Love, a Little of Anger*). *Dancing on the Shoulders of Death*, for example, epitomises the contradictory duality noted by Salām 'Abbūd as a defining feature of literary texts of the period, with 'beautiful destruction' and 'beautiful weeping' being key literary motifs.[81] The dancing motif is also used frequently as a symbolic gesture of defiance of death and mourning; families, especially parents of martyrs, are depicted as dancing at the funerals of their sons to celebrate their martyrdom.[82] This echoes Saddam's determination to 'dance on the wings of death' rather than give in to Iran.[83] Explicit titles were used as a strategy to maximise the use-value of ideological novels, as readers are exposed to the mobilising messages of texts in the most economical way possible, without having to read the text at all.

Ironically, despite being an overtly propagandistic text *The Third Troupe* is not on the higher end of the propaganda scale in terms of extremity. Nationalist themes and male camaraderie are less concentrated, watered-down versions of a novel like *Dancing on the Shoulders of Death* by Ādil 'Abd al-Jabbār, which claims to be the very first Iraqi novel of the Iraq–Iran War and is thus appropriately zealous given the belligerent atmosphere at the outset of the war. Camaraderie in *The Third Troupe* is represented by Khalid and Fa'iz's friendship, but this relationship is overshadowed (at least until Fa'iz dies for Khalid) by the love between Prishnak and Fa'iz. However, in *Dancing on the Shoulders of Death* there is more of an idealised nationalist camaraderie, where male–male relations take precedence over male–female relationships. The 'black' Khidr, Shihab, Safa' and the blond, blue-eyed martyr Abd al-Qadir form a kaleidoscopic entity which represents the Iraqi nation without the need for a strong female figure.[84] In fact, Shihab refuses to become romantically involved with Shayma, a girl Khidr is in love with, although he has the advantage of living in her house; and even when Shayma expresses her preference to Shihab, he not only refuses her advances, but also tries to scare her away by showing her that he is not a man of good character. Moreover, even at the height of what Shihab calls 'a one-sided rivalry', the two men are able to put aside all 'petty' personal grudges (including a past street brawl) and fight bravely and competently for the greater good of Iraq. On his deathbed, Khidr gives Shihab his blessing to marry Shayma, but instead Shihab slaps her on the face for being insensitive (read unpatriotic) and takes Khidr's lonely mother under his wing instead. Unconsummated marriages like Shihab and Shayma's in *Dancing on the Shoulders of Death*, Fa'iz and Prishnak in *The Third Troupe* and Sabah and Shatrin in Saddam's

The Fortified Castle seem to undermine (inadvertently perhaps) the utopian ideal of Iraqi unity on which state-sponsored texts rely. The mother who is given precedence here over a potential lover and wife, represents a national identity that is older and more rooted, whereas the fragile 'newness' of the nation-state as represented by a younger, frivolous woman is forgone.

Jāsim al-Raṣīf's last two novels *Khatt ahmar* (*Red Line*), published in 1987, and *Hijabat al-jahim* (*The Veils of Hell*), published in 1988, are both first-person civilian accounts of the war. One cannot underestimate the significance of this stylistic shift, as for the first time, the focus is now on the suffering of Iraqis on the home front which would legitimate the state's decision to end the war. *Red Line* depicts Iraq as a broken nation with minor and unconvincing flashes of camaraderie and solidarity, as well as a weak and anti-climactic conclusion predicting imminent victory. Written in one of the lowest years in book production during the war, and after initial excitement and Iraqi confidence had worn off, the novel immediately stands out for the absence of the word 'Persian' to denote the enemy, as by this stage in the conflict, the term had acquired an inflammatory quality, which did not sit well with the disillusioned political climate of Iraq in the late 1980s. Unusually, the term is also absent in al-Raṣīf's first novel *The Third Troupe*, unlike almost all other early war novels. Although a highly charged and propagandistically effective term, using *farisi* (Persian) or even *'ajami* (non-Arab) to evoke age-old historic animosity between the modern warring nation-states, would have inappropriately highlighted racial differences in a novel set in Kurdistan. In *Red Line*, the pejorative use of 'Iranian' instead of 'Persian' or 'non-Arab' nonetheless indicates an acceptance of Iran as a legitimate nation-state and represents a notable shift in consciousness with a return to a concrete military and political reality rather than a preoccupation with the glories of a hazy and intangible past. *Red Line* also exhibits other important departures from *The Third Troupe* and early war novels, notably the undermining of certain 'grand narratives', such as pan-Arabism, Iraqi nationalism and, significantly for women, the family as a microcosm of the Iraqi nation. This shift comes as disappointment and impatience with the war begin to mount and the strain on Iraq's infrastructure and economy begins to show.

The novel is divided into four parts, representing the first four years of war with Iran. The four parts of the novel correspond to its main characters, all natives of the town of Basra: Hamid 'Ubaid , a gardener and old widower with two children, Basma and Hassan; 'Abdullah 'Ali, a young air pilot; 'Adil Hassan a young marine officer who competes with 'Abdullah for the love of a girl named Shadha; and, finally, Zuhair Talib, Shadha's father, the drunk head of a dysfunctional family. Hamid 'Ubaid can be considered the 'hero' of the novel; he is described as 'Ayyub' the Arab name for the biblical prophet Job whose name is synonymous with patience in Arab culture. By the end of the novel Hamid 'Ubaid loses both his children Basma and Hassan and must draw on his namesake for comfort and peace of mind. Salām 'Abbūd notes the shift from the courageous and impetuous characterisations of both military and civil figures from the early war period to what he calls the 'Ayyubian model' of the later period, of which Hamid 'Ubaid is an example.[85] The absence of mothers, like Hamid's wife or older matriarchs is striking, as it points to the symbolic absence of national origins. Indeed, there is a prevailing sense of alienation, anxiety and loneliness which is prevalent throughout the narrative of Hamid 'Ubaid. Moreover, there seems to be an invasion of the private space that had hitherto been reserved for women, signalling the emasculation of men in the novel, whilst simultaneously signifying the absence of the female voice even in the traditionally feminine sphere of the home. Despite its civilian setting, there is a significant presence of soldiers on leave in *Red Line*, while all-female gatherings are notably absent, signalling the exclusion of the female voice and the dominance of men in the home, as well as on the battle front. Male dominance of war narratives even when civilian accounts were encouraged highlights the unease with which the state attempted to market the cessation of hostilities as a victory. Due to vastly limited funds compared with the beginning of the war, fewer new writers emerged and older more established writers were entrusted with expressing the state's message, delicately balancing celebration of Iraq's imminent and supposed victory and aversion for war, whilst directing blame for Iraq's suffering and impoverishment away from the Ba'th.

The jovial and almost celebratory mood at the beginning of the novel steadily deteriorates, as not only is the protagonist's son Hassan reported 'missing' on the battlefield, but also his daughter Basma is killed in a raid on their house just before the 'victory' at Huwaiza, and the half-hearted public parades of joy on the street which ensue. There is a striking lack of conviction and enthusiasm exhibited by all the characters regarding the war in *Red Line*; patriotic songs on the radio have a deflating effect in the novel, unlike in the novels previously discussed. However, this attitude towards the war is not framed in terms of cowardice, but rather a humanitarian distaste for war which encompasses both the public and the Iraqi leadership: 'the leaders were unwilling to expand the war front, in the hope that the Iranians would agree to negotiate soon'.[86] In a clear reference to Iraqi and Arab nationalism, Zuhair Talib, the novel's drunk protagonist/antagonist adds rather philosophically: 'what cursed creature dreamt of unifying a human species bent on exterminating each other'.[87] Also, on being disturbed at 4 am to go on a counter-raid, air pilot 'Abdullah 'Ali also angrily exclaims: 'can a man not sleep in a war?'[88] The war is referred to as 'this damn war',[89] rather than the holy war it was deemed to be in earlier novels. It is described as 'a badly played football game, the results well-known in advance', and the marines complain of the 'boredom and depression of service'.[90] In fact, Iraqi teenagers are the only ones depicted as genuinely excited about the war, and their enthusiasm, although commendable, is considered somewhat naive and immature. Furthermore, some young men who are not genuinely interested in the war as an ideology, but rather as a kind of empty macho display of strength to attract women, are depicted as show-offs.[91] Thus, 'Abdullah warns his brother that he should be careful with his gun as he may be tempted 'to flaunt it in front of the frightened girls', especially as he does not yet know how to use it. The 'childlike enthusiasm' of Hassan, a high school student, is almost comical as he gets into a brawl over a piece of glass which fell from an enemy plane at the beginning of the novel. He breathlessly tells his father: 'I will make you a rosary out of this glass. This is not just any old glass, look!'[92] This scene almost directly parodies an episode from *Dancing on the Shoulders of Death*, where the men in the cafe ask a soldier to bring them a memento from the battlefield.

Despite lacking any enthusiasm about the war, the usual marker of the 'merit' of a character in Iraqi war novels, Hamid 'Ubaid remains a positive character. He complains throughout the novel about the seemingly endless war exclaiming 'Until when my lord!? Until when!?',[93] and expresses his terror, and that of most of the citizens of Basra, of being killed in an Iranian air raid. This forms a marked contrast to the situation in *Dancing on the*

Shoulders of Death, where the whole city goes about its normal business in defiance, and children run up to the roofs of houses to watch enemy planes explode like fireworks. Nevertheless, Hamid 'Ubaid is commended for the sacrifices he makes for his children: from moving to Basra from his native town, to his refusal to remarry after the death of his young wife from typhoid. The absence of 'Ubaid 's wife and the mother of his children signifies the exclusion of women's voices even in civilian accounts and the traditionally 'female' space: the home, which is now a new space for men to exercise their power after the impotence felt in the war and its aftermath. This foreshadows many of the changes experienced in Iraqi society post-war, which can be explained by some theoretical findings on authoritarianism and patriarchy. Many feminist thinkers have explained the encroachment of men into the affairs and space of women as a 'compensating mechanism' to make up for the resentment and impotence felt by men vis-à-vis authoritarian power. In Iraq, the curtailing of women's rights and freedoms towards the end of the war became apparent, such as the introduction of a law forbiding a woman from travelling without the consent of her male guardian. The Ba'th's more conservative outlook on women's issues was influenced by political factors, such as Saddam's eagerness to tap into a new powerbase, tribal groups, as a dependable support force in the tumultuous period from the end of the war to the intifada in 1991.

As well as being a dedicated husband and family man, Hamid 'Ubaid is the quintessential Iraqi worker, and is used in *Red Line* as a means of expressing class conflict during the war, an issue which had never been discussed in the author's previous works, or in early war novels generally. The introduction of class as a marker not only of difference, but also as a marker of conflict and social schism within the supposed socialist utopia of the Ba'th, poses many questions regarding the Iraqi nation itself as a unified entity, and by extension, the 'enemy' which it seeks to eradicate. Hamid 'Ubaid comments bitterly that 'only the poor are crushed by war'[94] and is hurt when a client accuses him of lying about the cost of certain seeds for his garden:

> Even the 'new money' real estate's contractor, rat of the 'five-year plan', shouted in his face: 'you untrustworthy scum!' Who is untrustworthy these days? The poor who are blocking enemy fire with their chests, or the rich

> who are hiding their children from [military] service under various covers: medical reports, personal protection?! There is no trust in this world because the rich exist in it. He nearly screamed in the alleyway.[95]

When his only son goes missing in battle, ʿUbaid also bitterly reflects that 'the sons of barefoot workers in the palace of the rich are the fortresses of the nation . . . if you give us some money, then our children are giving your lives; so why this arrogance and empty pride?'[96] The inequality in the rights and obligations of citizens has a profound negative effect on the sense of national pride and camaraderie in the novel. Suspicion and distrust towards the corrupt rich prompt the drunk Zuhair Talib to be sceptical about the accounts of citizens' donations to the war effort publicised on state radio: 'gold and money – from where do all these people get this money during a war?'[97]

Despite its criticisms of certain sectors of Iraqi society and its detailing of some of the horrors of war, *Red Line* does not free itself completely from the ideology it espouses in order to achieve a full post-modern or 'fragmented' quality. Al-Raṣīf manages to avoid accusations of opposing the state by balancing criticisms with propagandistic elements and rhetoric. For example, in one of the rare moments of genuine self-sacrifice for the nation in the novel, a taxi driver friend of Hamid ʿUbaid loses his car in an Iranian air raid, and although it is his only source of income and he has eleven mouths to feed, he tells the neighbourhood men who try to put out the fire: 'let it burn. It is not worth one drop of blood from our soldiers in the East – let it be!'[98] Subsequently, all these men attempt to help him financially, thereby highlighting an idealised national solidarity, but exclusively among the working class. As with almost every Iraqi war novel, however, human and personal tragedies of war are dismissed in *Red Line*. When ʿAbdullah ʿAli's pilot friend Fahim, due to marry soon, is killed, Abdullah's superior reprimands him for showing excessive emotion:

> We did not send you on a picnic on the seaside in Basra so that you could cry over a comrade you lost there. We are in a war, and there are no emotions in wars. Orders – executing orders with precision – that is all. The homeland is above emotions, and I do not permit any of my officers to do what you are doing now . . . the homeland is above all these petty personal collapses.[99]

Dismissing emotion and privileging reason, the traditional binaries of female and male, is essentially a silencing of women, whom we do not see in mourning at all in the novel.

The kind of stoic rhetoric espoused by 'Abdullah 'Ali's commander would have been accepted unquestioningly by a character from a novel written at the beginning of the war, but is not as easily sustained in a novel published in 1987, and 'Abdullah is unconvinced:

> What kind of heaven will welcome you after being torn apart in the hell that is earth? And what can heaven do to bring together a soul as young as the earth itself? What heavenly celebration will occur when it is time for your sombre wedding which will never take place on this bombarded, corpse-filled earth? What grief will your departure leave behind? What gasp of longing will your mother moan when she sees your body wrapped in the flag?! What tears will your beloved shed? Lieutenant Sir! Is this how life ends in fleeting seconds in a report on battle?

Here even the religious rhetoric of heaven and hell is challenged as the 'martyr' is depicted as a tortured soul rather than an angel of heaven, despite the supposed 'legendary calm in the face of certain death'[100] of Iraqi soldiers. The novel does not conform to religious rhetoric and mocks it on several occasions, particularly towards the end, when mocking enemy religious zeal. Exclamations such as 'God is with us and with our children because we are right!'[101] are few and far between and are framed in terms of wishful thinking and self-reassurance rather than actual conviction. 'Abdullah sobs in his car in his grief at the loss of a friend and expresses his desire to 'cry in the arms of his mother like he used to as child', which is juxtaposed against the bombardment of 'incessant patriotic songs on the radio'.[102] These songs, which like Abdullah's superior, emphasise the community's wellbeing over that of the individual, seem empty and meaningless in the light of intense and personal human tragedy. Mothering images in this passage imply mourning and emotional fragility and serve as a reminder of the broken families and absent mothers in the novel. Moreover, the emphasis on maternal bonds seems to undermine national ones, as an image of a wounded motherland takes precedence over a potentially victorious fatherland.

The potentially resistive aspect of al-Raṣīf's novel is neutralised by his explicit alignment with the rhetoric of state propaganda. For example, internal threats to the state's hegemony are the object of uncompromising attacks in the novel. 'Adil Hassan turns his deserter brother Muhammad in to the authorities,[103] which is why he is named "Adil', 'the just one'. 'Adil bitterly discusses the shame and dishonour his brother has brought to the family after evading military service several times during the novel.[104] Also, 'Abdullah 'Ali's brother is shot by unknown assailants who are labelled 'mercenaries of the enemy',[105] thereby giving a general impression of Basra, the Shia capital of the south, as unsafe and treacherous. Basma, Hamid 'Ubaid 's daughter, reflects on this incident: 'she thought about the reasons why "unknown" attackers open fire on two young men on their way back from fulfilling a national duty. They are enemies then! Enemies who betray for a price; how awful it is for one to betray his people!'[106] The shift from focusing on the external enemy to the internal one as advised in state critical works, such as Mukhīf's, reflected the increasingly stifling atmosphere in Iraq, where the rise in the number of desertions among the armed forces led to draconian state measures to catch and punish deserters, whilst conflating military absenteeism and desertion with political dissent and treason.[107] Adel's fear about the potential soiling of his family's name due to the desertion of his brother reflects the genuine fear felt by Iraqi families who often disowned their children to avoid being punished for their desertion.

Material losses caused by Iranian inhumanity and disregard for innocent human life are measured according to the potential benefit they would have had on the lives of the poor. After saying that 150 Iranian planes had been shot down in the war so far, a friend of Hamid 'Ubaid says: 'they would have been better off buying bread for their hungry with that money'.[108] Also, reports of the death of a shepherd with his cattle herd north of Basra causes even the usually apathetic drunk Zuhair Talib to exclaim 'what putrid minds! If only they had made toys instead of planes, then they would have brought happiness to all the children of the world.'[109] Iranian war crimes are so heinous that a doctor almost loses his mind when his medical crew are unable to separate siblings who die in each other's arms when their house is bombed by an Iranian war plane.[110] Furthermore, a five-year-old girl becomes dumb after a bomb exploded killing all her family while they were having dinner.[111] Mounting civilian casualties provoke reflections on human beings' potential for evil: 'how can human beings dare to kill whole families, unarmed families merely out of hatred? Is this how war should be?'[112] The Iraqi response is to 'avoid civilian targets unless the Iranians continue to hit civilian targets',[113] which is an interesting shift from earlier novels in which Iraqis show restraint at all times.

The reference to casualties among children, and in particular female children, in a reportage style which does not humanise the victim, serves to channel the emotions of sympathy into outrage and anger against the enemy, which is precisely the aim of war propaganda. Cynthia Enloe notes how discourses during war deal with 'womenandchildren' [sic] together as one block thereby fusing women to the nation's collective future as a macrocosm of the family.[114] As collateral damage, women in *Red Line* serve as a symbol of Iranian barbarism, but at the same time the personal grief of individual women is not voiced as this would indicate national weakness. The management and control of expressions of sorrow and grief which are projected and voiced through men point to a crisis in masculinity which validates the need to reinforce the patriarchal order by stripping women of agency.

The use-value of literary accounts written from a civilian perspective to provide an outlet for public discontent and to prepare Iraqis for a peace that was pre-decided by the state was very high. However, instead of giving opportunities to new female writers to produce works from the civilian perspective, just as young and inexperienced male writers had done so at the beginning of the war, state-endorsed propaganda novels were produced by experienced male writers like al-Raṣīf in order to ensure that expressions of resentment or frustration were contained, and to guarantee that the delicately balanced messages of the state regarding the impending peace with Iran were conveyed as accurately as possible. Moreover, the war had exhausted the state economically, thus it was more efficient to entrust writers that were well known to the state with the task of marketing the war as a victory for Iraq. Male dominance of civilian war narratives is representative of the gradual male encroachment into the female sphere in order to regulate and control female activities, which would progressively increase after the war with the adoption of conservative discourses drawn from tribal values and Islamism. I have chosen to analyse works by the same author, supplemented by similar texts, to gauge this shift from 'progressive' to more traditional discourses on women, and to highlight the way in which pro-war texts followed state discourses regardless of their authors' personal preferences. The constant need to mobilise men and the traditional configurations of masculinity espoused by the state to meet the demands of war led to the marginalisation, and at times complete exclusion of the female voice and feminine responses to the war.

Notes

1. Kanan Makiya, *Republic of Fear: the Politics of Modern Iraq* (Berkeley: University of California Press, 1989), pp. 84–7.
2. Miriam Cooke, *Women and the War Story* (Berkeley: University of California Press, 1997), p. 221. Nadje Al-Ali notes that the state also provided free childcare and transportation to and from work, as well as generous maternity benefits for working mothers. Nadje Al-Ali, *Iraqi Women: Untold Stories*, p. 135.
3. For more on this, see Eric Davis, *Memories of State: Politics, History and Collective Identity in Modern Iraq* (Berkeley, University of California Press, 2005), pp. 161–6; and Makiya, *Republic of Fear*, pp. 84–5.
4. Rizk Khoury, *Iraq in Wartime*, p. 76.
5. Achim Rohde, 'Opportunities for Masculinity and Love: Cultural Production in Baʿthist Iraq during the 1980s', in Lahoucine Ouzgane (ed.), *Islamic Masculinities* (London: Zed Books, 2006), pp. 185–90.
6. In fact, the issue of female military service was a sensitive one, and when the first female combat pilots enrolled and graduated from the Air Force Academy (in no small part due to the pressure of GFIW) there was very little media coverage of the event. Rohde, *State–Society Relations in Baʿthist Iraq*, pp. 86–8.
7. Noga Efrati, 'Productive or Reproductive? The Roles of Women during the Iraq–Iran War', *Middle Eastern Studies* 35(2) (1999): 27–44.
8. Ibrāhīm Birjāwī, *Mushāhadāt ṣaḥāfī ʿarabī ʿalā al-jabhah: min zākhū ilā al-fāw* (Baghdād: Dār Wāsiṭ, 1987).
9. See Samir Al-Khalil, *The Monument: Art, Vulgarity, and Responsibility in Iraq* (Berkeley: University of California Press, 1991).
10. This 'defensive' Islamic shift occurs towards the end of 1986, but as Jerry Long and Ofra Bengio have noted, the 'appropriative Islamic stage' only really begins with the invasion of Kuwait. Jerry M. Long, *Saddam's War of Words: Politics, Religion and the Iraqi Invasion of Kuwait* (Austin, TX: University of Texas, 2004); Ofra Bengio, *Saddam's Word: Political Discourse in Iraq* (New York: Oxford University Press, 1998).

11. Davis, *Memories of State*, pp. 198–9.
12. See Ṭālib, *al- Ḥarb fī al-qiṣṣa al-'irāqīyya*, for a detailed list of all the short stories published in the first twenty months of the war, their date of publication, and which newspapers published them. Ṭālib, *al-Ḥarb fī al-qiṣṣa al-'irāqīyya*, pp. 111–31.
13. Ibid., p. 75 (my emphasis).
14. Erol Köroğlu, *Ottoman Propaganda and Turkish Identity: Literature in Turkey during World War I* (London: Tauris Academic Studies, 2007), p. xx.
15. 'Alī 'Abd al-Ḥusayn Mukhīf, *Fī qiṣṣat al-ḥarb: dirāsa naqdīyya* (Baghdād: al-Jumhūrīya al-'Irāqīya, Wizārat al-Thaqāfa wa-al-I'lām, Dā'irat al-Shu'ūn al-Thaqāfiyya wa al-Nashr, 1984), p. 12.
16. Cooke, *Women and the War Story*, p. 245.
17. Kadhim, 'Widows' Doomsday', p. 148.
18. Cooke, *Women and the War Story*, p. 241.
19. Wiebke Walther, "Review of Women and the War Story, by Miriam Cooke . . .', *Die Welt des Islams* 40(3) (2000): 425–8.
20. Rohde, *State–Society Relations in Ba'thist Iraq*, p. 13.
21. Rizk Khoury, *Iraq in Wartime*, p. 184.
22. Ibid., p. 9.
23. 'Abd al-Laṭīf al-Ḥirz, *al-Mustaḥīl fī al-adab al-'irāqī: istinbāṭāt al-naṣṣ al-jadīd wa rāhin al-mashhad al-thaqāfī fī zaman al-iḥtilāl*, silsilat gharīb 'ala al-ṭarīq (Bayrūt: Dār al-Fārābi, 2008), p. 30.
24. Ṭālib, *al-Ḥarb fī al-qiṣṣa al-'irāqīyya*, p. 77.
25. Ṭālib criticises the 'journalistic style' of writers several times, for example, on pp. 149, 162, 173 and 214 of *al-Ḥarb fī al-qiṣṣa al-'irāqīyya*. 'Alī 'Abd al-Ḥusayn Mukhīf also criticises the reliance on newspaper reports in Iraqi literature before the Iran–Iraq War during the Arab–Israeli wars. Mukhīf, *Fī qiṣṣat al-ḥarb*, pp. 26, 27.
26. Samah Selim, *The Novel and the Rural Imaginary in Egypt 1880–1985* (New York: RoutledgeCurzon, 2004), p. 67. 'Abbūd refers to this 'documentary' style as *al-tawthīq al-ikhabarī*, 'news documenting'. 'Abbūd, *Thaqāfat al-'unf fī al-'irāq*, p. 222.
27. There are many examples in modern literature, Arabic or otherwise, of great writers who are both journalists and creative writers, so I do not want to make the general claim that the spheres of media and literature should be mutually exclusive.
28. An example of this is 'Ādil 'Abd al-Jabbār's *Qirā'āt fī yawmiyāt muqātil*, which

is the subject of detailed literary analysis by Mukhīf's study. Mukhīf, *Fī qiṣṣat al-ḥarb*, pp. 75–87.

29. ʿAbbūd, *Thaqāfat al-ʿunf fi al-ʿIrāq*, p. 28.
30. Ṭālib, *al-Ḥarb fī al-qiṣṣa al-ʿirāqīyya*, p. 110.
31. ʿAbd al-Sattār al-Nāṣir, *al-Shahīd 1777* (Baghdād: Wizārat al-Thaqāfa wa-al-Iʿlām, 1981), p. 6.
32. ʿĀdil ʿAbd al-Jabbār, *al-Raqṣ ʿala aktāf al-mawt* (Baghdād: Dār al-Thawra, 1981), p. 196.
33. Aḥmad Qabbānī, *al-Sabʿ yaḍḥak* (Wizārat al-Thaqāfa wa-al-Iʿlām, 1985), p. 129.
34. Jāsim al-Raṣīf, *al-Faṣīl al-thālith* (Baghdād: Wizārat al-Thaqāfa wa al-Iʿlām, 1983), p. 241.
35. Suleiman and Muhawi, *Literature and Nation in the Middle East*, p. 229.
36. Mukhīf, *Fī qiṣṣat al-ḥarb*, p. 141.
37. Ibid., p. 181.
38. Ibid., p. 177.
39. Ibid., pp. 118, 127.
40. Ibid., pp. 137, 144, 136.
41. According to Mukhīf, war literature should propagate peace and highlight the lofty ideals and superior morals of Iraq. Ibid., pp. 6, 40, 71, 77.
42. Ibid., p. 93.
43. Ibid., p. 26.
44. Rizk Khoury, *Iraq in Wartime*, p. 58.
45. Riding the Islamic tide towards the end of the war entailed an abandonment of the 'secular' novel in the favour of a genre more amenable to Islamic themes, like drama. See ʿUmar Ṭālib, *Malāmiḥ al-masraḥīya al-ʿarabīya al-islāmīya* (al-Maghrib: Dār al-Āfāq al-Jadīda, 1987). A Baʿth Party manual had encouraged the formation of mobile theatre troupes as part of their programme of 'national agitation'. *al-Minhāj al-thaqafī al-markazī*: Ḥizb al-Baʿth al-ʿArabī al-Ishtirākī, al-Qiyādah al-Qawmīyah (Baghdād: Maktab al-Thaqāfah wa-al-Iʿlām, 1977), p. 281. During the Iran–Iraq War, there was a military theatre troupe *al-masraḥ al-ʿaskarī* which presented shows to the troops, as well as the general public through televised recordings of these shows. See, for example, at: http://www.youtube.com/watch?v=5PbAZSioEFc, last accessed 25 March 2019.
46. Jean Paul Sartre, *Qu'est-ce que la Littérature?* (Paris: Gallimard, 1948), pp. 24–8. Panegyric poetry was also produced during the war, and in line with Arab tradition. The use of the novel, however, was unprecedented.

47. Jāsim al-Raṣīf, *Ru'ūs al-ḥurriya al-mukayasa* (Bayrūt: al-Mu'assasa al-'Arabiya li-al-dirāsāt wa al-Nashr, 2007).
48. Available at: http://arraseef.blogspot.co.uk, last accessed 11 December 2018.
49. See at: https://www.kataranovels.com/novelist/%d8%ac%d8%a7%d8%b3%d9%85-%d8%a7%d9%84%d8%b1%d8%b5%d9%8a%d9%81, last accessed 1 November 2019.
50. 'Abbūd, *Thaqāfat al-'unf fi al-'Irāq*, p. 37.
51. Nadje Al-Ali, *Iraqi Women: Untold Stories*, pp. 265–6.
52. David Ghanim, *Gender and Violence in the Middle East* (Westport, CT: Praeger, 2009), p. 211.
53. Fatima Mernissi, *The Veil and the Male Elite: a Feminist Interpretation of Women's Rights in Islam* (New York: Basic Books, 1991), p.170.
54. The secret is divulged to the reader at the end of the novel, but it dies with the 'martyred' Prishnak who cannot inform her mother in time. Al-Raṣīf, *al-Faṣīl al-thālith*, pp. 333–4.
55. Ibid., p. 72.
56. Ibid., p. 207.
57. Ibid., pp. 141–2.
58. Al-Raṣīf does not depart from the norm when recounting acts of enemy cruelty, in this case perpetrated by Kurdish rebels, including various human rights abuses and collective punishment against civilians such as random shootings and bombings, and the burning of houses belonging to soldiers in the Popular Army. Ibid., pp. 194, 200, among others.
59. Ibid., p. 139.
60. Glorious or honourable women, a term used and popularised (but not necessarily coined) by Saddam.
61. Although there are young Kurds below the conscription age who try to join the Popular Army in the novel (al-Raṣīf, *al-Faṣīl al-thālith*, p. 160), these are mentioned casually and we do not actually meet any, which is unconvincing.
62. Ibid., pp. 131–2.
63. Ibid., pp. 137–8.
64. Ibid., p. 214.
65. Ibid., p. 265.
66. Ibid., p. 12.
67. Ibid., p. 17.
68. Ibid., p. 18.
69. Ibid., p. 16.

70. Ibid., p. 12.
71. Ibid., p. 316.
72. Ibid., p. 243.
73. Ibid., p. 212.
74. Ibid., p. 286.
75. Ibid., p. 213.
76. Ibid., p. 245.
77. Ibid., p. 219.
78. Ibid., p. 16.
79. Ibid., p. 300.
80. Ibid., p. 135.
81. ʿAbbūd, *Thaqāfat al-ʿunf fī al-ʿirāq*, p. 46.
82. Al-Jabbār, *al-Raqṣ ʿalā aktāf al-mawt*, p. 146. Another novel of the war was titled *al-Ḥidād lā yalīq bi-al-shuhadāʾ* (*Mourning is not Appropriate for Martyrs*).
83. Sharam Chubin and Charles Tripp, *Iran and Iraq at War* (London: I. B. Tauris, 1988), p. 21.
84. Benedict Anderson's comments on *Huckleberry Finn* are perhaps pertinent here as the friendship between the black slave Jim and white boy Huck is designed to represent a national reconciliation of sorts. Anderson, *Imagined Communities*, p. 203.
85. ʿAbbūd, *Thaqāfat al-ʿunf fī al-ʿIrāq*, p. 266.
86. Jāsim al-Raṣīf, *Khaṭṭ aḥmar*, al-Ṭabʿah 2 (Bayrūt: al-Muʿassasa al-ʿArabīya li-al-dirāsāt wa al-Nashr; ʿAmmān: Dār al-Fāris, 2000), p. 67.
87. Ibid,, p. 236.
88. Ibid., p. 156.
89. Ibid., p. 251.
90. Ibid., p. 351.
91. Ibid., p. 40.
92. Ibid., p. 56.
93. Ibid., p. 150.
94. Ibid., p. 178.
95. Ibid., p. 280.
96. Ibid., p. 367.
97. Ibid., p. 267.
98. Ibid., p. 222.
99. Ibid., p. 117.
100. Ibid., p. 143.

101. Ibid., p. 179.
102. Ibid., p. 144.
103. Ibid., p. 70.
104. Ibid., p. 261.
105. Ibid., p. 188.
106. Ibid., p. 196.
107. Rizk Khoury, *Iraq in Wartime*, p. 73.
108. Ibid., p. 153.
109. Ibid., p. 107.
110. Ibid., p. 197.
111. Ibid., p. 301.
112. Ibid., p. 47.
113. Ibid., p. 23.
114. Enloe, 'Womenandchildren'.

2

The Infamous Iraqi *Majidat*: Chastity, Chivalry and Collective Identity in the Novels of Saddam Hussein

Any study of the literary work of Saddam Hussein will inevitably be overshadowed by its author. In his review of *Ukhruj minha ya mal'un* (*Get Out, Damned One!*), Saddam's penultimate novel published posthumously in 2003, Iraqi novelist Fu'ād al-Takirlī explains that 'these days writing a review of a literary work does not draw any attention, but this review acquires a new meaning when its author is a man named Saddam Hussein'.[1] The politicisation of literary criticism, be it oppositional or state-sponsored, is symptomatic of the embattled nature of Iraq's cultural landscape under the Ba'th, where appraisals of literary texts became proxified attacks or vindications of political positions. Whether Saddam Hussein actually wrote his four novels, or whether this task was assigned to a single ghost writer or a panel is irrelevant, as the use of textual evidence to prove the dictator's intellectual capability represented the epitome of the state's appropriation of the novel as a symbol of national culture. By the time he had written the novels, Saddam was isolated politically, and Iraq was crippled economically after over a decade of sanctions which had severely affected all forms of publishing, including literary production, which had been so bombastic in the 1980s. The Ba'th's other symbolic marker of progress also experienced discursive and legislative setbacks. The regression in women's legal rights and social status in Iraqi society had persisted since the Iran–Iraq War and Saddam's appeasement, through conservative laws, of the tribal powerbase which had supported him during the 1991 intifada. In this vein, Adeed Dawisha asserts: 'women, too, would have their freedoms curtailed as they now, in this last decade of the 20th century, would be prohibited from travel abroad unless accompanied by a male relative from the paternal side of their immediate family. All this was done to a chorus of mounting emphasis on religious symbolism, which in itself constituted a repudiation of the modernism and secularism of city attitudes, so alien to tribal sensitivities.'[2] Ironically, Saddam Hussein's sudden espousal of the literary medium allowed for the re-adoption of 'liberal' discourses vis-à-vis women to enhance the cultured and progressive image that he desperately attempted to project in the face of mounting attacks against him as evil and barbaric. At the same time, literary narratives framed as 'stories', fell within the realm of the symbolic, and therefore maintained the disconnect between the symbolic adulation of certain types of women, and the implementation of real policies and legislation. The priority in terms of soft power towards the end of Saddam Hussein's reign seemed to lie in the novel as marker of progress and national culture, with 'liberal' discourses on women featuring as a supporting subtext in novels which harkened back to the revolutionary Iraq of the 1970s.

Babylon in Iraq: Saddam's Historical Fantasies and the Feminine Symbol in *Zabiba and the King* and *Get Out, Damned One!*

Saddam's first novel *Zabiba and the King* (2001) is a fictional historical allegory set in ancient Iraq. The novel tells the story of a love affair between a married peasant girl named Zabiba and a fictional King Arab. Zabiba, who represents the people of Iraq, is raped by her abusive husband on 17 January (the date US-led forces were deployed to force Saddam out of Kuwait) and dies with King Arab whilst defending their country from foreign invaders. In a crass re-enactment of Saddam Hussein's televised purge of the Ba'th Party when he ascended to power in 1979, the final section of *Zabiba and the King* features a parliamentary debate after Zabiba and Arab's deaths, during which characters that represent 'undesirable' ethnic or social groups are symbolically purged by being thrown out of the assembly.

It is clear from the very name chosen by Saddam for the female protagonist of his first novel that he did not intend to depict the character realistically. The name Zabiba, meaning raisin, is almost comical and highlights her insignificant status as a downtrodden peasant, in stark contrast to the king in the title. As a peasant, Zabiba not only represents the common people, but the nation itself, in its purest and most romanticised form. This echoes other texts from the modern Arab literary tradition, such as Mohammed Ḥussein Haikal's (1888–1956) *Zainab* (1913), in which the peasant heroine Zainab represents the 'real Egypt', which has remained unchanged 'from the time of the Pharaohs through the rule of Ismael to the present day'.[3] In almost all manifestations of totalitarian propaganda, dictators have positioned themselves as fathers to their peoples. Interestingly, the relationship between Saddam and the Iraqi people in his first novel is represented as one of equals between Zabiba (called 'daughter of the people', 'the beloved of the people' and 'the conscience of the people') and the king, rather than a father–child relationship. In line with his propagandistic claims at espousing democratic ideals, Saddam uses this love affair, first, to indicate a bond that is based on shared values and ideals rather than blood, and, secondly, to give more 'power to the people', as it is Zabiba who influences many of the king's decisions and even converts him to monotheism as a symbol of his redemption.[4]

The rape of Zabiba on the date US-led forces launched the offensive in 1991 which eventually drove Iraqi forces out of Kuwait, thus symbolises the violation of a nation and galvanises the king to wage war in her defence. Zabiba fights heroically alongside the king in the ensuing battle, and even sacrifices her life to save him, which represents the sacrifice of the Iraqi people in defence of Arabness or *'uruba*. In a letter written on her death bed, Zabiba exclaims 'I die but long live King Arab!'.[5] This depiction of female militancy forms a marked contrast to the state's reluctance to depict women as fighters during the Iran–Iraq War, for fear that this would lead to an emasculation of Iraqi men. However, as the novel seems to have been directed to audiences outside Iraq, female militancy is taken as a badge of honour and as a sign of equality between men and women in the country. It also serves as a potential warning to foreign invaders that all of Iraq could easily be galvanised to its defence. The author's tolerance of Zabiba's adultery can, on one level, be interpreted as stemming from his supposed liberal views on women, aided by the fact that the characters in the novel are not Muslim and so are not subject to the strict Islamic codes governing sexuality. But, on the other hand, Zabiba is merely a symbol in the novel, so the moral implications of her adultery are secondary considerations in the context of nationalist allegory. Furthermore, her marriage to an abusive husband (representing America and its allies) is awkward allegorically and is a glaring flaw in the plot. It would have made more sense, for example, to have an outsider rape Zabiba as a symbol of Western aggression, rather than joining the Iraqi people and the United States in a metaphorical marriage. Notably, like Zabiba, the king also commits adultery and this is justified given the treachery of his wife and her attempts to conspire against his rule. Ultimately, adultery on the part of both the female and male protagonists in *Zabiba and the King* does not compromise the moral fibre of the characters due to the fact that on the level of the plot, they are both living with unworthy partners, and on a symbolic level their relationship goes beyond the physical union of two individuals.

Zabiba and the King's cover (Appendix 2, Figure 1) marks the text as a historical fantasy as opposed to either an allegory or an authentically historical text. It comprises a mysterious woman in a flowing dress walking on water in what appears to be a garden, set against a mythical backdrop of an arch and columns at sunset. The cover bears no relation to the events of the story itself, especially Zabiba's identity as a peasant, and sends a contradictory message, as it inadvertently distances the Arab reader from the allegorical aspect of the novel. However, the cover does situate the novel firmly on a symbolic terrain which accords the author more freedom to discuss delicate issues such as adultery and political change. In her analysis *Zabiba and the King*, al-Muḥsin explains Saddam's purpose for writing the novel thus:

> The most important, practical and logical explanation for this was his desire to exploit writing and fantasy in the game of exchange and replacement *in which it becomes possible to manipulate factual and material truths and replace them with fantasy*. The novel's mission goes beyond mere mobilisation and constitutes a role reversal between word and reality . . . the process of brainwashing represented by speeches, slogans and everyday media hype signifies forcefully imposing an illusion in the place of reality. Herein lies the mission assigned to this novel (if it can indeed be called a novel): it attempts to prove its author's adherence to democratic ideals and the rule of the people; and although Saddam was not perceptive enough to be able to hide the inconsistencies in his text which prove otherwise, the work does indeed achieve its intended purpose which is to demonstrate his adoration for his people.[6]

In this passage, al-Muḥsin highlights the 'compensatory' function of the utopian discourses in *Zabiba and the King* which can equally be applied to some of Saddam Hussein's other novels. King Arab/Saddam's supposed dedication to women's rights, democracy and a harmonious multicultural body are discursive replacements of actual inequalities in Iraq under Baʿthist rule. In many ways the very function of ideology is the representation of the imaginary relationship of individuals to their real, often material, conditions of existence. Zabiba's sacrifice for her king constitutes one of the many inconsistencies of the 'democratic' discourse Fāṭima al-Muḥsin refers to, as ideally, it is the King who should sacrifice himself for the sake of his people and not the opposite. A feminist approach might equally question why selflessness and self-sacrifice are depicted as commendable feminine attributes, whereas selfishness in men is very often tolerated, if not celebrated, as will become clear in the analysis of *Men and a City*. The idealisation of Zabiba, Saddam's almost infallible heroine, highlights the tension between woman as symbol and woman as a realistic literary persona. Moreover, it also seems to highlight anxiety about Iraq as a nation: is it a vulnerable entity to be protected or is it a country of revolutions that will remain glorious with or without its King/Saddam?

After the deaths of Zabiba and Arab, a national assembly is formed to manage the country, and undesirables such as feudalists and foreigners are publicly humiliated and purged in a way which would have resonated with those familiar with Saddam's highly televised purge of the Baʿth Party on 22 July 1979 where members' names were called out and they were escorted outside the hall to be imprisoned and executed. This ending leaves the reader in doubt as to whether the proposed democratic transition of King Arab's country (encouraged by Zabiba) is actually viable or genuine given the reluctance to include minorities or different social classes. Although events in the novel take place in ancient Babylon, the text's symbolic plane is that of the modern Iraqi nation-state, which the characters constantly refer to as 'our country'. The crucial role of an 'immemorial' past in the construction of the 'myth' of the nation has been discussed by Benedict Anderson as providing a continuity and sense of authenticity to a newly constructed state. This 'myth-making' is especially strong in nations which assume a particularly 'glorious' ancient history such as Egypt and Iraq.[7] The 2004 translation of the novel even includes a map of Iraq, in which both ancient and modern cities are marked. The Iraqi nation-state is represented in the 'People's Assembly' scene at the end of the novel in which a number of 'good' and 'bad' characters are allowed to voice their opinions on their ideal ruling system. In the absence of the redeemed dead king from these discussions, the text conveniently finds new enemies to blame for the nation's troubles and dismisses them one by one. These include some of the 'eternal enemies' of the Ba'th: feudalists, communists and Zionists (often conflated with Jews), as well as specific members of Saddam's political opposition, such as the leader of the Iraqi National Congress (INC), Ahmed Chalabi, and senior leader in the Islamic Da'wa Party, Nuri al-Maliki, jointly referred to as Nuri Chalabi. Ironically, the author then projects the king's own 'crime' of being an absolute ruler on to the figure of Nuri Chalabi who is discredited as an imposter and described as a staunch monarchist.

Particularly strong criticism is reserved for land-owning feudalists in *Zabiba and the King*. Zabiba and her family work for a cruel Jewish landowner named Ḥasqil (Arabic for Ezekiel), who overworks them and denies peasants a decent wage. The feudal lord who is dismissed from the People's Assembly at the very end of the novel is described as a city-dweller (with a Jewish mother) who is concerned only with the 'harvest of the earth and not its roots'.[8] During this scene, a female peasant named Zahra' (a jarringly Islamic, and specifically Shia name) mocks this unnamed feudalist for his ambiguous origins, and lectures him on the importance of 'roots' and '*nasab*' using the metaphor of a tree: 'the fruit of a good (*tayyib*) tree is good and the fruit of a bad (*khabith*) tree is bad and he who does not know his paternal or maternal uncles can easily admit foreigners into our country under the pretence of being his relations'.[9] The religious connotations of this speech are clear, as this echoes the Qur'an: 'seest thou not how Allah coineth a similitude: a goodly saying, as a goodly tree, its root set firm, its branches reaching into heaven. Giving its fruit at every season by permission of its lord . . . and the similitude of a bad saying is as a bad tree, uprooted from upon the earth, possessing no stability'.[10] Trees in the text ultimately represent a nation's '*asala*' (authenticity) and deep-rootedness, as well as its sacredness. In some ways the country–city divide expounded in *Zabiba and the King* is a general socialist concern, completely in line with Ba'thist ideology, and is also a characteristic of nationalist writings. However, the divide also features in totalitarian propaganda generally in which a deep yearning is expressed for 'a womb-like purity and return to the earth'.[11] For example, in his short story collection *The Village the Village, the Earth the Earth and the Suicide of the Astronaut*, Libyan President Muammar Qaddafi also expresses his disgust at the 'nightmarish' city[12] and envisions a heavenly escape to the utopia of rural life.[13]

Despite the constant reference to the 'foreigners' inhabiting the nation, real conflict and treachery appears in the family unit, as those conspiring against the king are his wife, cousins and half-brothers (the sons of concubines, and so of decidedly inferior stock according to the author, and therefore more likely to engage in dishonourable acts).[14] Ofra Bengio notes how King Arab is loved by his sisters but hated by his conspiring stepbrothers, and believes this to be indicative of Saddam's own personal experiences of paternal abandonment and betrayal.[15] The text's redemption of the king in *Zabiba and the King* plays a key role in conveying its propagandistic message; although the revolutionaries affirm the evils of the monarchic ruling system, they admit that 'this King is better than previous kings'[16] (he has fewer wives, for example, an indication that he is progressive). They also bear him 'no ill will' because he fought alongside them and above all because 'Zabiba loved him'[17] in spite of his faults and gave him her blessing in a letter written on her death bed.

Whereas in *Zabiba and the King* conspiracies are directed against an individual (King Arab) from within his own family, this expands to become conspiracies against all Arabs and Muslims in *Get Out, Damned One!* This novel's symbolic plane is more expansive, which is clear from its quasi-biblical beginning, with the story of Ibrahim (the equivalent of the biblical Abraham in Arabic) and his three sons who represent the monotheistic religions of Judaism, Christianity and Islam. This family led a nomadic existence 1,500 years ago in Babylon, it says, despite the fact that Babylon predates the Arabs and the rise of Islam by thousands of years. Furthermore, the country presented in the text is essentially a collection of tribes, who are depicted as Arabic-speakers. The initial conflict in *Get Out, Damned One!* involves Hasqil, the character who represents the Jewish tradition, who is disowned and exiled by his father Ibrahim for his jealousy and attempts to hurt his brother Mahmud (representative of Islam). Hasqil then seeks refuge with a group called the 'desperate tribe', only to repay their hospitality by overthrowing their leader and bedding his foreign wife. The leader's daughter Ladha then organises a rebellion against Hasqil and the powerful foreign allies he has made to secure his power (labelled 'Romans' in the novel). The novel ends with the collapse of two towers built by Hasqil's allies in a suicide mission organised by the Arabs and their female leader. Significantly, Ladha (pleasure) changes her name and transforms into Nakhwa[18] (chivalry) to symbolise the shift in the Iraqi nation, from being 'used for pleasure' by greedy foreign powers, to acquiring honour and independence, and freeing itself from the shackles of imperialism.

Historical accuracy and consistency on the part of the author is replaced by a myriad of often contradictory cultural signifiers drawn from disparate discourses. Saddam's choice of a Babylonian setting in *Get Out, Damned One!* thus allowed him to depict an immemorial conflict between Arabs, 'Romans' and Jews in the same way the Iran–Iraq War was portrayed as part of an eternal struggle between Arabs and Persians. However, other potent discourses were also thrown into the mix, which highlights the Machiavellian quality of Baʿthist ideology, particularly its appeal to Islamic and tribal sensitivities when these discourses became ascendant. The weaponisation of tribalism, Islamism, Mesopotamian or ancient Iraqism and Arab nationalism came as part of Saddam's final showdown with the West, and the random amalgam of discourses concentrated in one text was designed to hit several birds with one stone in this, his last novel. Supposedly written as bombs were falling on Baghdad in 2003, pan-Arab and Islamist discourses are stronger in *Get Out, Damned One!* than in *Zabiba and the King*, as Saddam aimed to unite the Arab camp with the looming foreign threat from the United States and NATO. Moreover, an Islamic discourse is also utilised in the form of direct quotations and paraphrased excerpts from the Qur'an, in order to frame the conflict as a 'holy war' against the Romans/Americans (although there are a few hints at the collusion of some Arabs with the Roman enemy through the oil trade, which is a clear reference to the Gulf States). The novel ends with *Allahu Akbar!* literally meaning God is Great; a phrase that is commonly chanted by Muslims during wars to summon divine aid. Alongside its Arab and Muslim audience, the text is also directed at a Western audience, as a warning against a then imminent invasion, with the message that the bravery and resilience of Iraqis will never be defeated.

Get Out, Damned One! seems to be an extension of the Ba'th effort to 'Arabise' history (*ta'rib al-tarikh*), which often meant politicising history so it is relived in the present. The text 'Arabises' ancient Babylon, including the protagonist Ibrahim and his family who are depicted as Arabs (interestingly, rather than Babylonians or even Iraqis). After his attempts to 'castrate' Mahmud by bringing a hot coal close to his genitals, Hasqil is cursed by Ibrahim causing him to develop a lisp which prevents him from pronouncing letters from the Arabic language, especially the 'ra'.[19] This signals Hasqil's banishment and alienation from Arabism when he is deprived of his eloquence (*fasaha*).[20] The author drops the allegorical facade altogether when the 'Romans' propose a toast to Hasqil 'in 'a foreign language' using the word 'cheers'.[21] Hasqil and the Romans also greet each other with a handshake, unfamiliar to Arabs.[22] Symbolically, of course, Hasqil attempts to deprive Mahmud of his *rujula* (manliness), a concept that is essential to Saddam's neo-tribal discourse. As a result, it is he who loses his Arab authenticity (and by extension Arab values) when he no longer speaks Arabic. Language as a marker of Arab identity and *rujula* are intimately linked here, as non-Arab men in the text are depicted as effeminate, sexually perverse and cowardly.

The use of *furs* (Persians) or *'ajam* (originally meaning Persians but used for non-Arab-speakers generally) as derogatory terms has been a standard feature of the Iraqi novelistic tradition and political discourse since the war with Iran. Saddam uses both these terms in *Get Out, Damned One!* to denote a foreign menace and to allow himself to critique what he believed was an expression of *shu'ubiya*, defined by Ba'thist writer 'Abd al-Hādī Fukaykī as 'hatred of the Arabs and the desire to suppress their uniqueness'.[23] In many ways *al-shu'ubiya* is the ideological antithesis of Arab nationalism, and is personified in the novels by enemies living amongst the Arab community: the Jews and the Persians, who are depicted as slaves of Western imperialism. Interestingly, the term *'ajam* in the novel seems to refer to those who have mixed with the Arabs through marriage or those living among them, such as Ladha's mother and paternal grandmother, whilst the term *furs* is reserved for those outside the Arab nation. The danger of the *'ajam* is that they threaten to contaminate the racial purity of Arabs, thereby compromising Arab integrity, and this happens primarily through marriage to non-Arab women. Although Nakhwa is entrusted with leading revolutionaries to victory against Hasqil and his foreign allies, the underlying message of the novel is one of intolerance towards foreigners, and in particular, foreign women. This contradiction seems to stem mainly from structural weaknesses in the text, rather than deliberate nuance or ideological ambiguity.

The emphasis on Arabism has a direct impact on the representation of women as symbolic markers of the nation's honour and purity. Hasqil's moral bankruptcy is attributed to the 'foreign blood' passed on to him from his maternal uncles. The author uses the term '*irq najis*',[24] literally meaning 'impure vein' to denote this foreign blood. Likewise, Ladha's promiscuity is attributed to her *'ajami* origins. When she refuses his sexual advances, Ladha tells Hasqil that Arab women are not promiscuous like *'ajami* women, referring to her own mother who had readily acquiesced to having an affair with him. Although the mother is eventually redeemed for refusing to continue her affair with Hasqil, and is subsequently murdered for doing so, it remains ironic that Ladha should attack *'ajami* women because, of course, she too is of 'foreign blood', and from both sides of her family. Ladha's paternal grandmother is also *'ajamiya* which explains the shameful cowardice her father displays in battle. Despite inciting violence and schism, Hasqil is also too cowardly to participate in the fighting, and instead stays in the tribe to take advantage of its leader's absence, replacing him both as political leader and as the head of the house by bedding his wife; the ultimate act of betrayal. The moral of the story of *Get Out, Damned One!* is spelled out clearly: 'you should not let a foreigner manage your affairs'.[25]

There have been several published Arabic editions of *Get Out, Damned One!* and the paratextual information on the respective covers of each edition has managed to correspond to specific propaganda messages at the time of publication. Editions published after the US invasion of Iraq contain a clear intention to appropriate the text for the purposes of mobilisation, and instead of the anonymous 'by its author', Saddam's name appears clearly on the covers (Appendix 2, Figure 2) and the blurb of the book contains a dedication by Raghad Hussein to her father, which situates the text as resistance literature par excellence. This edition would privilege and emphasise the allegorical interpretation of the novel, aligning Nakhwa the heroine with Raghad Hussein. However, the illustrations on the cover of this edition do not give primacy to the female heroine rather to her male counterpart, thereby shifting emphasis to male, rather than female heroism. In contrast, the first edition emphasises the symbolic centrality of woman as an expression of the nation, as the female form occupies the largest and most visually powerful space on the cover (Appendix 2, Figure 3). This particular edition was published shortly before the US invasion of Iraq and provides a familiar nationalist trope which would have been easy for the Iraqi reader to recognise.

Although *Get Out, Damned One!* is a historically inaccurate mishmash of Islamic, ancient and modern Iraqi elements (especially local proverbs and tribal traditions and poetry), it reflects the multilayered and adaptive quality of Baʿthist nationalist ideology and agenda. Furthermore, it also reveals that propaganda literature does not seek to persuade the rational mind with coherence or consistency; rather it aims to illicit an emotional response and strike a chord with the sensitivities of its target audience through emotional resonance. This is why litterateurs are better propagandists than either politicians or journalists, and probably why Saddam turned to the novel genre after exhausting every other medium for his propaganda. Propaganda has generally not been deemed worthy of serious scholarly attention because it is considered ubiquitous and crass. Not only this, but propaganda is also thought to 'taint' any artistic medium with which it comes into contact, thereby devaluing propaganda literature as an object of serious critical study. This means that texts like *Get Out, Damned One!* and *Zabiba and the King* will always fall between the cracks of several academic disciplines or risk being ignored altogether.

Holding Back: Machismo and the Dilemma of 'Real' Women in *The Fortified Castle* and *Men and a City*

Published in 2001, Saddam Hussein's second and longest novel *Al-Qalʿa al-hasina* (*The Fortified Castle*) is a prime example of what Elie Podeh termed 'cultural thickness',[26] which conceals beneath its confident expression of nationalist discourses a genuine crisis in Iraq's identity, as well as unease with the supposedly natural and strong bonds between Iraqis. In a Foucauldian sense, in which silence does not necessarily mean repression, and verbosity does not naturally entail freedom, the 'over-language' which characterises this novel, as well as literary production in Saddam's Iraq generally, is indicative of both state malaise and state hegemonic practices. By producing an overflow of cultural, literary and media discourses, the former Iraq regime was able to monopolise language and impose its own discourse from above, thereby achieving a degree of control that straightforward silencing or censorship could not accomplish alone. *The Fortified Castle*'s long-winded stressing and re-stressing of the unity of Iraq and its people in 700 pages (double the number of pages of each of the other novels) of exaggerated and grandiose prose typical of propaganda, has made for a particularly boring and repetitive read. This may be the main reason why it is the most neglected it of all the novels presumably authored by the former Iraqi dictator.

Set in the University of Baghdad during Iraq's invasion of Kuwait, *The Fortified Castle* contains the most extensive reflections on male–female relations in all four of Saddam's novels and is framed as a romance in the author's preface, beginning with a short eulogy to love: 'Love is God's [most] beautiful symphony on earth. All the colours and melodies bear witness through it, be it in success or failure, in movement or inertia, in climbing upwards or downwards. All shapes find themselves in it or in opposition to it, either at its peak or at its bottom.' The Ba'th's ideological father Michel 'Aflaq had previously emphasised that love of the Arab nation is a central tenant of the *qawmiya* aspect of Ba'thism.[27] The *Fortified Castle* tells the story of a potential union of Arab and Kurdish student protagonists Sabah and Shatrin, representing a thinly veiled political allegory (and a weak one at that) as by the end of the novel the reader is uncertain as to whether the marriage will actually take place. The text's ultimate question is whether one 'can live without a cause?'[28] Sabah, a former soldier and war hero from the Iran–Iraq War, asserts that only a revolutionary can know the meaning of true personal love because of the deep affection he feels for the cause of his nation. He confesses his love to Shatrin primarily because of her faith 'in the great Ba'th Party',[29] a party which considers the improvement of the status of women in Iraq among its greatest achievements.[30] When Sabah lists the sacrifices made by patriotic men for their country, the indignant Shatrin responds by mentioning the names of female martyrs to highlight the discursive equality between the sexes under Saddam's rule, including the way women's contributions to the revolution should be remembered and acknowledged:

> But you did not mention the name of a single woman? It is as if Iraqi women have not made sacrifices . . . do you not remember Firyal who was martyred

> at the beginning of the conflict with the monsters of Iran when their agents of Iranian origin threw bombs at students while they were congregating in al-Mustansiriyya University in the spring of 1980? Do you not remember Mosul's martyr Hafsa al-ʿUmari, who was hung on an electricity pole by communists during Qasim's era? . . . what about the bride of Mandali, who was martyred in her wedding gown and the martyr-artist Layla al-ʿAttar?[31]

As the longest of Saddam's four texts, the compensatory function of *The Fortified Castle*, where large sections of political oratory are voiced mainly through the male protagonist, interrupt narrative discourse in an attempt to 'write over' the social and legal struggles facing Iraqi women and other subaltern groups in the nation.

In many ways the novel attempts a geographical mapping of Iraq in an idealised allegorical representation of the nation: Sabah (which means 'morning', alliterates with Saddam, but also comes from the same root as Sabha, Saddam's mother's name), a war hero from the eight-year conflict with Iran, comes from a rural village near the Sunni capital of the north, Mosul. His lover Shatrin is a Kurd from the city of Sulaymaniya, who not only represents the nation, as is often the case with women in nationalist fiction, but her union with Sabah also symbolises the bond between Iraqi brethren, Arab and Kurd, villagers and city-dwellers. The protagonists Sabah and Shatrin are law students who receive their compulsory military training at the University of Baghdad, and at the hands of commander Husayn bin Ali[32] (an explicit reference to the grandson of the Prophet Mohammed and the second Shia imam), who is a native of Basra, the Shia capital of southern Iraq. The protagonists are then deployed for military service in Mosul, a city whose symbolic meaning is again made explicit: 'Mosul, as its name implies, is a link (*halaqat wasl*) between countries that used to trade with Iraq, and between the north and south of the country.'[33] In its unprecedented explicitness, the text leaves nothing for the reader to decipher, and forcefully imposes imaginary bonds of idealised nationalism onto a situation of real inequality, or what Fāṭima al-Muḥsin refers to as the ideological game of exchange and replacement.[34] In this sense, it also conforms to the needs of propaganda, which cannot afford to be subtle, lest its message be misinterpreted.[35] In his introduction to the novel, a state literary critic called Ali Salman praises the explicitness of this text, 'which does not occupy the reader with questions, or the search for reasons behind those questions, because it simply puts him in a prayer alcove, in which he hears nothing but the praises and pangs of a soul rebelling against hesitancy and confusion, for the sake of nationalist, pan-Arab and religious ideals'.[36]

The cover of *The Fortified Castle* (Appendix 2, Figure 4) is an important paratextual element as it provides a visual summary of the novel's nationalist themes. It comprises the Dome of the Rock and several missiles, which are swept by the wind to form the peak of a triangular structure, possibly a mountain. There is also a large female face further down the page, which dominates the cover, and other male and female faces, which look up lovingly and with pride at this strange edifice, with its target clear in sight: the liberation of Jerusalem. Saddam had claimed that his invasion of Kuwait was a precursor to the liberation of Jerusalem, which won him much popular support on Arab streets, and the Palestinian question often features in political discussions in the novel.[37] The introduction to *The Fortified Castle* by Ali 'Abd Allah Salman lavishes farcical laudatory praise upon the novel, which is described as an 'epic' that a normal mind cannot conceive.[38] The novel also represents, according to Salman, 'a spontaneous dialogue with truth, which we have not seen in novels produced in the mid to late twentieth century'.[39] Of equal importance here is the disclaimer, present in all four of Saddam's novels, which asserts that:

> after all this (literary) achievement, the author refused that his work [should] see the light of public publishing, except under 'by its author', humbled by the sacrifices made in the past and present by the chivalric women and men of Iraq during two wars, one waged against villains, and the other to build their future, which has been destroyed by those villains.[40]

This strange combination of arrogance and self-depreciation is, according to Salām 'Abbūd, a prominent feature in the psyche of Iraqi state writers which reveals inferiority complexes and a deep sense of subjugation.[41] This is most clearly expressed in *The Fortified Castle* with the oxymoron 'humble pride'.[42] This complex and contradictory psychological state is further revealed in a rare and brief moment in the novel, in which Fa'iz repents for feeling as confident in victory as a mountain, but then justifies this arrogance, by saying it stems from a deep faith in God.[43]

Saddam's novelistic discourse in *The Fortified Castle* contains many echoes of his political speeches, which highlights the instrumentalisation of literature for propaganda purposes, and genre confusion, which literary critics have noted in their discussions of his novels. I would not, however, recommend using this as absolute proof of Saddam's authorship of his novels, for as noted by Radi Ja'far in his book *Uslub al-ra'is al-qa'id: al-bina' al-khariji wa al-madamin al-balaghiya* (*The [Rhetorical] Style of the Leader President: Form and* Rhetoric, 1991), a generation of Iraqi writers emulated Hussein's style, and some of his idioms even became part of the daily vocabulary of the masses, used to support a view,[44] or, in the case of writers, to appease the regime. An example of the convergence of Saddam's political and literary discourses where Saddam recounts a meeting with members of the High Committee of the North, during which he was asked: wherein lies the state's greatest victory in the North? Saddam responded by saying:

> Our greatest victory to date is that we did not fire a single bullet at an individual in the opposite trench if he ran out of ammunition and surrender[ed]; and our greatest victory to date is also that we did not rape a single woman during our military operations or loot (which commonly took place in the past). Our greatest victory is that, despite the shedding of blood, those who surrendered after running out of ammunition could come and eat together with a soldier from the same plate, as if nothing happened.[45]

The author comments that this piece of wisdom surprised Saddam's listeners and 'filled their hearts with admiration and esteem'.[46] Echoing the theme of Iraqi nobility highlighted in this excerpt, is a scene in *The Fortified Castle* where, after his capture by Bedouin shepherds, an American pilot is permitted to share their meal.[47] In another episode, upon attempting to escape his humane and hospitable captors, a British soldier comically says (in broken Arabic): 'why should I be ashamed of attempting to escape after you treated me so well? Loyalty is not a characteristic of Anglo-Saxon people, only of Arabs, so I am not obliged to conform to your standards.'[48] The emphasis placed on the Englishman's 'broken Arabic' brings to the fore the issue of language as a marker of Arab authenticity. In *The Fortified Castle*, the English language is attacked as the language of imperialism, which should be prevented from insidiously creeping into public parlance and academia.[49]

Contrasting the English soldier's immorality and cowardice, Iraq's soldiers are almost indestructible, losing battles and men only when they are stabbed in the back. They are repeatedly referred to as the lions and eagles of Iraq,[50] who hunt their prey with lethal efficiency coupled with infinite mercy, and display superhuman courage. Husayn, the group's Shia military leader does not duck for cover when American bombs fall on the group, and Shatrin is embarrassed (and, as a woman, excused) for showing weakness and losing consciousness in the same scene.[51] The contrast between the enemy's depravity and the excessive and idealised nobility of Iraqi soldiers outlined above, is not only typical of war propaganda generally, but also replicates a popular theme from Iraqi fiction during the Iran–Iraq War. *The Fortified Castle* definitely reads like those novels, particularly its propagandistic elements. This is because propaganda under totalitarian regimes like Saddam's is produced with machine-like efficiency, and relies on sheer bulk and incessant repetition to achieve its desired effect. Rather than a diversity of material or a polyphonic kaleidoscope of narrative voices, we therefore end up hearing the same robotic voice, with no personal idiosyncrasies. In this case, it seems that in their eagerness to emulate the president's rhetorical genius, war-mongering writers and novelists from the Iran–Iraq War may have ironically produced literary works that could well have been written by the dictator himself, thereby pre-empting *The Fortified Castle*. In its extreme zeal, and the intensity of its emotions (particularly love of the nation and hatred of its enemies), the novel regresses to the style of so-called immature accounts of the early Iran–Iraq War period such as ʿĀdil ʿAbd al-Jabbār's *Dancing on the Shoulders of Death*, the war's first novel. These novels were critiqued by ʿAlī ʿAbd al-Ḥusayn Mukhīf, a state literary critic, for being slightly unrealistic, and by opposition writer Salām ʿAbbūd for theatrically mirroring scenes from 1980s American cowboy movies, in which the hero kills scores of enemies without so much as a scratch. It is ironic that Saddam began writing his novels after claiming that Iraqi cultural production during the war was disappointing, yet he was not able to outdo or surpass it himself, and produced *The Fortified Castle*, in many ways a mere replica of those novels.

In an emphatic declaration of Iraqi unity, Sabah cries: 'I am a Kurd, as well as being an Arab. I represent the Kurdish people . . . because I am Baʿthist . . . isn't every Kurd an Arab in the depths of his heart, as well as being specifically a Kurd within Iraq?'[52] Sabah also asserts that the Kurdish language has Arabic at its heart,[53] and expresses his love for all of Kurdistan: 'I love Sulaimaniya, Irbil and Dahuk. I constantly yearn for the waterfalls of Bikhal, Klaw and Hassan, and the peak of Mount Gara . . .'[54] At the beginning of the novel, Sabah also asserts that 'every citizen in the South would like to know more about Nineveh's civilisation, just as all Northerners in Iraq strive to learn more about Basra . . . its ports . . . and the battles that our brave army led against the armies of Iran which were defeated, including the one in Faw, named the city of sacrifice and gateway to the great victory, which lies 80 kms south of Basra'.[55] But not all areas in Iraq are given equal commendation. The author's undoubted preference for his own rural Sunni Arab origins permeates the text (for all its talk of the unity and brotherhood of the Iraqi state, in 700 pages the novel does not visit either the Kurdish north or Shia south. In fact, those who visit the north like Shatrin's father are considered traitors). For example, on their way to Mosul for training, the group pass the city of 'Awja south of Tikrit, the birthplace of Saddam Hussein, which is glorified above and beyond all the cities of Iraq mentioned in the novel. Travelling in the novel allows Sabah ample time to give textbook-like detail about Iraq's history and the glory of its ancient civilisation. When the group alight in the city itself, a Tikriti sheikh tells the group that the city's history is no less than 4,000 years old, and that Tikritis are well known for their courage and refusal to surrender no matter what the odds. For example, Salahuddin al-Ayyubi who defeated the Crusaders (the group's name is significantly the Salahuddin Brigade[56]), Ahmad Hassan al-Bakr and Saddam Hussein were all born in Tikrit.[57] Notably, Saddam's name is mentioned no less than fifty times in the novel, compensating for his refusal to own the text by putting his name on the cover.

In a visit to the countryside, Sabah praises the hospitality of Bedouins and the extensive freedoms supposedly given to their women.[58] Bedouins have a reputation for being hospitable in Arabic culture generally, but the focus here is on generosity as a 'pure' Arab trait, as opposed to the miserliness of non-Arab characters in Saddam's other novels, such as the Jewish Hasqil in *Get Out, Damned One!* The focus on Bedouin culture is one of the primary means through which a neo-tribal utopianism is expressed in the novel and marks it firmly as a product of the conservatism of its time. The revival of 'neo-tribalism' and folk culture in the 1990s signified a return to reassuring pre-national identities in Iraq at a time when the very existence of the Ba'thist state was under threat. The country and rurality is thus glorified as the original and authentic nation, thereby reinforcing Sabah and Saddam's *asala* in terms of their *'uruba*.[59] This rural authenticity is almost always symbolised by the deep-rooted tree, and, as with other nationalist novels, the tree often expresses a utopian desire to return to purity and origins. In *The Fortified Castle*, Sabah asserts that the fruit of a foreign (Turkish) tree tastes better when the soil is Iraqi,[60] which at first seems to provide an inclusive and accommodating view of national belonging, but it is one which is not maintained in a coherent way throughout the text. Furthermore, we are even told that Sabah loves the earth more than Shatrin,[61] which is a clue for what is to become of their engagement. The harmony between national union through marriage and attachment to the earth is not maintained in the text due to the inherent unease with the Kurdish Question. The fear of racial contamination and of compromising Arab purity and perceived values may provide a possible answer as to why Sabah in *The Fortified Castle* does not marry his Kurdish fiancée: Sabah's children's maternal uncles would be Kurds residing in the autonomous north, rather than authentic Iraqis like himself (and Saddam) had the union taken place. This is probably why there are hints in *The Fortified Castle* that Sabah and Shatrin will each marry their cousins, signifying that blood and kinship ties are more important than essentially 'fabricated' national bonds. In this sense the novels of Saddam have regressed from those in the Iran–Iraq War in their inability to include Kurds through marriage.

The idealism of the Arab–Kurd relationship is undermined early on in the novel, as Shatrin's father returns to the autonomous north seeking medical treatment because he has more trust in Western doctors than in Iraqi ones (Shatrin disagrees with her father's immoral decision to travel outside the borders of the legitimate state but accompanies him anyway). Authorial bias is clear in the way blame for problems in the relationship is placed on Shatrin and not Sabah, for example, she is revealed to be stubborn: 'is it because you are Kurdish?' Sabah asks,[62] in a telling moment of ethnic stereotyping. Perhaps the novel's only true moment of perceptiveness comes when Sabah tells Shatrin that their private love has no symbolic meaning, and thus it cannot rectify any of the 'problems' caused by autonomy in the north. Towards the end of the novel, Shatrin becomes less physically attractive because she puts on weight, which upsets Sabah. This small detail in the novel illustrates that liberal discourses notwithstanding, there remains a preoccupation with and a desire to control the female body and to judge it. However, what really worries Sabah is Shatrin's irreligiosity as she does not fulfil her religious obligations, for example, she does not pray, whereas as an exemplary Baʿthist in the 1990s and child of the 'Faith Campaign', Sabah prays regularly and even yearns to go to *hajj* (which is not presently possible due to what he calls the American 'occupation' of the holy cities of Mecca and Medina). However, the nail in the coffin, so to speak, of the engagement (and by extension the utopian 'marriage' between Iraq's different ethnic components) is Shatrin's eagerness that the 'castle', Sabah's family estate, is divided after Sabah's hitherto absent father's death, in a clear nod to Kurdish autonomy. It is Sabah's mother Salha (meaning 'pious one', but also rhymes with Sabha, Saddam's mother's name) who has the final very strong stance on the subject when she emphatically says:

> we inherited this castle and land, and no one has ever bought it from us, and the only person in true possession of it is he who guards it with his blood and keeps it safe. This is how we inherited it, and this is how it will stay . . . and he who disagrees with this has no other choice but to beg at the doors of foreigners who will either throw him bones or pelt him with stones.[63]

Sabah's entitlement to the land as a Sunni Arab male allows him to objectify Shatrin by likening her to the nation in a physical sense. He provides voyeuristically detailed and sexually explicit descriptions of parts of the female body, which are compared with the mountains and valleys of the nation. Positive jealousy, or *ghira*,[64] a quintessentially tribal Arab concept, is a recurrent theme in the novel, for just as Sabah is uncomfortable with Shatrin's loud feminine laughter and her tight revealing clothing worn in public, he contends that those men who do not possess *ghira* over their nation are like those who do not care if their lover's nakedness is exposed. In the words of Yuval-Davis, 'proper behaviour, proper clothing embody the line which signifies the collectivity's boundaries'.[65] The preoccupation with racial purity finds its natural extension in the sexual relationships of the biological producers of that nation, which makes Shatrin's small acts of transgression all the more suspicious. Propaganda cannot betray self-doubt, yet *The Fortified Castle*'s unrelenting expressions of an overblown national pride expose the cracks in the utopian union of Sabah and Shatrin, highlighting how discursive excess is symptomatic of ideological anxiety. This is corroborated by the resolution, or lack thereof, of the plot, namely, the failure of the two to marry (although the engagement is still in place by the end of the novel). Indeed, the text ends in a surprisingly abrupt manner, as if its author suddenly lost interest in the work, preferring instead to start his next novel, and perhaps hastily proceeding to publish this one.

In its extravagant promotion of Saddam Hussein's cult of personality, the former dictator's third novel *Men and a City* (2002) can most accurately be described as a self-obsessed modern hagiography. Ironically, however, the novel is framed as the work of a humble author, which serves to shed light on Saddam's curious decision not to publish his name on all four of his works. *Men and a City* is a fictionalised autobiography which uses rhyming or alliterating pseudonyms to recount the story of Saddam Hussein's childhood up until his involvement, at the age of twenty-two, in the failed assassination attempt of Iraq's Prime Minister Abd al-Karim Qasim on 7 October 1959. It focuses on the physical hardships faced by Salih (the character who represents Saddam in the novel) and his role in the rise of the Baʿth Party, supported by his Tikriti clan. Born in Al ʿAwja in 1937 to parents Sabha and Hussein, Saddam was the only surviving child from that marriage, as his two older brothers had died in infancy. Hussein the father had died while Sabha was pregnant with Saddam and she remarried after his death. Biographical accounts mention that at around the age of ten Saddam fled the abuse of his stepfather Ibrahim al-Hassan to his maternal uncle Khairallah Talfah's house in Baghdad, whose daughter Sajida he was to later marry. Khairallah Talfah (called Mal Allah Rabbah in the text) was an Arab nationalist and veteran of the Anglo-Iraqi War of 1941, who was imprisoned and expelled from the army due to the role he played in the army revolt against the Iraqi monarchy (which was supported by the then-occupying British forces). Talfah became a father figure to Saddam and introduced him to members of the nascent Baʿth Party, including strengthening ties to Talfah's brother-in-law and Saddam's cousin, Ahmad Hassan al-Bakr, who would later become Iraq's fourth president. Despite doubts regarding the extent of Saddam's involvement in the assassination attempt of Abd al-Karim Qasim, this event would become the stuff of legend, to be repeated and embellished ad nauseum by various Iraqi media outlets. A novel recounting the events was even commissioned and published in 1978 under the title *The Long Days*, and a highly publicised film of the same title was released in 1980 starring Saddam Kamel, Saddam Hussein's cousin, as the lead.

From his fatherless childhood to the first major milestone in his political career, Saddam presents himself as a hero who triumphed against all odds to achieve his destiny as the saviour of Iraq. *Men and a City*'s lengthy introduction describes the protagonist as 'a shining star in the space of Iraq',[66] and 'a compass for the Arab nation, guiding it towards a destiny of greatness'.[67] Moreover, the author conflates Saddam's supposed singularity with his belonging to a downtrodden Iraqi mass, adding that the life of this 'Arab knight' mirrors the historical trajectory of his nation and his people,[68] and was 'inspired by the spirit of history and the courage he had inherited from his brave family and clan'.[69] The anonymous writer of the preface adds that the narrator of the text was alive and witnessed the great events that have unfolded in recent history: 'events unlike any other in history, just as the knight is unlike any other, and his generation is also unlike any other generation'. He asserts that what makes the novel unique is that it is a clear expression of the personality of its author, as well as being a 'mirror' of the life of the nation, so much so that it almost speaks out loud.[70] The preface also praises the selflessness of the author who 'has refused to write his name, just as he did before with *Zabiba and the King* and *The Fortified Castle*',[71] and like all his works, explicitly states on its back cover that all proceeds from sales of the novel will go to the poor, the needy and orphans.

The novel is a structural mess of randomly collected memories, albeit in a roughly chronological order. The shift from third- to first-person begins a third of the way through the novel, with 'Salih says . . .'[72] followed by a long first-person narrative. The third-person narration returns around twenty pages later during an episode about an outbreak of malaria with: 'Salih, whose memories we will use to recount those events said . . .'[73] However, the shift is not as clean as the observation above may imply, as there are points during the third-person narration when a first-person perspective also creeps in, such as the description of Salih's stepmother Amina about whom the narrator comments: '*we* used to love her very much' (my emphasis). It is as if the author had become so engrossed in the act of writing that he simply forgot to maintain consistency in his experiments with narrative voice. Moreover, it is also evident that the work has not been edited at all, either by the author himself or by a professional editor as it is full of grammatical and spelling mistakes. By the end of the novel, the illusion of a third-person narrator objectively mediating the events is dropped completely and is fully replaced by a first-person narration.

Attempts to resolve the contradiction between the humility of the text and the self-aggrandisement necessary to Saddam's cult of personality expose the author's dilemma in the inconsistent use of the third-person narration, and the presence of a confused narrative voice. In the context of propaganda, which requires crystal clarity of the message (if not crude brashness) to reach its intended audience, a third-person narration allows for the exaggerated commendation of Saddam in the preface, whilst at the same time barely preserving the thin veneer of supposed humility, which a first-person narration could not sustain without being virtually unreadable. In terms of genre, the decision to write a third-person novel rather than a first-person autobiography is also determined by the requirements of propaganda. The preface maintains that the text is a novel based on true events, and that the fictional characters are true to their 'real' counterparts,[74] yet in the words of Stephen Guth, the author refuses to sign an explicit *pacte autobiographique*.[75] According to Jameson: 'genres are *institutions* or social contracts between a writer and a specific public, whose function is to specify the proper use of a particular cultural artifact',[76] that is, a means of controlling interpretation. By 'packaging' his autobiography as a novel, Saddam was able to hit two birds with one stone: give an additional personalised depth to the utopian nationalism of his other novels and highlight his humility in refusing to explicitly 'own' his story. It is this 'personal' aspect of *Men and a City* which makes it the best out of Saddam's four works, surpassing even the 'professional' account of his life titled *The Long Days* (1978) which he had commissioned as vice-president.

The trilogy titled *The Long Days* by novelist Abd al-Amir al-Muʿalla begins its narration at the point where *Men and a City* ends: the failed assassination attempt on Abd al-Karim Qasim. As the text was produced before the real ideological mobilisation of Iraqi society had begun (and even before the ideology of the Baʿth as state discourse had fully crystalised), it is less ideologically or polemically charged than *Men and a City*. In that novel Saddam is renamed Mohammed al-Saqr (eagle), an interesting subversion of Mohammed Baqir Al-Sadr, the Shia Ayatollah murdered with his sister Bint al-Hudā by Saddam's regime in 1980. Unlike *Men and a City*, the novel also attempts to conform to the norms of literary writing in its linearity and accurate division of chapters, but remains a distant and at times subtle third-person account, lacking the immediacy and urgency of Saddam's account of events, which is deemed superior even by political opponents like ʿAbbūd. Ironically, the preface to *Men and a City* characterises the style of the novel, despite the impulsiveness attributed to its author, as 'free from the rhetorical zeal present in other novels *of this kind*'.[77] This is probably a dismissive nod at *The Long Days* and a claim of superiority over that novel. Just as Saddam had first lavished praise on the committed Iraqi novel of the Iran–Iraq War, and then when he came to publish his first novel said that he was motivated to write it because Iraqi literary production had thus far been disappointing.

As for the title of the text, it bears little or no relation to the content of *Men and a City*, and seems to be the only 'inaccurate' title out of Saddam's four works; the novel is mainly about one man, not many, and does not primarily take place in the city. According to Samah Selim, due to the 'centrality of the peasant and land question in modern nationalist consciousness and the ideology of the state . . . even properly urban fiction is almost always haunted by the presence of the village, as an intensely problematic geographical and historical place of origins'.[78] However, according to Gérard Genette, all paratexts are 'at the service of a better reception for the text',[79] even this seemingly incongruous title which uses the plural to indicate that Saddam is not arrogant enough to write a book entirely about himself (although it is in fact dedicated entirely to him, and should have more accurately been called *Man and a City*). In contrast, the blurb on the back cover of *The Long Days* states that it is: 'a novel based on the recent historical events in Iraq. It records the struggle of the young men who moulded the new Iraq. It is a drama of real life.'[80] *The Long Days* provides the perspectives of other Ba'th cell members in separate chapters, particularly leading up to the assassination attempt, but Saddam's role is given primacy.

Ultimately, the question remains: why did Saddam decide to author an 'autobiography' when there was both *The Long Days* the novel and the film adaptation? A possible answer may lie in the content of the work itself which focuses on the author's childhood and coming of age like a true *bildungsroman*, and gives us no details beyond the author's early involvement with the Ba'th Party. There is a strong element of nostalgia in an old Saddam looking back on his childhood, and this nostalgia in turn fuels utopian propaganda in the novel. According to O'Shaughnessy, nostalgia becomes propaganda only when it is strategically mobilised.[81] Perhaps it might be overstating it to say that this is perhaps the part of Saddam's life he was most genuinely proud of, as writing any autobiography is inextricable from a sense of pride and achievement.[82]

A closer look at *Men and a City*'s paratexts may serve to illuminate the utopian mechanisms of the novel's message. The novel is signed by an anonymous 'baghdadi' or son of Baghdad and a title in bold visually divides a city from the countryside, from which an Arab knight in traditional garb rides his steed; above him is the Ka'ba and images of holy Shia sites in Iraq. Interestingly, the cover (Appendix 2, Figure 5) provides a rare moment where the city is portrayed in a positive light, as the rays of faith emanating from Baghdad labelled 'the mother and not the lover' meet the rays of Mecca and Damascus. It is only in this abstract, Islamicised sense that Baghdad can be idolised, rather than in its social realities, which are critiqued in the novel as contaminated urban sprawl.[83] The cover also includes the prayer: 'Dear God protect your servants, the freedom fighters' in an emblem of the sun in the right-hand corner of the cover, and a declaration of awe at divine creation: 'praise the most merciful' in the shape of a heart beneath an eagle draped in the Palestinian and Iraqi flags. These religious symbols and Islamic prayers complement both the author's claims to Hashemite descent and the upright religious persona adopted by Saddam in the novel. Notably, this is the only cover that does not include an image of a female face, marking it as a conservative novel compared with the author's other three works. The preface of *Men and a City* uses the *basmallah*, which is notable given that

The Fortified Castle, the novel that preceded it, begins with a (secular) love poem. According to Ofra Bengio, the *basmallah* only appeared in official Iraqi political discourse after 1979 to counter Iran's claims to religious legitimacy.[84] However, the *basmallah* was not used consistently in either political or cultural discourses under the Baʿth, but was in fact strategically placed in certain contexts. *Men and a City* also ends in a rhetorically sloganistic way with: 'long live Iraq, Palestine and the Arab nation', and like *Zabiba and the King* and *Get Out, Damned One!* with 'Allahu Akbar!' The preface describes Saddam as 'a man who believes that life is a cause',[85] but unlike *The Fortified Castle*, this cause is an exclusively male endeavour, which is not discursively configured to include women.

Lineages and bloodlines are a central theme in *Men and a City*, which contains an emphatic statement on the importance of matrilineal lineage, using a traditional Iraqi proverb: 'if you want your son to protect your land and home then ask about his maternal uncle'.[86] By transferring primacy to maternal rather than paternal blood relations, Saddam in this novel reconnects to an alternative cultural basis (present in Levantine culture) for glorifying and belonging to his mother's side of the family. Apart from reiterating claims to a paternal Hashemite descent at the beginning of the novel, Saddam has very few anecdotes or personal stories to tell about his father's side, compensated in part by the fact that his parents were in fact cousins. However, when Saddam does mention his father, he does so with an impersonal reverence, as one would refer to a saint, with a focus on one particular (neo-tribal) trait: *ghira* or positive jealousy. *Ghira* allows men a greater sense of selfhood by defining themselves as guardians of female honour. The prefaces of both *Get Out, Damned One!* and *Zabiba and the King* describe their author as a *najib ghayur* (an intelligent man who is jealous for the honour of his country/his women kin). In *Men and a City*, a man who possesses *ghira* is called *abu ʿamsha* or *akhu hadhla*, meaning that he is the father or brother of an honourable woman. According to Beth Baron, the use of kin idioms allows for the imagining of the nation as a fictive household, highlighting the mobilisation of familial rhetoric for political purposes. Another term, which appears exclusively in this novel and which was popularised by Saddam's wars, is *majidat* meaning 'glorious women', designed to resonate with Iraqi audiences at times of national crises. In *Men and a City*, unlike Saddam's other novels, there are no female protagonists, and *ghira* becomes an essential means of envisioning a nation that is vulnerable and must be protected from violation, just like the women in the text.

At the beginning of the novel, Hussein the father is described primarily as the protector of the honour of women; his help is sought by an old neighbour who fears being cuckolded by a man who constantly harasses his young wife. Hussein then devises a plan to catch the culprit in the act and beats him, but in conformance with tribal values does not alert the authorities or the rest of the village in order to safeguard the reputations of the neighbour and his wife. This long anecdote may perhaps constitute an attack on the (false) rumours circulated by his enemies who have labelled Saddam as the son of a prostitute.[87] In fact, the author painstakingly explains that his mother adhered to local tribal traditions by immediately disclosing her pregnancy to her male and female relatives: 'Every woman must disclose her pregnancy, even at the earliest stages, so that if her husband were to die, she would not be accused of fornication or adultery.'[88] This point is so important that the author did not change the names of his parents in line with his use of pseudonyms elsewhere: 'everyone knew how much Sabha loved Hussein and how faithful she was to him',[89] and for this reason very few dared to ask for her hand after she was widowed. As an extension of his father's machismo, Saddam presents himself as equally chivalrous; in his early youth he even threatens men on a bus at gunpoint for not offering their seats to standing girls,[90] an act of chivalry that is exaggerated to comical proportions. His comrades also protect women during nationalist demonstrations against monarchists and communists.[91]

In the opening pages of the text, the narrator asks his mother for forgiveness for writing about the inappropriate subjects of pregnancy and childbirth, saying that he did so only at the behest of 'those who have insisted I write something about the subject [of his life], even if it is in the form of a novel'.[92] This is the only moment in the text that explicitly refers to the act of writing, and thus merits a pause. Saddam's claim that, rather than stemming purely from his ego, he was *forced* to write an account of his life is part of the propaganda campaign to 'market' himself as humble, much of which is affirmed by the paratextual information in all the novels: from the refusal to print his name on the covers of all four works, to the claim that all financial proceedings from sales go to the poor. However, this exaggerated coyness at discussing marriage and childbirth (in by no means explicit terms) forms a stark contrast to the explicit sexual references in *Zabiba and the King* and *The Fortified Castle*. Furthermore, the novels were written in such close succession that this episode cannot possibly indicate a genuine shift from a secular discourse in the first two novels, to a religious discourse in the last two. Saddam was ultimately a leader of realpolitik, adopting a variety of personas in the public sphere in any way that would maintain his legitimacy and power. Aware of the innate power of religion and its discourse of morality, the upright persona adopted by Saddam in his last two novels has indeed remained a most powerful one and constitutes the favoured narrative by pro-Saddamists today propagating the 'myth' of the martyr-president.

Men and a City paints a perfect picture of familial bliss in the idyllic marriage of Sabha and Hussein the father, despite abject poverty and lack of adequate sanitation and medical care which result in the tragic death of their first child Anwar at four months. In his article 'Why Novels not Autobiographies?', Stephan Guth asserts that fiction, rather than 'autobiography-proper'[93] is more suited to conveying the general failure of society as opposed to the individual'. In fact, he adds that 'the novel which comes closest to autobiographical reality is essentially a story of success'.[94] Not only does *Men and a City* describe the success of Saddam the individual, but this 'success' is made possible only in the context of a perfect family and clan, rather than in an individualist sense, where the 'hero' rebels against the shackles of tradition and social and familial restraints. Saddam generously uses the 'novelised' autobiography as an ideal means of social criticism, in particular, his detailed descriptions of the hardships of rural life. In a long passage reflecting on his experiences working as a menial farmhand, he remarks: 'life in the country is cruel, miserable in fact',[95] adding that dogs in the city live a better life than the people in the country.[96] This powerful evocation of the miserable life led by millions of Iraqis makes the need for a saviour from amongst 'the peasants' more urgent. The protagonist Salih says he learnt 'everything a peasant should know',[97] and his rural roots function as a manly source of pride in the author's past, like his uncle Mal Allah's scars of battle, and distinguishes him from the physically weaker and less courageous city-folk, who are described in 'feminine' terms.

The novel combines elements of a 'neo-conservative utopia', where traditions must be upheld through the prism of tribal values, and a socialist one which advocates *ishtirakiya* as exemplified by the Ba'th (for example, the protagonist and his uncle prefer not to go to weddings in order to leave extra food for the needy).[98] This is because the socialist utopia of the Ba'th has already been established from the perspective of the author (writing in the present) and has now been transformed to a stagnant 'conservative' utopia keen on maintaining the status quo. For this reason, the detailed 'social realism' and criticism of certain political and social realities does not extend to the intimate world of the home or the tribal values of the village. In fact, the author is determined to prove that he is the product of a loving and healthy extended family, refusing even to 'blacken the name' of his violently abusive stepfather, towards whom he is not only respectful in the text, but reverent. The author refers to his stepfather Ibrahim (who interestingly, is not given a pseudonym) as 'tall, strong, good-looking, trustworthy, brave, *ghayur*, with yellow-green eyes'.[99] Furthermore, Saddam is also apathetic towards Ibrahim in the section where he runs away, saying that he did so because he was simply not permitted to go to school, and not because he was beaten or abused. He then leaves on foot in the middle of the night, without the permission of his stepfather, facing many dangers on the way.[100] The author is dismissive of conflicts within the family, and declines to provide any anecdotal details of even the smallest of arguments, which are glossed over by the repetition of the compensatory 'but we were a happy family'.[101] This provides an indication that there is something amiss, lurking behind the author's idealised depiction of his family, which he would rather ignore. The author even stresses the harmony between Ibrahim's two wives and, between himself and his step brother: 'they always got along, except a few squabbles which must necessarily occur between step wives'.[102] In any case, the private and the public converge as the author's nostalgia for the past undermines the utopia that has supposedly been established by the Ba'th in the present, particularly his yearning for an older and more committed generation of revolutionaries. He says that some Ba'thists have changed from the 'good old days', but most were faithful to the Party. This echoes Sabah's nostalgia for more committed Ba'thists in *The Fortified Castle.*[103]

The reiteration of his supposed Hashemite descent enables Saddam to sanctify his family in a way that would have otherwise been difficult to sustain. The narrative begins by saying that Sayyid Hussein the father belonged to a family of Husayni Sayyids.[104] Hussein the father says at the beginning of the novel that he will call his first child Fatima if it is a girl. In Iraqi public political discourse, Saddam's claim to Hashemite descent appeared quite suddenly in 1995, as part of what Ofra Bengio calls the 'deliberate Islamic flag-waving' period. Saddam also had genealogists produce a family tree to prove this, saying he had not mentioned his noble lineage before due to his humility. Humility of course, is the main reason why Saddam claims he did not want to write his name on the covers of all his novels, replacing it with 'by its author' instead. In another part of the novel, the author glorifies this noble family and even links *siyada* to Arab nationalism: 'Husaini Sayyids are well known for being pious and God-fearing, and for their love of Arab nationalism, without which Islam would not have achieved what it has [achieved].'[105] This conflation of Islam and Arab nationalism is very much typical of Iraqi Ba'thist ideology in its latter stages, but in the context of Saddam's cult of personality the strong religious undertones of *Men and a City* add another dimension to the author's understanding of chivalry and masculinity.

Salih (meaning 'pious one'), the literary persona standing for Saddam in the novel comes from a male line that is characterised by uncommon bravery in the face of foreign invasions. In fact, one of the author's earliest memories is being taken to the cemetery by his mother who shows him the graves of his forefathers who were all freedom fighters killed by a series of brutal enemies.[106] His maternal uncle Mal Allah Rabbah is said to have 'slaughtered Ottoman soldiers who tried to invade our city'[107]; Rabbah is described as a war hero against British colonialism and bears the scars of war which he frequently flaunts 'as signs of heroism and sacrifice'.[108] During his imprisonment, Rabbah breaks the ribs of a government spy 'like a lion',[109] and in 1948, he gave up his rifle for the war effort in Palestine, at a time when Salih says Arab leaders treacherously did not allow anyone to volunteer against Israel.[110] According to 'Abbūd, 'Saddam deliberately confuses heroism with cruelty; heroism in the vernacular sense is synonymous with 'manliness' *rujula* which Saddam truly believes he is destined to embody'.[111] The title of the novel underscores the importance of 'manliness'; a mythologised social construction, central to the author's understanding of himself and others. For example, when his uncle and mentor is imprisoned, Salih asserts that prison is for men, and (referring to his uncle) tells the reader: 'remember he was from Iraq and a man!'[112]

Indeed, as the son of an honourable tribe, the hero is unable to escape the destiny of his manhood, which his mother attempts to weaken him by making him wear earrings for fear of losing him like other male members of her family. Having also lost two children in infancy before him, Salih's mother frets excessively for his safety, and is terrified when, as a baby, her brother used to playfully throw him up in the air. This 'normal' depiction of motherly anxiety nevertheless forms a stark contrast to the image of the all sacrificing mothers propagated by the Ba'th during the Iran–Iraq War. As if anticipating this problem, the young Salih 'convinces' his mother Sabha that something must be done to save Iraq: 'Mother, Iraq is burning! The English have burned Iraq! The country has fallen prey to wolves.'[113] Finally, he coaxes her into expressing her dedication to the country in a clichéd form: 'I want you to be an eagle my son.'[114] 'Abbūd comments on the earrings episode thus: 'but the mother could not change the course of destiny. Saddam believed in only two things in his life: Saddam the individual, and his eternally loyal friend: destiny.'[115] This contradictory depiction of his mother reveals an author that is torn between an ideologised utopianism of propaganda and the 'realism' of an autobiography. Women in *Men and a City* are often petty, capricious and neurotic, standing in the way of the hero achieving his destiny. They exist in 'real life' to be protected and safeguarded en masse, unlike in Saddam's two allegorical novels, where as mere symbols they can take on a revolutionary leadership role.

As an extension of his brave family and clan, Salih does not complain of physical pain even as a child, just like his uncle and forefathers before him, who were all wounded in battle (one is bitten by a snake and never once moaned).[116] Hussein the father is even said to have been known for killing the wild wolves which attacked him.[117] In fact, wolves appear frequently in the novel as metaphors for Iraq's enemies, as well as asserting the agricultural/religious image of Salih as a 'good shepherd'. In the climactic episode at the end of the novel, Salih insists a bullet is removed from his leg despite the unavailability of anaesthetic by invoking his fearless forefathers and summoning their superhuman feats of bravery, physical strength and fortitude. Saddam had previously told an Egyptian journalist (about the 1980 film *The Long Days*) that he had instructed the director to make the film 'didactic, truthful and historically accurate, as well as accessible to the majority of viewers'. The journalist replied that the film certainly met that criterion, except for one scene in which a comrade cuts into Saddam's leg, using a razor blade to get a bullet out. He added, addressing Saddam:

> the actor playing your part only grimaces. I think he should scream in pain. It would be more realistic to show people that you, as a human being, have physically suffered. Saddam, keen to advertise his heroic qualities, then commented: 'I didn't think it was realistic either. I wanted the director to reshoot the scene because I remember the day when it happened. I did not grimace or move an inch until the bullet was out.'[118]

The glorification of cruelty and physical fortitude and the disdain for the weakness associated with the 'feminine' make *Men and a City* the most ideological and uncompromising of Saddam's novels. Conservative political views are matched with traditional views on gender roles, allowing for the critique of 'others' through the projection of feminine attributes onto them. Salih's city-reared comrades and accomplices in the assassination attempt on Abd al-Karim Qasim's life are described as physically and emotionally weak; they faint at the sight of blood and, due to excessive pity, do not want to abandon an injured comrade, despite it being an unwise decision that could cost them their own lives. Salih has the final call, and after cruelly taunting them, imperiously commands the group to leave the fallen comrade.

The superiority of 'the rural' and the inferiority of 'the urban' is a recurrent theme in all four of Saddam's novels, but predictably features most strongly in *Men and a City*; city-dwellers are physically weak and arrogant, including Salih's city-reared cousins and bride-to-be Sajida, who scratches the young Salih upon his arrival at their house (however, the author says he was chivalrous and did not hit her back as this would not have been considered a manly thing to do). City-folk are also depicted as being 'contaminated' through intermarriage with foreigners and undesirable social elements, such as 'regime cronies who eagerly wait for crumbs from those in power, mawalis remaining from the Ottoman invasion and Jews with their Iranian partners'.[119] Conversely, a Syrian comrade is treated by the author as an adopted son of Iraq, saying that 'anyone who smells the air of Iraq and drinks its water is an Iraqi'.[120] This contrasts his not-so-accommodating view of Iraqis of Persian or Turkish origins that are treated with suspicion. The city-folk/country-folk divide is further ideologised in the classic style of Ba'thist socialism in the reference to feudalists who 'usually descend from the armies which invaded Iraq'.[121] Salih's stepfather, for example, is imprisoned because he objected to the pressure of his landlord to work harder, at the behest and pressure of colonial powers to produce more cotton.[122] Bruce King's description of nationalism seems pertinent here:

> Nationalism is an urban movement which identifies with the rural areas as a source of authenticity, finding in the 'folk' the attitudes, beliefs, customs and language to create a sense of national unity among people who have other loyalties. Nationalism aims at . . . rejection of cosmopolitan upper classes, intellectuals and others likely to be influenced by foreign ideas.[123]

Inclusivity and exclusivity in the formation of bonds is a crucial function of ideological novels. The delicate balance between accommodation and exclusion is given varying degrees of emphases according to the potential audience and generic framework. The purity of rural women is key in *Men and a City* towards the preservation of essentially Iraqi Arab tribal values, which is why conservative discourses about women, race and rurality seem to go hand in hand.

Concluding Remarks

Ultimately, Saddam's novels depict women who are viewed as symbols of crass nationalism rather than as individuals. This leads to potentially problematic representations of women in Saddam's autobiography in particular, in which he depicts his mother as excessively fretting for his safety, and his female kin as obstacles to achieving his destiny. At the same time, these women are placed on a pedestal and revered as idealised symbols of the Iraqi nation and representative of 'all Iraqi women'. *The Fortified Castle* contains the only Kurdish female protagonist out of the texts and calls her 'the human being and symbol'[124]; however, after initially idealising Shatrin, the narrator struggles to accept her marriage to the Arab male protagonist Sabah, thereby symbolically severing the idealist national ties which bind Kurds and Arabs as equal citizens in the Iraqi nation-state. It is no coincidence, then, that Shatrin remains the least favourable of all Saddam's heroines. The dilemma of the feminine ideal seems to extend to the texts' expressions of a utopian Iraqi (and at times Arab) nationalism, where there is great uncertainty about the collective identity of the nation itself: how inclusive/exclusive it should be, how liberal or conservative? And how culturally and racially diverse? Also of interest is the projection of modern nationalist values onto the 'pre-national' protagonists Zabiba and Nakhwa, implying that just as Iraq has remained unchanged from 'time immemorial', to use Benedict Anderson's expression, so too have the women of Iraq, who have retained the same values from ancient times to the modern day: chaste, devoted to Arabism and their male kin, and courageous when facing the state's enemies.

Beyond the polemic surrounding the novels, taken together the four works of Saddam represent the culmination of contradictory state views on women over almost three decades. Zabiba is idealised in spite of her promiscuity, whilst the Kurdish heroine Shatrin in *The Fortified Castle* is harshly reprimanded for her unrestrained and attractive feminine laughter in front of men. The chaste women of *Men and a City* are respectfully kept behind closed doors, whilst the heroine of *Get Out, Damned One!* (said to represent Saddam's eldest daughter Raghad) leads an entire army against foreign invaders. Saddam's novels were written in such quick succession (four novels in as many years) that it is not possible for there to have been genuine ideological shifts in his views towards women, resulting in the 'random mix' to which al-Takarli refers in the title of his article. According to Mikhail Bakhtin, genre should be privileged as the central prism through which texts should be interpreted. Indeed, genre determines the context in which women are viewed and how accommodating the state can be regarding female sexual behaviour, providing a clue towards a better understanding of these discrepancies. *Zabiba and the King* is marketed as a romance and, like *Get Out, Damned One!*, is an allegorical narrative set in ancient Babylon, where women are not subject to the moral codes of a post-Islam world. For this reason, it becomes easier for the author to incorporate more liberal views on women, and to even discuss women's bodies in a more frank and explicit manner.

On the other hand, *The Fortified Castle* and *Men and a City* are decidedly more conservative; the latter in particular, as an autobiography of sorts, contains by far the most conservative views of women, and is the only text out of the four that lacks a credible female protagonist, precisely because the women in the novel are based on *real* women, however symbolic their role may be. Female chastity is idealised in the novels set in modern Iraq because the destiny of the nation is tied to both its longevity and demographic growth, meaning that as bearers of the nation's future, women have the potential to shape the identity of the nation. In *Men and a City*, subtle hints about the potentially unfaithful Kurdish protagonist Shatrin reveal deeper anxieties about the so-called national treachery of the Kurds, and the fear of adultery becomes directly analogous to treachery in a political sense and racial contamination. However, Shatrin does not go as far as infidelity, as Saddam is torn between depicting a harmonious multi-ethnic nation under the Ba'th in the way that it was expressed before Kurdish rebellions began during the Iran–Iraq War and the sedition of Iraqi Kurdistan, and venting his anger against the Kurds as potential foreign agents and 'pollutants' of the nation's purity.

The utilisation of the status of women as a means of demarking the boundary between barbarism and civilisation is an oft-used orientalist stereotype in discourses about the Arab and Muslim world, particularly during contentious political crises. In an article published on the website of the BBC, it was claimed that Saddam's novels expressed contempt for women as 'deceptive adulterers'.[125] This reading (a personal attack possibly intended to further discredit Saddam before an impending American and British invasion of Iraq) overlooked the fact that the depiction of female figures is overwhelmingly positive in Saddam's works, and that the adulteresses referred to in the article are in fact redeemed. In Saddam's debut novel of 2001, for example, the adulterous 'Joan of Arc'[126] of the novel Zabiba is justified in her preference for King 'Arab over her brutal husband. Moreover, Saddam's penultimate novel *Get Out, Damned One!* expresses an idealisation and trust of Arab women, and it even redeems the morally compromised (and foreign) Um Ladha (meaning the Mother of Pleasure in a nod to her hedonism) who is murdered by Hasqil, the Jewish antagonist in the novel when she regrets committing adultery with him. Ironically, the novels that are most forgiving of the sexual misbehaviour of women, namely, the first and fourth novels, were precisely the works that received the most media attention and were subject to the least nuanced or objective critical readings, particularly regarding the stance they express on women. This chapter argues that the novels of Saddam Hussein functioned differently according to the chosen genre: the historical fantasies *Zabiba and the King* and *Get Out, Damned One!* were directed at Saddam's enemies in the West, first, as a reminder of Iraq's cultural superiority and ancient glory, and, secondly, as a rebuttal of accusations that Iraq's treatment of its women was 'backward'. Both novels feature strong militant female characters that defend their people against foreign invaders, highlighting the political salience of texts that were marketed as 'resistance literature'. As for his second and third novels, *The Fortified Castle* and *Men and a City* set during Iraq's tumultuous modern history, these were inward-looking texts directed at Iraqi and Arab audiences which expressed explicit nationalist metaphors through personal and collective narratives. As such, these novels are less forgiving of potentially transgressive female behaviour and struggle to balance the liberal discourses on women which are historically appropriate to the texts' spatio-temporal setting and the conservative climate in Iraq at the time of the their production.

Torn between supposedly progressive Ba'thist discourses and practices regarding women, and political and economic changes which led to more conservative approaches to the 'Woman Question', the novels of Saddam Hussein exemplify the mixed messages on women perpetuated by the Ba'th. This chapter has argued that there is a dilemma inherent in depicting the feminine ideal, in which woman as symbol contradicts woman as real individual or believable literary character. This dilemma is in many ways an artistic question regarding plot, allegory and characterisation, but as propagandistic texts, the novels more importantly shed light on extra-literary debates. Ambiguity in depicting women in Saddam's novels often translates into anxiety regarding Iraq's national identity, where the focus on female chastity metamorphoses into an obsession with the purity of the nation; its roots and rural origins and identity. Saddam was, above all, a pragmatist, and was neither an advocate for women's rights nor strictly a reactionary misogynist.

Notes

1. Fu'ād al-Takirlī, 'Qirā'a fi riwāyat ṣaddām ḥusayn "ukhruj minhā yā mal'ūn" (1–2): khalṭa 'ashwā'iya bayna al-tārīkh wa al-siyāsa bi-ramziyya fajja', *al-Sharq al-Awsaṭ*, 13 September 2004.

2. Adid Dawisha, *Iraq: a Political History from Independence to Occupation* (Princeton, NJ: Princeton University Press, 2009), p. 238.
3. Mohammed Ḥussein Haikal, *Zainab*, trans. John Mohammed Grinsted (London: Darf Publishers, 1989), p. 15.
4. *Zabība wa al-malik*: riwāya li-kātibihā (Iraq: s.n., 2001), pp.70, 97.
5. Ibid., p. 121.
6. Fāṭima al-Muḥsin, 'al-ra'īs wa tajalīh al-riwā'ī', *al-Thaqāfa al-Jadīda*, available at: http://www. althakafaaljadeda.com/fatma_almu7sen.htm, last accessed 4 October 2018 (my emphasis).
7. Anderson, *Imagined Communities*, pp. 7–10.
8. Ibid., p. 49.
9. *Zabība wa al-malik*, p. 158.
10. *The Meaning of the Glorious Quran*, trans. Mohammed Marmaduke Pickthall (New York: A. A. Knopf, 1930), 14: 23–6.
11. O'Shaughnessy, *Politics and Propaganda*, pp. 38–42.
12. Mu'ammar al-Qadhdhāfi, *al-Qarya al-qarya, al-arḍ al-arḍ, wa-intiḥār rā'id al-faḍā' wa-qiṣaṣ ukhrā* (London: Riad El-Rayyes, 1995), p. 11.
13. Ibid., p. 28.
14. *Zabība wa al-malik*, p. 25.
15. Ofra Bengio, 'Saddam Husayn's Novel of Fear', *Middle East Quarterly* 11(1) (2002): 9–18; and Salām 'Abbūd, 'al-Diktatūr yarwī sīratahu: mukhaiyilat al-'unf bi'athar raj'ī', 9 January 2006, available at: http://www.iraqmemory.org/INP/view.asp?ID=68, last accessed 20 December 2018.
16. *Zabība wa al-malik*, p. 42.
17. Ibid., p. 132.
18. *Ukhruj minhā yā mal'ūn*: riwāya li-kātibihā (Baghdād: Dār al-Ḥurrīyya li-al-Ṭibā'a wa al-Nashr, 2003), p. 67.
19. Ibid., p. 10.
20. In his analysis of the linguistic elements of Jahiz's thinking, Yasir Suleiman outlines Jahiz's classification of audible (*natiq*) objects into *fasih* (those who are intelligible in any language, i.e., human beings) and *a'jam*, i.e., other animals. What distinguishes being *fasih* in the Arabic language is the clarity or *bayan* of its speakers, something which Hasqil loses in this scene of the novel. According to Jahiz's configuration, this would align him in a dehumanising way with unintelligible creatures (*a'jam*). The fact that a'jam and '*ajam* (non-Arabs) are so similar linguistically, and are often used interchangeably in discourse, points more generally to the association of Arabic with the higher human faculties of

logic and reasoning, alongside the value-laden association of Arabic with chivalry and honour present in this novel. Yasir Suleiman, '*Bayān* as a Principle of Taxonomy: Linguistic Elements in Jāhiz's Thinking', *Journal of Semitic Studies* Supp.14 (2002): *Studies on Arabia in Honour of G. Rex Smith*, John F. Healey and Venetia Porter (eds) (Oxford: Oxford University Press, 2002).

21. *Ukhruj minhā yā malʿūn*, p. 88.
22. Ibid., p. 168.
23. ʿAbd al-Hādī Fukaykī, *al-Shuʿūbīya wa al-qawmīya al-ʿarabīya* (Bayrūt: n.d.), pp. 20, 52, 111.
24. *Ukhruj minhā yā malʿūn*, p. 29.
25. Ibid., p. 154.
26. Elie Podeh uses this term to refer to the 'fullness' of the Baʿth state calendar, which he says is indicative of a crisis in Iraq's national identity. Podeh, 'From Indifference to Obsession'.
27. Michel ʿAflaq, *Fī sabīl al-baʿth* (Bayrūt: Dār al-Ṭalīʿah lil-Ṭibāʿa wa-al-Nashr, al-Ṭabʿa 7, 1972), p. 50.
28. *Al-Qalʿa al-ḥaṣīna:* riwāya li-kātibihā (Baghdād: Dār al-Ḥurrīya, 2001), p. 9.
29. Ibid., p. 203.
30. Ibid., pp. 219, 236.
31. Ibid., p. 108.
32. Ibid., p. 33.
33. Ibid., p. 49.
34. Fāṭima al-Muḥsin, 'al-Ra'īs wa tajjalīh al-riwā'ī'.
35. O'Shaughnessy stresses the need for propaganda to be explicit and clear, 'unlike other forms of advocacy', *Politics and Propaganda*, p. 16.
36. *Al-Qalʿa al-ḥaṣīna*, p. 7.
37. For example, ibid., pp. 658–9.
38. Ibid., p. 6
39. Ibid., p. 5.
40. Ibid., p. 8.
41. ʿAbbūd, *Thaqāfat al-ʿunf fī al-ʿirāq*, p. 227.
42. *Al-Qalʿa al-ḥaṣīna*, p. 30.
43. Ibid., p. 14.
44. Ibid., p. 5.
45. Ibid., p. 64.
46. Ibid.
47. Ibid., p. 166.

48. Ibid., p. 504. This Englishman had previously tried to bribe the Bedouin women who had captured him with money, in order to secure his release, and was a spy trained in Lebanon, the author says.
49. Ibid., pp. 356, 407–8.
50. Ibid., p. 490.
51. Ibid., pp. 149–52.
52. Ibid., p. 160.
53. Ibid., p. 308.
54. Ibid., p. 540.
55. Ibid., p. 40.
56. Ibid., p.26.
57. Ibid., pp. 65–6.
58. Ibid., pp. 157–8.
59. *Al-Qal'a al-ḥaṣīna*, p. 228.
60. Ibid., p. 212.
61. Ibid., p. 246.
62. Ibid., p. 557.
63. Ibid., p. 713.
64. A positive type of jealousy closely connected to honour, *ghira* is located outside the male self but often defines him. The feeling can most accurately be described as a refusal to allow others to violate a female entity connected to men, usually female kin but symbolically the nation.
65. Yuval-Davis and Helm, *Gender and the Nation*, p. 46.
66. *Rijāl wa madīna:* riwāya li-kātibihā (Baghdād: Dār al-Ḥurrīya li-al-Ṭibā'a, 2002), p. 4.
67. Ibid., p. 5.
68. Ibid., p. 4.
69. Ibid., p. 3.
70. Ibid., p. 4.
71. Ibid., p. 6.
72. Ibid., pp. 92–3.
73. Ibid., p. 119.
74. Ibid., p. 5.
75. Stephen Guth, 'Why Novels not Autobiographies', in Robin Ostle, Ed de Moor and Stefan Wild (eds), *Writing the Self: Autobiographical Writing in Modern Arabic Literature* (London: Saqi Books, 1998), p. 139.
76. Jameson, *The Political Unconscious*, p. 106.

77. *Rijāl wa madīna*, p. 6 (my emphasis).
78. Selim, *The Novel and the Rural Imaginary*, p. 2.
79. Genette, *Paratexts*, p. 2.
80. Abdul Ameer al-Muʿalla, *The Long Days* (Pt 1), trans. Mohieddin Ismail (London: Ithaca Press, 1979).
81. O'Shaughnessy, *Politics and Propaganda*, p. 43.
82. Stephen Guth asserts that 'the novel which comes closest to autobiographical reality is essentially a story of success', Guth, 'Why Novels not Autobiographies?', p. 142.
83. *Rijāl wa madīna*, p. 294.
84. Bengio, *Saddam's Word*, p. 182.
85. *Rijāl wa madīna*, p. 3.
86. Ibid., p. 10.
87. Said K. Aburish, *Saddam Hussein: the Politics of Revenge* (London: Bloomsbury, 2001), p. 11.
88. *Rijāl wa madīna*, p. 20.
89. Ibid., p. 46.
90. Ibid., p. 193.
91. Ibid., p. 205.
92. Ibid., p. 46.
93. According to Guth, all autobiographies are fictionalised accounts of reality: 'Writing an autobiography means producing a fictional account. It gives a life a meaning which is not inherent in this life itself.' Guth, 'Why Novels not Autobiographies?', p. 147.
94. *Rijāl wa madīna*, p. 142.
95. Ibid., pp. 92–3.
96. Ibid., p. 94.
97. Ibid., p. 132.
98. Ibid., p. 96.
99. Ibid., p. 62.
100. Ibid., p. 162.
101. Ibid., pp. 81–2.
102. Ibid., pp. 90–1.
103. Ibid., p. 335.
104. Ibid., pp. 37–8. The literal meaning of *sayyid* is master (derived from the gerund *siyada* meaning dominance or control). However, in some Arab communities, particularly those with Shia populations, the term sayyid has come to

mean descendant of the Prophet Mohammed, and more specifically through his grandson Husayn (rather than Hassani sayyids who are predominately Sunni, and who are often referred to as sharifs).

105. *Rijāl wa madīna*, p. 218.
106. Ibid., pp. 73–4.
107. Ibid., p. 28.
108. Ibid., p. 85.
109. Ibid., p. 87.
110. Ibid., p. 170
111. 'Abbūd, 'al-Diktatūr yarwī sīratahu: mukhaiyilat al-'unf bi'athar raj'ī'.
112. *Rijāl wa madīna*, p. 114.
113. Ibid., p. 191.
114. Ibid., p. 189.
115. 'Abbūd, 'al-Diktatūr yarwī sīratahu: mukhaiyilat al-'unf bi'athar raj'ī'.
116. *Rijāl wa madīna*, pp. 107–9.
117. Ibid., p. 28.
118. Geoff Simons, *Iraq: From Sumer to Saddam* (Basingstoke: Macmillan, 1996), p. 273.
119. *Rijāl wa madīna*, p. 86.
120. Ibid., p. 295.
121. Ibid., p. 99.
122. Ibid., pp. 174–5.
123. Brennan, 'The National Longing for Form', p. 53.
124. *Al-Qal'a al-ḥaṣīna*, p. 482.
125. Available at: http://news.bbc.co.uk/1/hi/entertainment/arts/2981394.stm, last accessed 3 October 2018.
126. Bengio, 'Saddam Husayn's Novel of Fear'.

PART 2

3

Fighting Fire with Fire: the Islamic Novel in Iraq and the Battle for Hearts and Minds

The wide scale and organised production of written material for the consumption of a growing readership meant for the first time in modern history people, the Iraqi people, especially women, were exposed to a plethora of texts which explicitly or not served the ideology of the state. This chapter argues that the appropriation of the novel by Shia women writers with an Islamic agenda was a pragmatic endeavour designed to woo young girls away from the secularising effects of the modern novel and its pertaining nationalist discourses as advocated by the Ba'th. In so doing, authors aimed to re-privatise the female space and female sexuality at a time when the state was steadily encroaching upon the traditionally female space of the home for the sake of building and developing the nation-state. The push for the economic utilisation of women during Iraq's economic boom in the late 1960s and 1970s meant that women were more and more visible in the public eye, and public discourses on women by the Ba'th called for equality between the sexes, an agenda pushed by the female branch of the Ba'th Party: the General Federation of Iraqi Women (GFIW). As such, the seemingly reactionary discourses of the authors in question, however conservative when viewed from a modern, liberal and eurocentric world view, in fact represented a challenge to Ba'thist legitimacy at a particular moment in the history of the Party, that is to say, when it was at its most 'secular'. It is important to remember that once the economic need for women had been expended during the war, and the threat of Iran's Islamic revivalist discourse had become apparent, Ba'thist state discourses became just as, if not more, conservative than the authors here, calling on Iraqi women to resume their true roles as mothers and daughters, and encouraging them to have at least four children each to boost the war effort in order to address the demographic gap between Iraq and Iran. According to Nada Shabout, the focus on mothering, and the return in Iraqi culture of women to the position of mothers signifies a setback in women's rights and discourses on women more generally.[1]

The politicisation of women's role as bearer of children has ramifications for their generative qualities and potential role in bearing culture. Therefore, to characterise marriage and childbearing as purely regressive in the context of women's empowerment tends towards an over-simplification of the symbolic representation of Iraqi women in discourse. This chapter argues that the language used to signify 'progress' and 'regression' is often steeped in a religious–secular polemic which does not accurately represent the complexity of power configurations and contestations.

As has been expounded in previous chapters, the Ba'th sent contradictory messages regarding women throughout the decades. However, sexual purity remains a key feature of all these discourses: sex and sexual consummation through marriage in early nationalist works represented a pure nationalist allegory without moral implications, as it symbolised the formation of nationalist bonds. In later discourses, sex and marriage were framed within the honour–shame paradigm rather than a strictly moral or ethical one. The Islamic appropriation of the novel genre was symbolically powerful and also used marriage allegorically. In these texts, marriage is extolled as an institution that could safeguard the chastity of young girls and initiate them back into a traditional familial and community structure. This ultimately challenged the state's perceived intrusion into the female space and its supposed liberation of women through economic opportunity and lax moral codes. Although religious sermons had played a vital role in the education, guidance and ideologisation of young Iraqi women in the build up to the Iranian revolution, the adoption of the novel was deemed necessary to combat what was seen as the innate voyeurism of the genre. For early Islamic authors, secular novels presented a new threat to the minds of young virgins. The fear of young girls indulging in novels filled with innuendo and sexual allusions; of being seduced by the furtive, and almost promiscuous pleasure of novel reading; this fear constitutes the driving force behind the emergence of female Islamic novelists in the late 1960s and 1970s. In *Mudhakarat mughtariba* (*Memoirs of a Student Abroad*), Khawla al-Qazwīnī (1955–) attacks 'love stories, romances and explicit magazines',[2] which she fears will sexualise young girls, leading her to engage in a textual battle between good and evil for the hearts and minds of women.

The rise of a female readership, the first generation of its kind in modern Iraqi history, was deemed as an opportunity by the state to spread and inculcate its values amongst its populace. Several liberal women's magazines emerged, often with women in bathing suits on the front covers, and many young girls from middle-class families grew up on a steady diet of popular romance novels translated from Western languages. This was a trend which affected women from all sectors of Iraqi society, including the country's Shia majority. According to Rohde, 'eroticised pictures of women highlighted contempt for religious sensibilities in the early days of the Baʿth'.[3] It is against this backdrop that the emergence of an Islamic novel pioneered by women must be understood. According to the authors treated in this chapter, and in line with broader religious discourses, women were seen as most vulnerable to the cultural onslaught of Western imperialism as represented by Arab socialism, which infused written materials with its alien values; values that were explicitly encouraged by the state to corrupt Iraqi women and turn them away from God and Islam. The interest in novel writing as a didactic and pedagogical tool by religious Shia women in Iraq was based on assumptions about women as subjects amenable to persuasion and influence, as well as understandings of the role of the newly emergent novel genre in shaping en masse the world views of young girls and women. The idea that young girls were fickle, shallow and easily manipulated informs much of the characterisation aspect of Islamic novels, particularly the characterisation of antagonists.

Public debates about women's dress, modesty codes and attempts to challenge taboos on sexuality formed part of the cultural atmosphere in Iraq in the 1960s and through the 1970s, and the hijab rarely featured in these. For example, Achim Rohde notes that there were debates as to whether very short skirts should be permitted on university campuses.[4] With the rise of Islam as a political power in neighbouring Iran and the emergence of conspicuous markers of religious devotion in the hijab, Baʿthist representatives of the GFWI were even sent to female religious gatherings to encourage women to abandon 'backward' religious practices, including donning the veil and the abaya specifically.[5] According to Zahra Ali 'Shia Islamicization with its gender norms (hijab and sexual morality) and religious rituals (*Arbaʿin*, *'Ashura*)[6] became tools to resist the Baʿth'.[7] The onslaught of modernisation and secularism threatened the power of Shia scholars and literati as keepers of ancient knowledge, and the centralisation of education had shifted power away from the *hawza*, the traditional centre of learning in Shia culture. Secular modernisation also threatened 'heritage' elements of Shiism and certain ritualistic elements of the sect, such as the annual commemoration of the martyrdom of Husayn, including public processions. These were banned in the fear that they could develop into full-blown revolts as they had in Iraq's recent history. Rizk Khoury notes that 70 per cent of participants in Shia rituals in 1983 were women, making them symbolic and actual holders of a new 'cassette culture' which democratised scriptural knowledge for lay people.[8]

According to Sabry Hafez, modern literature 'violated the symbolic domain of Islam'.[9] One reason for this is that the older community of religious scholars and notables is often excluded from the processes of modernisation and the 'democratisation of knowledge' which granted power to the powerless through language and literary form. According to Hafez, literary texts are open, whilst scripture is closed, as a reflection of Islam's status as the last Abrahamic religion. Hafez contrasts the monophonic voice of religious texts to the polyphony he sees as inherent to modern narrative structures. He stresses that the Islamic *umma* is seen as an essentially fixed concept with set poetic genres, whereas the '*watan*' nation is new, subversive and more complex in terms of genre. In Iraq, attempts to replace the religious concept of the Islamic *umma*, first with Arab nationalism, and then with a more specific Iraqi nationalism, clashed with calls to revitalise political and cultural connections through Islam in the late 1970s and 1980s. The penchant towards totalitarianism and the erasure of religious experiences from public discourses produced a secular homogenising voice, rather than the polyphony that characterises the novel genre proper, according to Bakhtin and others. This is met with an equally uncompromising and authoritative religious voice in Islamic novels.

Modern Islamic literature as a genre has not been extensively produced or studied, as it often falls in the gap between the study of history, literature and cultural studies. The corpus of works by religious Arab women seems to warrant a different, more interdisciplinary approach, as methods drawn from traditional literary analyses of canonical works seem to fall short of providing a full understanding of their social impact and political significance. The use of realistic fiction for instruction was not new. In pre-modern Arab prose traditions, didactic prose, for example, anecdotal writing in the *adab* genre often straggled boundaries between fiction and non-fiction. As for Islamic writing by women in the modern world, perhaps the earliest instances of 'pure fiction' didactic writing by an Arab Shia woman was Dalāl Khalīl Ṣafadī's *Hawadith wa ʿibar* (*Events and Morals*) published in 1935 in Lebanon, and republished two years later in 1937 by the al-Raʿi Press, Najaf. In 1965, Safadi also published *Arbaʿun qissa haqiqiya waqiʿiya* (*Forty Real-life Stories*) from her new home in Canada. These kinds of short stories signalled the emergence of a new literary genre headed by Arab Shia women, which would develop into novellas and full-length novels under the author credited with establishing the female religious novel, Āmina al-Ṣadr, famously known by her pen-name Bint al-Hudā. In their seminal compilation of Arab female writers, Ferial Ghazoul and Radwa Ashour mention three Islamic female authors in addition to Safadi, all of whom are Iraqi or have ties with Iraq: Bint al-Hudā, Khawla al-Qazwīnī and Ma'ida al-Rabiʿi.[10] Although other popular novelists were not included, the anthology addresses a gap in scholarly recognition of Islamic-leaning writing by women. Islamic novels by women fall outside the canon in many ways primarily because they do not espouse the values associated with modernity and liberalism. As such, these niche works do not have transcendental value and would not appeal to a wide range of audiences or literati. Widely read by unmarried Muslim women at an important historical juncture, but not given enough critical attention, the educational texts in this chapter bear the hallmark of ideological texts that are 'of the moment', emerging in spurts according to the ebb and flow of the political Islamic tide.

Islamic discourse in religious novels by women in Iraq falls between the doctrinal and heritage function, as expounded by Sabry Hafez. Core Islamic beliefs seem to be unquestionable and are not discussed except the hijab and sex outside marriage as, first, being deemed issues that particularly affected women, and, secondly, because they were easily amenable to instrumentalisation by capitalising on the symbolic and social significance of issues related to female sexuality and male–female interactions. By marking out sexual promiscuity as an issue that primarily affects women, and by making explicit links between women's dress and sexual activity with social corruption, and by extension, the corruption of the whole country, women are used as an allegory for corruption to attack the Baʿth. According to the authors in this chapter, the modern Iraqi woman was a product of Baʿthist corruption under a thin veneer of sexual liberation. The female body often functioned as a site of contention in political and cultural discourses in Baʿthist Iraq, and this manifested itself particularly as a struggle between various utopias symbolised by woman. Islamic writers yearn for the utopia of a righteous society free of vice, at the centre of which is a rethinking of the place of women, and, perhaps more importantly, the appearance of women. According to this discourse, Islam keeps women from being exploited by the sexualising forces of modernity and secularism, and preserves female dignity through the emphasis on chastity (represented by the hijab) as a protective barrier shielding the body from the onslaught of foreign ideas and foreign men. Similarly, virtuous books are intended to shield the mind from the impure thoughts and twisted values of Western culture.

Conversely, the Baʿth also saw itself as a liberal and progressive utopia for women, and adopted policies that served female empowerment when Iraq's 'golden generation' of women were needed to help boost the economy in the 1960s and 1970s. In the novels discussed in this chapter, being home-bound is a form of resistance; it is to resist being part of a new economic and social order at the heart of which are oppressive governments which do not fear God, and which revel in depravity and corruption. Where empowerment in the 1970s and early 1980s signified the Baʿth female contribution to the economy and less emphasis on the home as the 'natural' space for women, the Islamic writers in this chapter envision the sanctity of the home as the ultimate form of happiness and fulfillment, with protagonists leaving the home only to pursue knowledge or visit relatives, which is regarded as a religious obligation. In *Memoirs of a Woman Abroad*, the protagonist's scholarship to America becomes a missionary quest, and she spends most of her time either at university or at home. Indeed, it is only in the interest of spiritual growth and connection to her Islamic roots that the protagonist visits the house of a devout Lebanese woman and her widower brother. These visits revolve almost exclusively around religious discussions regarding the dilemma of being a Muslim in the West, but also lead to the development of a love interest which is not fulfilled.

The rise of the hijab from the late 1970s onwards was not only a marker of political Islam, but was also a symbol of resistance to state encroachment into the female sphere. In one personal account, noted by Nadje Al-Ali in her oral history project, one woman expresses the idea that donning the veil was a sign of resistance for women of her generation.[11] Donning the veil allowed for the re-privatising of women's lives at a time when traditional notions of female sexuality and space as private were being challenged. Indeed, the most striking feature of Islamic novels is their restraint, which is evident in the authorial voice and tone of the text, as well as its characterisation and theme. The authors examined in this chapter attempt to make their characters relatable by providing access to their inner thoughts by using stream of consciousness techniques, but these thoughts are transmitted through a narrow filter of ideology. Similarly, the hijab functions as a stylistic device that forms a barrier between the reader and the characters; the latter are not 'violated' by the prying eyes of the reader, as their private lives remain private, as they would be if a guest visited their house for the first time, for example. The idea of 'closed' and 'open' texts is useful here, as prescriptive or didactic texts often do not allow for multiple interpretations, especially as there is often self-censorship on the part of authors in order to produce ideologically coherent texts. The act of closing the text by not allowing the reader access to the inner thoughts of characters is a means of restoring appropriate social order, respectability and propriety that the author feels has been lost in Iraqi society.

'As if there is a War': the Battle over Morality in Bint al-Hudā's *Virtue Prevails* and Khawla al-Qazwinī's *When a Man Thinks*

Educated at home in a family of religious scholars, Āmina al-Ṣadr (1937–1980) published her novels in the years building up to Saddam's ascension to absolute power from among the ranks of the Ba'th Party. Al-Ṣadr helped to established several religious schools for girls in the holy city of Najaf and al-Kadhimiya, a Shia suburb of Baghdad, and wrote for *al-Adwa'* (*The Lights*), an Islamic magazine published by the religious *'ulama* of Najaf, under the pen-name Bint al-Hudā meaning 'Daughter of Guidance'. She also participated in the mobilising efforts of the Shia uprising of 1977 in the month of Safar, called the 'Fortieth Uprising' instigated by the Baʿthist authorities' attempts to deny the faithful from visit rights to the shrine of Husayn, which prompted a severe backlash.[12] This activism and political support of her brother was probably what made her a threat to the state and not her novels as such. Both Āmina and her brother Sayyid Mohammed Baqir Al-Sadr were tortured and executed in 1980 on the orders of Saddam Hussein, and their bodies were not returned to their family, presumably as a deterrent to other Shia to toe the state line. Bint al-Hudā was, and in many ways still is, the most prolific and popular writer of modern Islamic fiction. Her works went into multiple editions and were distributed across the Gulf among Arab Shia communities, as well as in Lebanon and Iraq. There are also several collected volumes of her works, both fiction and non-fiction. By the year of her death in 1980, her most popular novel *al-Fadila tantasir* (*Virtue Prevails*, 1969) was in its sixth edition; sales no doubt boosted by the author's execution at the hands of Saddam Hussein's security forces. Read by generations of women and young girls, many Shia Arab readers attribute their first exposure to literature to her, as conservative parents considered the novels ideal forms of entertainment for young adults.

Bint al-Hudā chose the novel for ideological reasons, rather than as an artistic or creative choice.[13] In the introduction to her short story collection *Laytani kuntu aʿlam* (*I Wish I Had Known,* 1978), the Beirut-based publisher hopes that the stories 'can save the souls of the new generation'.[14] This latent fear of the corrupting influences of socialist ideologies on women is then used as a proxy to attack the political system, which may explain why Bint al-Hudā's books were eventually banned in Iraq. However, the most potent signifier of all was probably her name, as the ultimate marker of identity and clerical authority, which posed a real challenge to the state – even if that name was to be found on something as innocuous as a novel. After 1980, the al-Sadrs symbolised martyrdom and injustice, an extension of the martyrdom and oppression of the family of the Prophet, to which they, as sayyids, belonged. Crucially, Bint al-Hudā's pen-name was used instead of Āmina al-Sadr, but there was no doubt as to her identity. The choice to use a pseudonym remains significant symbolically; it is out of modesty that al-Sadr does not mention her name, as the spirit of her writings is more important.

Interestingly, the author's aversion to fame or glory is a motif taken up in a similar way by Saddam Hussein in his novels, albeit pushed to theatrical proportions.

If Only I had Known is a good example of titles being used as mirrors of textual intent in ideological texts, indicating a pre-*sahwa* (religious revival) consciousness that sees the secular world as being in a state of ignorance comparable to that of pre-Islamic Arabia (*jahiliya*). The feeling of regret inherent in the title of the novel echoes Qur'anic discourse which paints a picture of the afterlife in which human beings constantly regret not having sought or listened to the truth (biting fingers out of sheer regret). The author here attempts to save the souls of as many women as she can before it is too late, and by 1981 there were already four editions of this book. In the publisher's peritext, the literary space is depicted as a battleground between good and evil, where committed writers use the genre to guide readers towards higher values, and where irresponsible authors deliberately use the novel to poison the minds of the young. In another text titled *al-Bahitha 'an al-haqiqa* (*The Seeker of Truth*), the novel is depicted as a means to an end, and the author's aims always extend beyond art into philosophical, political, social and religious debates as a way of saving the new generation from corruption and waywardness.[15] A copy of this book was kept in Baghdad's national library in 1979, meaning that religious texts written by women were not seen as threatening probably even after the Safar uprisings and the political activism of the author's brother, Ayatollah Mohammed Baqir Al-Sadr. It thus seemed that an outright ban of Bint al-Hudā's works was unnecessary, as news of her execution at the hands of the regime sent a clear enough message from the state.

In 'Kalima wa da'wa' ('A Word and a Call'),[16] a collection of sermons by Bint al-Hudā, all the sermons begin with 'Dear Sister', as the anonymity of the author extends to the audience of the sermon, leaving the reader to focus on just the message rather than the transmitter or recipient. She applauds the missionary role of nuns, which is favourably compared with religious Muslim women, who are not doing enough for the young and do not preach openly due to the fear of being ridiculed or censored. In the prologue to *Virtue Prevails*, her most famous novel, al-Sadr begins: 'I am not a novelist or story writer; I have never tried before this to write a story.' She claims to want to paint a realistic picture of everyday life in Iraq where 'the forces of good and evil collide', and where *'aqida* (religious creed) is battling against 'the culture and behaviour of imperialism and imperialists'.[17] Although any work of fiction necessarily involves imagination, Bin al-Hudā explicitly aims at *waqiʿiya* (realism), not in the sense of the realist movement in literature as she seems somewhat detached from modern literary tradition in Iraq, the Arab world and the wider international novelistic tradition. The emphasis on *waqiʿiya* in almost all Bint al-Hudā's novels represented a way of challenging the predominance of secular culture in state representations of the 'average' Iraqi household. In contrast, the 'realistic life' or 'realistic love' supposedly depicted in the novels represented highly stylised attempts to portray the 'real Iraq', with a conservative Shia perspective at its centre. There was, of course, no single Iraq, whether secular or religious, however an 'ideal' Iraq was projected onto the national imaginary by the state, which attempted to ethnically and religiously homogenise the nation-state in public discourses. Bint al-Hudā and other religious writers challenged and resisted this process by giving a voice to what can be considered a subaltern discourse, and in so doing, aimed to force the state to acknowledge the existence of religious sensibilities as part of the nation. Herein lies the importance of using the novel genre as a national allegory and the pertinence of Bint al-Hudā's choice to turn to narrative genres rather than traditional ones like poetry, which she also wrote.

According to Sabry Hafez, before speculating about Islam in a text, its role or centrality, 'significant textual investigation' must be done. The concept of simulacrum is central to understanding the utopian elements of propaganda literature generally, and ideological Islamic texts specifically. For Islamic authors life should imitate the ideal, which necessarily leads to a clash between competing utopias: the secular Baʿthist utopias outlined in previous chapters and a potentially more dangerous discourse, threatening to state hegemony, which is the Islamic utopian ideal. The promise of heaven, and the use of the so-called 'Golden Age' of Islam to prove that utopias can be achieved make Islamic discourses particularly potent. Hafez states that 'simulacrum is the opposite of representation, as it turns religion into politics'.[18] Indeed, Bint al-Hudā's *waqiʿiya* is not really representation, rather it is utopia as a stylistic device that politicises imaginary events as 'the way things should be'. The performative aspect of Islamic novels lies in the creation of examples of exemplary behaviour; fictitious role models with no inner conflict or contradictions. Piety is performed for the emulation of the reader in the context of a domestic drama genre which supposedly reflected the realities of Iraqi society. In fact, the novels present a simulated reality stripped of nuance to galvanise the faithful into action, as they are given a choice between two opposing world views.

Virtue Prevails tells the story of a mature sixteen-year-old named Naqa' who is engaged to be married to Ibrahim, an upright man from a devout family. Naqa''s blissful happiness at the match is interrupted by her maternal cousin Su'ad, who is irreligious and jealous of Naqa' as she had hoped to marry Ibrahim herself. Su'ad's husband Mahmud is rich and spoiled and the couple lead a disreputable life of parties and affairs. Out of vengefulness, Su'ad attempts to ruin Naqa''s reputation by directing her unsuspecting husband to woo and seduce her. She tells him that Naqa' is merely dressed as a saint but is in fact a woman of ill-repute. However, once Mahmud approaches Naqa' at a public park, he realises that she is not the woman his wife painted her out to be. He is gradually influenced by his conversations with Naqa' and learns to change his ways to lead a more religious life. The novel's end thus echoes its title, with virtue (represented by Naqa') prevailing over sinfulness (as embodied by Su'ad) who is threatened with divorce.

Naqa' is held up as an example for other women; marrying young, she is innocent and pure *tahira* and has the angelic halo of a saint. Naqa' is not really a human being, rather she is 'a pure angel'[19] and a shining star who embodies chastity and virtue.[20] The author calls her 'the sister' who performs sacred duties and says that Naqa' shows that perfection can exist in human beings. As previous chapters have shown, a utopian sensibility often evolves into narratives of purity that issue damning indictments against those who cannot attain perfection or do not view it as such. Naqa' is an unattainable role model, however inspiring, which means she is not a relatable character. However, Naqa' is representative of discourses of purity which extend to wider issues about cultural authenticity, imperialism and East–West dichotomies, where the female body must not be polluted by even entering the West, for example. Naqa' refuses to honeymoon in Europe, despite the numerous anecdotes provided by Su'ad hailing the West as a beacon of liberty and progression,[21] and although he visits Europe often on business and for study, Ibrahim tells Naqa': 'If Europe was a pure place with a genuine authentic culture, I would have taken you there.'[22] He adds that girls are polluted by the 'poisonous germs'[23] of the West, which is why they must be protected within the private realm; whereas men seem to have a natural guard which protects them from Western influence. It is important to note that there were no explicit religious fatwas forbidding women from visiting the West, and many of Bint al-Hudā's followers sought religious guidance from her and her brother whilst studying or working abroad. Literary discourses and their symbolic power were used to deliver scathing political critiques through the proxy issue of women and marriage, and as such should not always be taken at face value.

Virtue Prevails embodies the contradictions inherent in the life of modern-day Muslims in Iraq, particularly women. An East–West dichotomy is established at the outset; one represented by virtue (*fadila*), while the other is marked by vice (*radhila*). The author signals the text as religious by invoking spiritual guidance and success from God (*tawfiq*) through the use of the basmallah: the traditional opening for chapters in the Qur'an which was and still is unusual for Arab novels. The conflict in the novel between Naqa' (purity) and her Westernised cousin Suʿad, meaning happy female or bringer of luck, is entirely symbolic. Although not a specifically religious name, Naqa' became very popular in Iraq as a result of its popularisation through the novel, which went into multiple reprints. On the other hand, the antagonist is given a secular name with no religious or moral connotations. For Suʿad, the pursuit of pleasure is a right and she is depicted as a hedonistic temptress who indulges in bodily and worldly pleasures in her pursuit of happiness. In her conversations, Suʿad uses very mild sexual innuendos and tells dirty jokes to her cousin which are meant to shock conservative female readers. Indeed, language and behaviour (particularly dress) are closely linked as markers of conformity or transgression.

Interestingly, al-Ṣadr has linked the protagonist and antagonist Naqa' and Suʿad by blood through their mothers and not their fathers, as the purity of Naqa' is maintained through her father's line and name. Purity is primarily defined as not having contact with men, sexually or otherwise, in line with certain interpretations of Islamic and specifically Shia religious discourses.

One example of this from Shia cultural heritage (although by no means an authenticated source), is the story of Zainab the daughter of Ali Ibn Abi Talib, who when she walked the streets of Kufa, men could not even see her shadow. Naqa' says that she does not receive men at home without the presence of her husband, does not attend mixed gatherings[24] and declines an invitation to Su'ad's wild birthday party.[25] Moreover, in a hyperbolic gesture of excessive zeal, Ibrahim implores Naqa' not to contaminate her photograph album by placing her cousin's picture next to her own. To oblige him she takes a step further and completely destroys Su'ad's photo, symbolically severing familial blood ties if they do not conform to her strict moral code.[26] There are several instances in Islamic novels of the severing of blood ties, action that is specifically condemned in the Islamic tradition. However, the emphasis on piety provides moral justification for this action and allows for the formation of new supranationalist bonds in the place of blood bonds.

Naqa' and Su'ad disagree as to what constitutes a happy marriage; whilst Naqa' seeks 'a realistic happiness'[27] with the 'pragmatic' Ibrahim, Su'ad asserts that a successful marriage should be built upon the principles of modern culture. Realism is advocated as an antidote to unrealistic expectations in novels and other printed material directed at women, particularly those arguments which advocate complete equality between the sexes in their rights and obligations or the division of labour inside and outside the home. What Naqa' sees as a 'happy nest',[28] Su'ad views as an imprisonment in line with post-war Western-inspired views on women's liberation in the 1950s. Su'ad is depicted from the very outset as being polluted by Western culture, a perverse temptress; she is labelled 'Satan', and her moral failings are attributed to the absence of a viable female role model in her life, as she lost her mother at a young age. On the surface, Iraqi society is to blame for the moral failings of women like Su'ad, victims who are predominately female and therefore, according to the author, more impressionable and easily mislead. However, taken in its political context, the act of bemoaning the corruption of society and 'foreign ideas' is an indirect attack on Arab socialism and its insidious attempts to marginalise Islam and Islamic values under the guise of freedom and women's rights. The author highlights the need to provide guidance to young girls through her novels, and she adopts a mothering and chastising role using the third-person narrator. Su'ad's 'poisonous words'[29] fall on deaf ears, as Naqa' determines to ask her fiancé about the status of women in Islam, and to get back to her cousin accordingly. Here, primacy is given to male authority, as Naqa' does not have the privilege of seniority or gender to be able to respond to Su'ad's arguments. In the ensuing episode, Ibrahim's dialogues with Naqa' are basically speeches or extended monologues, as he is the vessel through which the text's conservative discourses are voiced. Vessel characters of this kind are typically found in ideological novels, be they resistive or collaborative, and highlight the primacy of the message over literary style or form. Naqa', like Ibrahim, also takes on a symbolic role, but not a dominant one, signifying the female religious ideal of chastity and meekness in her deference to those older and wiser than herself, rather than being opinionated or strong willed.

Naqa's fiancé Ibrahim is described as being a young man of noble origin '*'ariq al-asl, rafi' al-manbat*'.[30] The use of pastoral imagery is a common literary trope of the Arab novel, invoking the pure unadulterated origins of the nation. Moreover, the idea that bloodlines are imbued with a sacred quality emanates from a specifically Shia religious understanding of lineages, given the fact that succession to the Prophet Mohammed is connected to his descendants through his daughter Fatima. It is notable that the name Ibrahim appears in several ideological novels across the political spectrum in Iraq, which is testament to the symbolic power of this name as a potential bridge between Iraq's various ethnicities and religions. Here, Ibrahim is a symbol of the origin of faith as the father of the three monotheistic religions and is said to be 'the dream of every believing virgin'.[31] The emphasis on virginity as an ideal in females that should be relinquished only to a deserving husband for the purposes of procreation, depicts women as mere vessels to carry the 'seeds' of men.

The use of origin as a marker of individual merit poses several questions: does Ibrahim's nobility stem from his faith or family? Is merit (primarily meaning piety in a religious context) inherited or is it acquired? Notably, *Virtue Prevails* was written before the Iranian Revolution, therefore it is less radical than expected in terms of its understanding of class and social hierarchy. Instead, the text follows the trajectory of Islamic tradition which conflates religious merit and compatibility in marriage. Compatibility is a central issue that goes beyond the individualistic or social effects of marriage, rather, it points to the espousal of values on a macro-cosmic scale. The idea of more companionate marriages emerges in later Islamic works as it represents the destiny of the nation and its ideological choices to either become secular in identity or religious. These later texts often involve a 'change of heart' where a secular (usually male) character transforms into a practising Muslim and marries the devout female protagonist. However, in the nascent stages of the Islamic novel, as exemplified by *Virtue Prevails*, marriage from the woman's perspective forms part of a kind of guardianship relationship, where the husband assumes the role of guide, protector and financial supporter.

The text reveals that Suʿad had secretly desired Ibrahim, and that he had scorned and rejected her because she was not upright and religious enough for his tastes. Suʿad's husband Mahmud is spoilt and jobless and is emasculated by the narrator by being financially supported by his father. The traditional configuration of masculinity as defined by the ability to provide is indicative of the author's conservative fictional agenda which she believes is supported by Islamic teachings. Suʿad plans to use her husband to tempt and ruin Naqa' to take revenge on Ibrahim for not choosing her. According to the author, she is 'like thousands of girls' tricked into pursuing hedonistic Western lifestyles to their ruin.[32] By 'ruin' or 'downfall', the author is referring directly to sexual promiscuity as symbolised by Suʿad's failure to dress modestly. The consumption of alcohol is also directly linked to sexual promiscuity and Westernisation due to its prohibition in Islam as the root of all sins. Suʿad's secret desire to marry Ibrahim seems at odds with her liberal character and reveals not only a blind jealousy of Naqa', but also a deep insecurity that she is a defiled woman with an instinctive yearning to possess something pure in her life. The idea that humans were all born with a *fitra*, an inherent inclination towards good, is reflected in the redemption of wayward characters in the novels of Bint al-Hudā specifically, and in the Islamic female novel more generally. Suʿad is not redeemed per se, but she is still afforded a chance to repent. Interestingly, however, her husband Mahmud is completely redeemed and is depicted as a victim of his wife, whom he loves but who has led him astray. The name Mahmud (the praiseworthy one) is also a popular name in ideological novels, first, for its ideological ambiguity or neutrality, being neither an explicitly religious or secular name, and, secondly, due to the name's moral connotations.

Naqa''s conservative beliefs lead her to relinquish her independence and mobility, and she even says that she does not need to learn to drive as she would not want to leave the house without her husband.[33] Moreover, despite being an avid reader, we know little about Naqa''s formal education, or whether she even attended school; a reflection, perhaps, of the author's own life as a home-schooler. In contrast, Ibrahim is said to be a doctorate student in France and, interestingly, it is only when Ibrahim leaves for Paris does Naqa' venture out; her first appearance in public is at the airport to see her husband off on a business trip. Suʿad attacks Naqa' for her isolation at home and her failure to integrate into wider society saying: 'and is this pathetic lifestyle you love and the isolation you have imposed on yourself part of your personal faith?' Naqa' replies that she is not interested in being integrated in a corrupt society and asserts that she has her own society of 'innocent relations and pure friendships'.[34] Naqa' is eager to challenge Suʿad's understanding of society, which she says is fundamentally flawed. When she responds to her cousin that she is not a social outcast or a recluse, but is in fact part of a larger community of believers, Suʿad exclaims: 'What is [this] society? Why can't we see them publicly, these millions who share your views.'[35] This exchange is significant to our understanding of the discursive power struggle that was taking place in Iraq at the time, as it highlights the predominance of secular values in the public sphere and the marginalisation of religious communities and their relegation outside what is considered 'normal' or 'moderate'. As Foucault has observed of power, dominant values attempt to pass themselves off as natural and neutral, whereas opposing values are considered extreme or fanatical. The text pits society (secular) against community (religious), however, in so doing it perpetuates the angel–whore stereotypes which do not recognise the diversity of female views and perspectives.

Although we are told that Naqa' leaves home only for the absolute essentials, such as fulfilling her religious duty by visiting relatives, she does go to a local park to read in solitude. The park represents a space for reflection on the beauty of God's creation; it is a means to an end and that end is almost entirely spiritual. While in public, Naqa' is deliberately introverted, and the act of reading is designed to block the undesirable advances of men. When Suʿad's husband Mahmud, spurred on by his wife, approaches Naqa' with the intention of seducing her, Naqa' transforms this encounter into a missionary quest and manages to 'convert' him into a God-fearing Muslim. Convinced by his wife that Naqa''s piety is merely a performance, Mahmud is shocked when he realises that her righteousness is not a façade; for when she loses her diamond earring at the park, Naqa' saves a beggarwoman who is caught with the jewels from arrest by claiming that she had in fact gifted it to the woman, and hands her the second earring.[36] When Mahmud observes this noble act, he apologises to Naqa' for harassing her and desperately asks her for help to reform his depraved lifestyle, which he claims is primarily caused by his wealth.[37] Naqa''s advice is for Mahmud to find himself a new community of believers who will support and guide him, asserting that her words are 'but one melody among thousands of pure and beautiful voices'.[38] Mahmud and Naqa''s relationship set a precedent in Islamic novels for the kind of interactions that were religiously permissible between unrelated men and women. Ultimately, contact between the sexes without the presence of chaperones seems to be acceptable only if it involves a higher purpose of guidance to the truth.

Virtue Prevails uses intertextuality by referencing verses from the Qur'an to discuss the unity of the Muslim *umma* in the face of an onslaught of Western ideas; the protagonist attends prayers in the grand mosque in Damascus, signalling a different kind of unity to the one advocated by Baʿthist pan-Arabism, when Syria and Iraq briefly joined to form the United Arab Republic from 1958 to 1961. It is important to comment on the setting of the text, which is deliberately ambiguous in the sense that the reader would assume that it is Iraq until the mention of Damascus once in the text. Hints of a Syrian setting are convenient, as Syria was similar enough to Iraq culturally and shared its political heritage as the birth place of Arab socialism which developed into Baʿthism. The author's insistence on realism is thus maintained but without explicitly attacking the Baʿth at home or angering state censors. Another ambiguous clue regarding the novel's setting is the name of the park that Naqa' frequents: *muntazah al-jumhuriya* (Park of the Republic). All in all, however, *Virtue Prevails* remains devoid of local colour and elevates the text beyond its localised perspectives to what the author sees as a universal parable. In so doing, she emphasises the importance of nonsectarian supranationalist bonds in the road to achieving a spiritual renaissance in Iraqi society. The bleeding out of local colour and the deliberate lack of specifity in terms of social and historical context are all hallmarks of propaganda art, which we find in other chapters in this volume, such as the novels of the Iran–Iraq War and the novels of Saddam Hussein.

According to Wiley, Bint al-Hudā offered a middle ground between unequivocal and erroneous practices considered part of Islam and complete Westernisation. Hers was a third option that was not available before, and so for Wiley, al-Ṣadr's voice was one of moderation.[39] Indeed, what may seem to modern readers as patronising, reactionary or polarising, is in fact a form of symbolic resistance to state discourses. As mentioned before, some of the extremism evident in the literary discourses of Bint al-Hudā do not in fact correlate with her social and political activities to enable women through education and financial independence. Moreover, given the intense divide between Shia religious communities and the modernising processes of the secular Iraqi nation-state, Bint al-Hudā's espousal of relatively liberal values whilst maintaining religious legitimacy was groundbreaking for Iraqi women from conservative backgrounds. In *Virtue Prevails* Naqa''s harsh mother is reprimanded for her uncompromising views of her niece Suʿad, and the author expresses her disdain for extremism which she claims pushes young people away from Islam.[40] Ultimately, the pragmatic realism Bint al-Hudā claimed to espouse can be interpreted in modern terms as a kind of centrism given the intensely polarised political climate in which she lived. But what was perhaps her most important legacy, Bint al-Hudā also set a precedent for Shia women that it was not only acceptable, but even commendable to write.

Discursive battles in narratives carry symbolic meanings that are often divorced from an author's actual stance on important issues. There were three issues on which Āmina al-Ṣadr, the most important figure in the history of Islamic fictional writing by Shia Arab women, appeared more conservative in her novels than in reality: marriage, the hijab and women working. In the case of the hijab, there even seems to be a contradiction between the discourses present in the writer's novels, and her stated position in other works. Adamantly and vocally encouraged in her novels, the hijab was seen in a more flexible manner when it came to its practical application outside the Muslim world. Wiley notes that when asked about the necessity of wearing hijab abroad whilst on a scholarship to study medicine if this is likely to affect the student's welfare, the response from Bint al-Hudā at the time was a lenient one.[41] It is unclear, however, if she had the official backing of her brother Sayyid Mohammed Baqir Al-Sadr, who was Iraq's premier religious authority and object of emulation (*taqlid*)[42] at the time. The emphasis on the hijab as a resolute religious obligation, whose failure to uphold eventually became a punishable criminal act according to the laws of the new Islamic republic in neighbouring Iran, was essentially a political decision which used women's clothing as a marker of the identity of a new nation. It exemplified the use of women as elevated nationalist symbols, whilst simultaneously denying individual women free choice regarding their appearance in public.

It is crucial to note that no other Iraqi Shia woman had done as much as Bint al-Hudā for the economic empowerment of working-class women, especially those women at the head of households, so her extolling of the virtues of staying at home should not be taken at face value. The author herself lived alone with her mother in a female-led household, as she never married, and so was aware of the specific challenges facing single women in similar situations. Written before the war between Iran and Iraq had erupted, her novels should be considered within the context of a '1970s' Ba'thist strategy to utilise women in the economy and as such 'staying at home' for well-to-do females was a way of resisting state imperatives. However, Bint al-Hudā actively encouraged the economic betterment of women by supporting projects to teach handicrafts and other skills to help make women financially independent, whilst gaining the support of the religious establishment to allow girls from conservative families to attend school. Seen from this perspective, the confinement of almost all Bint al-Hudā's fictional characters to the home seems to be a symbol of the isolation of conservative Shia communities from the wider, more secularised Iraqi society, rather than an explicit command to not work or study.[43]

More political and expansive in scope than any of Bint al-Hudā's works, in part due to the bellicose rhetoric of the text's setting in the 1980s, *'Indama yufakir al-rajul* (*When a Man Thinks*, 1993) by Khawla al-Qazwīnī, is described as an attempt to 'combat globalization and cultural imperialism; to spread awareness and enlighten'.[44] Born in Iraq to a conservative family of mixed Iraqi and Kuwaiti origins when borders were not fully demarcated, Khawla al-Qazwīnī, like her role model Bint al-Hudā, wrote Islamic texts prolifically and is currently the most popular and famous of all Shia Islamic novelists. Unlike Bint al-Hudā, al-Qazwīnī states on her official website that the main audience for her works are young male and female readers, although she is overwhelmingly read by women.[45] Indeed, the enduring appeal of *When a Man Thinks* (its third edition was published in 2009) is perhaps due to the fact that is read by both genders. However, al-Qazwinī's recent change in direction towards more domestic themes, marital consultations and romance genres seems to have somewhat alienated male readers. Al-Qazwīnī posits *al-adab al-multazim* (engaged literature) or *al-adab al-Islami* (Islamic literature) specifically as a substitute for trashy women's magazines with hidden ideological agendas.[46] In an online article titled 'On Islamic Literature', she defines Islamic literature as having a proselytising quality aimed at 'converting' the reader through *al-wa'dh al-mubashir*[47] (direct preaching). Al-Qazwīnī sees Islamic literature as a form of worship and devotion, and by implication her texts are restrained in tone and content despite their romantic themes and often cliched plot lines and dialogues, which are clearly designed to attract teenage girls. This combination of political interests, romance genres and religious preaching are reflected on her website, which includes a section on religious fatwas, marital consultations, and a selection of media articles on or by the author. In an effort to encourage a new generation of religious youth to contribute to the Islamic literature genre, al-Qazwīnī also welcomes submissions from new writers in the Islamic literature genre, but these are inevitably of low quality. It is noteworthy that some of the miscellaneous pieces of marital advice given through al-Qazwinī's novels and online articles can be seen as anti-feminist, such as her encouragement of women to always smile for their husbands, and to never greet their husbands with frowns. However, depictions of women in *When a Man Thinks* are decidedly more varied, despite falling into stereotypical categories and not being well developed or nuanced.

Similar to Bint al-Hudā, al-Qazwīnī says that she draws inspiration for her educational works from real life. She believes that her calling in life is to 'light a candle in the midst of darkness', and to guide others towards 'perfecting values and morals'.[48] Al-Qazwīnī claims inspiration from various authors, so she situates herself within a tradition of Islamic writing and a trajectory of modern Arabic literature, including writers that have been critical of the religious establishment such as Naguib Mahfouz. Victor

Hugo is given special mention by both Bint al-Hudā[49] and al-Qazwīnī; *Les Miserables* is cited as being of particular inspiration, as it resonated with the way the Shia characterised themselves at the apex of revolutionary fervour as *al-mustad'afun* (the downtrodden), which was a key term that emerged from Iran. That al-Qazwīnī and Bint al-Hudā saw themselves as revolutionaries might seem incredible given the conservative rhetoric they propagate. However, once contextualised within a political climate which, first, seemed to favour imported Western ideologies such as socialism over a traditional way of life, and, secondly, to violently suppress the uniqueness of the Shia religious experience, it is unsurprising then that there would be a rhetorical alignment with a kind of anti-imperialist 'revolutionary third-worldism'. Its manifestation in Iraq seemed to conflate political leftism in the public realm with religious conservativism in discourses about private morals. Likewise, stylistic inspiration in terms of 'form', which was supposedly derived from giants in world literature, basically meant the adoption of the novel genre, as Islamic texts showed little ingenuity in terms of content compared with the canonical texts that supposedly inspired them.

When a Man Thinks tells the story of Muhammad, a young devout political science university student in an unidentified Arab country. Muhammad marries his incompatible cousin Manal to please his mother, and in return for her allowing his sister Fatima to marry the revolutionary poet Ali, Muhammad's best friend and comrade. Muhammad is politically active in the Islamic youth movement and finds a job as a journalist at a local newspaper, where a plot against him is concocted by a combination of Arab and Western intelligence services. Muhammad is sent to Russia to a conference with Suzanne, a secretary at the newspaper who is assigned the task of seducing him in order to tarnish his reputation and that of the Islamic youth movement. However, Muhammad refuses Suzanne's advances and harshly admonishes her for allowing herself to be objectified as a sexual object for men. Upon their return, Suzanne commits suicide in mysterious circumstances and Muhammad is publicly accused of being implicated in her death. Muhammad's wife Manal does not stand by him and believes the rumours surrounding his involvement with Suzanne. She subsequently divorces him and does not allow him to see their son. Broken-hearted, and subsequently imprisoned and tortured, Muhammad's citizenship is revoked and he is banished to Turkey. The novel ends with Muhammad leaving the country to continue his postgraduate studies at Oxford University, whilst continuing to work as a journalist for an Islamic newspaper based in London. At the end of the novel, Muhammad falls in love with the committed Kawthar, a student and researcher and marries her. However, his newfound happiness is cut short on a trip to France for a conference, where he is assassinated by unknown gunmen at his Paris hotel.

When a Man Thinks was first banned in Kuwait due to its blatant proclamation of political Islam, which was deemed to be threatening due to its latent link to Iran, and fears in the Gulf of a Shia revivalist movement in their countries inspired by the Iranian Revolution. Written at the peak of Islamic discourses and, specifically, at the apex of Shia revivalism, in *When a Man Thinks* Islam is posited as the logical solution to the social and political ills rampant in Arab society. According to the author, the liberation of Palestine, as the ultimate worldly goal, can be achieved only through the espousal of Islamic values, and responsibility for embodying these values is accorded to both men, as 'active' citizens in this imaginary *umma*, and 'passive' women as supporters of their husbands and as vessels carrying the new generation and shapers of the consciousness of the youth. The symbolic function of women means that a virgin–whore polemic permeates the text, with Muhammad's sister Fatima representing the ideal Muslim wife and Suzanne the secretary representing the wayward temptress. However, there is also a third group of women that al-Qazwīnī portrays; these women are fickle and relatively harmless, but they are also politically disengaged and indifferent to the wider issues affecting the Islamic *umma*. Completely absorbed by her 'feminine' pursuits and rituals of beautification and socialisation, Muhammad's wife Manal, falls into this category. First described as an 'empty', 'spoilt' and 'selfish' girl who is used to having her own way,[50] Manal's behaviour towards Muhammad is depicted as irrational and erratic, and her jealousy and pride lead her to deny Muhammad access to his son after the divorce she had pushed fervently for. Moreover, she later bombards him with letters after their divorce begging him to get back together with her, otherwise she will not even send him any photographs of their child. The author's burgeoning interest in marriage counselling is evident in this, her first book, as there is a tendency to homogenise male and female responses within a wider system of thought based on the view that men and women are inherently different.

The book functions as a parable or cautionary tale warning young readers of the dangers of marrying on a whim, or at the behest of one's parents or family if there is no compatibility. Muhammad is emotionally blackmailed by his mother, who insists on his marrying her niece, stressing that her beauty will make him happy. Interestingly, and just like *Virtue Prevails*, wayward cousins are always on the mother's side and not the father's. Muhammad expresses filial loyalty and devotion at the expense of his own happiness and accepts marrying Manal as part of what Fatima calls 'the ugliest of compromises'[51] in which his mother would allow his sister Fatima to marry his best friend Ali, the politically engaged poet. In the introduction to the novel, the author asserts that it is impossible for a man to possess two loves: 'for it is either the love of the self or the love of others'.[52] Muhammad sacrifices his own happiness for the sake of his mother, sister and the infatuated Manal, but is ultimately rewarded with a truly compatible spouse in Kawthar. He warns Manal that he is different from other men: 'I have married my work and responsibilities and do not consider marital life a priority . . . or any other minor personal preoccupations for that matter'.[53] In a foreshadowing of his fate as a martyr, Muhammad imagines Manal as a widow mourning his death: 'he could hear from far away the sounds of prisons and hangman's nooses, of pain and deprivation'.[54]

Change is primarily initiated by men in *When a Man Thinks*, which is not common in Islamic texts, where the norm is that women are the primary catalysts for positive change in society. This can be explained by the text's political themes, which posed a dilemma for female Islamic writers more generally. Faced with pressing political issues from which they were excluded, devout female writers who were perhaps more comfortable with domestic dramas nonetheless felt that they had to be politically engaged, and al-Qazwīnī shows herself to be extremely well read through elaborate references from world literature to political thought and current affairs. Direct political activism was not the norm amongst devout women and the torture and murder of Bint al-Hudā sent shock waves that seemed to deter religious female activism indefinitely. The violation of the conservative female body through imprisonment, torture and potential rape, a body that is considered so sacred that it must be covered from the male gaze itself, had serious repercussions for religious men and represented a real threat of emasculation and humiliation of their honour. As a result, disapproval of gender mixing coupled with traditional notions of female roles meant that religious female political activism does not feature in any of the Islamic novels surveyed. The university attended by Muhammad and his comrades in *When a Man Thinks* is representative of the public space; it is essentially an ideological battleground, which determines the direction of the new generation and, by extension, the identity of the unnamed state itself. As such, there are no religious female students at the university, and so the responsibility falls on Muhammed and his male comrades to fight for the ideals of Islamic revivalism. Despite losing the student elections to the secular students, Muhammad is hopeful that the seeds of change are sewn and an ongoing struggle is begun. Westernisation as the polar opposite of Islamism is critiqued through the use of an archetypal character in al-Qazwinī's oeuvre: the politically apathetic and superficial man or woman. This is signified through dress and language in the text, for example, Muhammad's Palestinian colleague student wears a gold chain which is prohibited in Islam for men, and walks in a narcissistic way in order to attract attention and in blatant contempt of humility as a religious value.[55] Muhammad is outspoken in his criticism of what he sees as his colleagues' and lecturers' betrayal of Islamic values and constantly challenges those around him: 'they don't know the truth about religion' he says, in half monologue, half speech, 'which will always be a stronger force than all other ideas . . . only God is eternal, only God remains after all human civilizations are gone'.[56] Muhammad is ultimately, a vessel for the author's message and is too idealistic to be a fully rounded or believable character, as he is completely self-sacrificing and engrossed in the cause.

The symbolic role of women is significant in the text, despite the absence of religious women at the university, and by proxy, the public space. Muhammad's sister Fatima is the ideal useful wife, who did not pursue higher education, preferring instead to study for a diploma in sewing at an all-female vocational college.[57] In her later works, al-Qazwinī's female protagonists are more bookish and less domestic, owing to social changes and trends. In *When a Man Thinks*, however, Fatima is housebound and cares for the domestic and personal needs of her widowed mother. Her brother recommends her as a wife to his friend Ali because she would be the ideal support for him whilst studying abroad in Egypt, and marriage is framed primarily in terms of how it can benefit the man, rather than the woman. It is no coincidence that the ideal couple are named Fatima and Ali, as this would strongly resonate with a Shia audience. As the Prophet Muhammad's cousin and son-in-law, Ali Ibn Abi Talib is seen as the rightful successor, or *khalifa*, of Muhammad, and has a saint-like almost legendary status in Shia Islam, not least due to his marriage to Fatima, the daughter of the Prophet and his role in preserving the lineage of the Prophet by fathering a line of 'imams' or spiritual leaders for the Shia faithful.

When a Man Thinks is essentially about the intellectual capacities of men and their ability to defend the Muslim *umma* from the ideological onslaught of imperialist ideas. The novel details Muhammad's conference visit to Russia accompanied by the temptress figure Suzanne (called 'the female snake'[58]), the secretary at the newspaper he works at, who was deployed as part of a plot to dishonour him in an 'Islamist scandal'. Suzanne is sexually exploited by the head of the newspaper who uses her in his shadier tasks, and is more or less without agency, objectified by men and not in control of her destiny. She takes photographs of the unsuspecting Muhammad and sends copies to his wife as proof of his infidelity. Suzanne explains to Muhammad that she is a lost woman who needs guidance, but Muhammad's treatment of her is strikingly cruel, which is in contrast to Naqa''s accommodating attitude towards Mahmud in *Virtue Prevails*. Muhammad reprimands Suzanne for the 'cheap' way she dresses and tells her to 'keep her flesh in a clothes wardrobe' so that he can speak to her.[59] To show that she is not really a bad woman, Suzanne agrees to tell Muhammad the details of who is behind the conspiracy to ruin his reputation. However, she is murdered by unknown assassins before she can expose 'the foreign hands' involved in the plot, and her death is framed as a suicide, exploited to further implicate Muhammad. Despite her guilt, Suzanne is not given a real chance to redeem herself, which is a common pattern in religiously committed novels, where men are more easily forgiven for their transgressions. Moreover, descriptions of the appearance of women who are unveiled like Suzanne and Su'ad in Bint al-Hudā's *Virtue Prevails* are uncompromising and condemnatory, and directly link dress to sexual promiscuity and licentiousness. Because women's dress and bodies are proxy discourses, female characters must necessarily be depicted in black/white terms representing the forces of good and evil. There is no room for nuance, subtlety or more complex representations of female religiosity or even personal preference in dress, be it modest or otherwise. Sex is also linked to a more political understanding of corruption, hence, the obsession with covering. Whilst in exile in Turkey, Muhammad discusses the weaponising of sex in political and cultural contexts: 'During the Second World War the Japanese would throw photographs of naked women at American soldiers from their aircraft, and likewise the Germans did the same to distract British soldiers with sex and physical pleasure. The more an individual is preoccupied with this kind of deception, the more likely it is that human devils will pillage his country, steal its wealth and enslave and humiliate his people.'[60]

Like the works of Bint al-Hudā, *When a Man Thinks* is set in an ambiguous geographical and cultural space, which points to a universal message, but in so doing compromises local colour and descriptive details. Interestingly, the author makes explicit the national identities of certain characters: Suzanne and the uncommitted student critiqued by Muhammad are both Palestinians, but they represent the loss of the cause due to their espousal of secular values. On the other hand, Muhammad's soulmate and wife Kawthar, whom he meets in London, is also a Palestinian. However, Kawthar is a 'real' Palestinian, as she grew up under Israeli occupation and experienced suffering and trauma. After he professes his love to her, Kawthar tells Muhammad in a letter that she is scarred by the murder of her younger brother who was shot in the head by an Israeli soldier,[61] and that she feels that 'her blood is different from that of other women'.[62] Kawthar represents the symbolic alignment of Muhammad (representing political Islam) and the Palestinian cause, which is why the author had to make clear Kawthar's nationality, whereas Muhammad's remains unknown. In fact, from the very beginning Muhammad's isolation and out of place-ness are emphasised; his soul is different from others[63] the author says, and his path in life is described as being 'full of thorns' and obstacles which he has to overcome alone.[64] However, once forcibly removed from his country, Muhammad is able to establish bonds with like-minded comrades that transcend race and nationality. This network includes committed Arabs, Turks, Muslim Russians, as well as, potentially, English converts to Islam, who are the objects of Kawthar's research. This family of believers is the Islamic *umma* incarnate, with its different races and even sects, although references to Shiism are very rare some of Muhammad's readings are clearly part of Shia heritage. Ultimately, the author's choice to mark the national identity of characters in *When a Man Thinks* is at the service of the symbolic meanings and the political message of the text, be it the universal aspect of the Islamic cause or its symbolic relationship to the Palestinian question and other struggles.

'The Cause Needs Money': Practical Matters in May al-Ḥusaynī's *And Darkness Dissipated* and 'Alyā' al-Anṣārī's *A Travel Ticket*

May al-Husaynī's *Wa inhasar al-zalam* (*And Darkness Dissipated*), published in 1987 (and republished in 1993), is a text that epitomises some of the didactic features found in the works of other Islamic authors. Life on this lowly earth (*dunya*, the Arabic noun for the world or life and the adjective for lower) is described as a mirage which appears as a cool drinking fountain designed to ensnare and deceive human beings with worldly temptation. Moreover, and like all Islamic novels, *And Darkness Dissipated* is written in modern standard Arabic in order to elevate it to the status of an eternal parable in its pitting of darkness against light and the wayward path versus the path of truth. The avoidance of the use of the Iraqi dialect not only makes the painting of local colour impossible, but also has a symbolic significance in its privileging of the linguistic homogeneity and unity provided by *fusha* over the fragmented voice of dialect as representative of a nationalist sensibility. On the other hand, however, al-Ḥusaynī's novel reveals a preoccupation with the practical and material issues facing Iraqi women, such as earning a living and the possibility (but not necessarily the desirability) of self-exile, issues which had not previously been prioritised by other Islamic novelists.

Despite being written in the late 1980s, the religious discourses of *And Darkness Dissipated* remain relatively unchanged compared with earlier Islamic works. From the outset, the author asserts that 'a good righteous marriage and pure motherhood is the best jihad for a woman'.[65] 'Ayda, the first female character introduced to the reader, is described as childlike in her innocence, whilst her husband Hamid is an ideal devout believer who 'has never sinned'.[66] The belief in infallibility is a unique feature of Shia Islam, which regards the Prophet Mohammed, his cousin and son-in-law Ali and his daughter Fatima, along with a genealogical line of imams, as the 'Fourteen Infallibles'. This may provide an explanation as to why devoutness is often framed in hagiographical language in Shia religious novels, as infallibility is seen as something which is possible to attain. Hamid's *kunya* is Abu 'Isam, as is customary in the Arab world, to name someone after their first (often male) child, and 'Isam is derived from the gerund *'isma* which means infallibility.

'Ayda loses her parents in one of many freak accidents which appear in the text as a form of divine tribulation, echoing the Sixth Shia tenet of belief, which is to believe in fate whether good or bad. She then gives birth to two boys and a girl, and her husband Hamid predicts that his eldest son 'Isam will have a bright future ahead of him. Ironically, 'Isam grows to be blinded by a poisonous and dark life in the West and meets a tragic end. When her parents die, Raja' (meaning hope) bears all the responsibility for her younger brother in the absence of 'Isam, who has left the country. This establishes her as head of the household, which was not uncommon towards the end of the Iran–Iraq War when many men simply did not return home.

Long didactic monologues by the narrator reflect on death and instruct the faithful to prepare through good deeds for judgement in the afterlife. In a style that is akin to female religious sermons recited at funerals and Shia religious gatherings to mourn dead saints, 'Ayda is commemorated on her *arba'in*, the fortieth day after her death. Repetitive authorial interjections highlight the encroachment of the non-literary into the literary, and the eagerness of the author to express her religious message. The 'Shia-ness' of the characters is not overstated in the text but is not hidden either, which is unsurprising considering that *And Darkness Dissipated* was published outside Iraq in Beirut, Lebanon. It seems, however, that even with the freedoms afforded to Shia authors abroad, there is a reluctance to express a sectarian identity that would unnecessarily alienate devout Muslims more generally. The idealistic bond of religion remains unchallenged by the bond of sect at this stage of Islamic revivalism.

The protagonist of the novel Raja' is homebound, but is invited to tutor her rich neighbour Nada, whom she eventually serves as mentor, guiding her towards a more devout life. The trope of an authoritative female authority figure guiding others (often away from the authority of men, as in the case of Nada's brother Sami) develops into a profession in its own right, as Raja' is sought as a professional *da'iya* (lit. 'female caller to Islam') by her community. One of the most significant threats to the Ba'th was Hizb al-Da'wa al-Islamiya (Party of the Islamic Call), which had at its core a proselytising mission to bring the masses back to God, believing that it was a religious duty to enjoin the good and forbid the evil. In *And Darkness Dissipated* Raja' is able to support herself and her brother financially, first, through tutoring and then by giving paid sermons to young girls at the behest of parents and clerics. Bint al-Hudā had bemoaned the state of female missionaries in Islam, whose efforts she claimed, were far less developed than their Christian contemporaries. The response was the rise in female missionaries, both real and fictional, and the archetypal female mentor seems to be modelled after Bint al-Hudā.

Complete isolation from society is not advocated by Raja', as she says women can still actively engage with the outside world within the limits of honour, purity and modest dress in order to be protected from 'human wolves'.[67] The public sphere in the Islamic novel is one of increasing threats and danger; it is a discordant world characterised by an inherent duality established by God who had created good and evil, night and day, and male and female. The author details the traditional gender configuration of needs and responsibilities that Islam proposes: 'man needs woman's affection, while she needs his strength and financial support'.[68] This forms a marked contrast to the idealism that came at the beginning of the Iranian Revolution, where material sacrifices were made for the cause and financial considerations were secondary (many women of that generation made concessions in terms of dowry, for example, insisting that a copy of the Qur'an was enough, and that a believing young man should not be rejected in marriage for financial reasons. They quoted the oft-used verse from the Qur'an: 'accept them in their poverty, then God will enrich them through his bounty').[69]

The assumption that a secular upbringing is completely debauched leads to the conflation of religion and morality in the text, as Raja' critiques the hedonism and pursuit of pleasure which characterises her tutee's household, commenting that Nada's family taught her that 'life is a delicious meal to be enjoyed'.[70] Written at a time of great financial hardship and austerity, the text struggles with ideas from previous generations that associated wealth with corruption. Using religious discourses to emphasise men's financial obligations towards women, the author allows the poor Raja' to marry Nada's brother, the rich Sami who had previously been angered by the changes in his sister's belief. She states in sermon style that 'spiritual deprivation is worse than economic deprivation', insisting that Raja' does not marry Sami for his money, rather for his convictions.[71] As a result, all Sami's past sins are forgiven, and Raja' is conveniently relieved of the financial burden of providing for her family; her newfound material security allows Raja' to better resist the secular lifestyle led by upper and middle classes in Iraq, the representatives of power in the novel.

Aware of the new situation in Iraq, where the deaths of hundreds of thousands of Iraqi soldiers during the war left many women exposed and unsupported, the author also makes a point to criticise the way in which contemporary marriages are conducted, especially the 'selling of women by associating dowries with a woman's worth'.[72] She adds that 'girls these days are materialistic', unlike Raja' whose piety and devoutness earns her worldly success in marriage. The text ends with stylistic conventions of the novel: 'completed by the grace of God' and 'He who trusts in God is never forsaken', which seems to be the message behind the novel. As for Raja''s eldest brother ʿIsam who had left Iraq to study in an unidentified European country, he is punished for favouring the godless West over the land of Islam. Just as Iraq is not explicitly identified as the setting of the novel, so it becomes unnecessary to identify its antithesis in the West as both function as symbolic opposites. During his time abroad, ʿIsam marries a promiscuous Western woman and feels trapped and empty, prompting him to commit suicide and leave behind children who will be lost after him. Occidentalist interpretations lack nuance and paint the West as a dystopia and mirage rather than a haven, luring ʿIsam to forgo his responsibilities at home and abandon his sister and younger brother who are left to fend for themselves after the death of their parents.

In line with Islamic tradition, Raja' contends that people should be judged only according to their adherence to religious values, rather than education, family standing and material wealth. However, the dissonance between theory and practice, between the symbolic value of equating humility with piety and the practical needs of women in dire economic circumstances leads to plot changes in the author's attempt to narrativise real and pressing survival issues. Raja''s 'conversion' of and marriage to Nada's brother

Sami seems forced, especially given Sami's initial horrified reaction to his sister's newfound religiosity and his parents' strong opposition to the marriage. Persuaded by Raja''s rhetorical eloquence to abandon his upbringing and follow strict religious teachings, Sami's sudden attraction to Raja' is a convenient plot device to reward her for her piety and supporting financially what has remained of the family.

The idea that good modest girls will always be rewarded with a rich husband is a relatively new development in the trajectory of the Islamic novel, almost certainly shaped by the new economic realities in Iraq, and also features in ('Alyā' al-Anṣārī's novel *Tadhkirat Safar* (*A Travel Ticket*), written in 1999 but set in the late 1960s and 1970s. The novel tells the story of Bahr and Hind, a brother and sister forced to leave their small fishing village for the city to escape a tyrannical uncle who has terrorised their community and monopolised its wealth. Despite the hardships faced by the siblings in their new home, Bahr works hard to support his sister financially and also manages to continue his studies. His sister Hind also attends university where she meets the liberal Khalid whom she 'converts' and eventually marries against the wishes of his parents. The promise of material security for well-intentioned religious girls may not have been realistic but was clearly an attempt to provide motivation for young girls, and to stress that opportunities for marital felicity are not diminished by dressing modestly. As such, female protagonists like Hind in *A Travel Ticket* are encouraged to leave the home and the university becomes an acceptable public space for religious girls to frequent.

A Travel Ticket begins with an allegorical power struggle in a small fishing village in the south of Iraq, a change from the domestic urban setting of most Islamic novels, and a microcosm for a totalitarian Iraq. The fishermen organise a revolt which is framed as an epic battle between truth and injustice, corruption and faith. The essential conflict is also expressed through a Cain–Abel dichotomy which is explicitly spelled out to the reader. Adnan the antagonist is a mafia leader and his cronies vandalise the fishing boats of revolting fisherman allied to his brother Salim, who dies in mysterious circumstances. Will his cause die with him?[73] the author asks. The anticipated return of the prodigal son does not take place in the novel, as Salim's children Bahr and Hind leave for the city and never return to confront their uncle.

This flaw in the narrative due to lack of closure and the discrepancy between beginning and end highlights the way in which artistic concerns are often secondary to ideological aims in religious novels. Likewise, dramatic and narrative conventions converge in the text, which reads like a play in parts and does not seem to have undergone any copy-editing. This harks back to the novels of the Iran–Iraq War, which were often riddled with spelling errors and narrative gaps due to the speed with which they were produced to maximise their use-value at certain points during the war.

The revolution 'against corruption',[74] a grandiose label for what is essentially a family argument at the beginning of the text, emphasises its allegorical quality, as justice and truth are pitted against corruption and injustice. Reflections on injustice are a clear reference to authoritarianism:

> Yesterday it was just Adnan and his cronies defending him, now he has the silence of people and their submission; that silence that makes him feel secure and gives him power. Yes, a dictator would never be able to tyrannise if others had not allowed him to do so, for injustice never lasts unless there is silence in the face of truth and submission in the face of injustice. These are the ways of the world and that is how injustice began from the beginning of time to infinity.[75]

Bahr also reflects on the nature of injustice when his sister asks him why Cain killed Abel: 'We are unjust to the earth and time when we blame them for these corrupt times. In fact, we are the problem. We label time "polluted", call the earth "treacherous" and the days "cruel", when it is the human wolves that have ruined the world.'[76] In *A Travel Ticket* the author asserts that injustice exists in the village and the city,[77] and this might be why it is not necessary for Bahr to return home to challenge his uncle; rather, jihad in the city, the source of corruption, is more significant than a localised family squabble. Bahr's abandonment of his ancestral homeland is framed as a kind of *hijra*, paralleling the Prophet's journey from Makkah to Madinah which marked the beginning of the Islamic calendar. Bahr (meaning sea) is the embodiment of a committed youth, working during the day to support his sister and the kind widower Ismail who has provided them with shelter, and studying in the evenings.

The university setting emerges yet again as a space where conflicting ideologies vie for ascendency, similar to *When a Man Thinks*. Bahr prepares his sister for being potentially brainwashed at university, for example, one of his lecturers once said that conflict and bloodshed were imminent, as the world exemplifies Darwin's survival of the fittest where 'we have to either be eaten or eat each other'. Moreover, the university gradually becomes a dangerous space, where religious youths are monitored by pro-government spies that threaten to report them to the authorities.[78] However, the university is also depicted as a space for opportunity, particularly in terms of marriage for single girls. Due to her charisma, strength and intelligence, Hind catches the eye of fellow student Khalid and rebukes him harshly for approaching her without the presence of a chaperone, as she has dated views on male–female interactions. Hind's friend reprimands her for her 'extreme' views and judgemental attitude towards non-religious students at university and is encouraged to socialise with them in a friendly manner.[79] She also encourages Hind to get to know Khalid and offers to act as a chaperone on their first date at the university coffee shop. Interestingly, extremism in the text is equated with secular, rather than religious discourses. Khalid's mother's Widad's prejudice against girls who wear the hijab is the most explicit vocalisation of extreme secular views on religiosity. She tells her son that those girls who don the veil are 'backward and uncultured'[80]; that they look frumpy in their loose clothing and would be an embarrassment in their social circles. The class dimension, which is notably absent in early Islamic novels, appears in texts in the 1990s, in particular associating religiosity with the poor and downtrodden in a way that lends a revolutionary quality (believed to be inherent to Shiism) to being devout and working class. Hind and Khalid's marriage is ultimately held up as an example in the text of the union of the two worlds: secular and religious, rich and poor, in a way that asserts the harmony and balance of moderation and rejects extremism on both sides of the political spectrum.

The shift towards depicting a flawed protagonist alongside nuanced and tolerant depictions of the 'other' is a significant one in the history of the female Islamic novel. Hind's uncompromising views on 'liberals', and especially women who put make up on and reveal their bodies, are nipped in the bud by Bahr who encourages her to see less religiously inclined individuals as victims who should be helped and encouraged to be more pious, rather than confronted or censured.[81] Notably, Hind's name has no ideological or symbolic meaning, which marks a significant development in the Islamic novel and affords the protagonist the luxury of imperfection which previous religious protagonists did not have. Moreover, the angel–whore dichotomy is not present in this novel and although the characters do roughly fall into the 'good' or 'bad' categories, the author does attempt to add complexity beyond black–white stereotypes or views. Her stance on gender mixing is decidedly more lenient than previous authors, particularly Bint al-Hudā whose views were essentially reactive to what Sabry Hafez calls the process of discrediting, rationalising, accommodating, secularising and questioning of Islam which spanned the 1920s–1960s. Although the 1990s are generally considered a continuation of the 1970s reversal in the secularising processes of modernisation in Arabic literary culture, those texts with a religious sensibility written towards the end of the decade are decidedly less zealous and polemical precisely because secular discourses were no longer ascendant.

In *A Travel Ticket*, there is even a moment of textual self-reflection when Bahr is jokingly told by a friend that he talks about the ills of society 'as if there is a war',[82] which is in fact how the epic battle between good and evil had been expressed in earlier religiously committed novels. The text's serious tone derives mainly from the urgency of its 1970s context, which only becomes evident two-thirds of the way into the text when the author describes the 1970s as the decade when religious awareness was on the rise and Al-Ṣadr and his sister Bint al-Hudā's names are mentioned explicitly. In line with its 1970s setting (which the author calls 'the age of commitment'[83]) the rise of political Islam is given a Shia dimension in *A Travel Ticket* that does not feature in texts written in the actual historical context of the plot as resistance to the Baʿth had to be expressed in a coded manner, such as through the use of tradition and heritage. Shia identity is more pronounced in Islamic novels emerging in the late 1980 and 1990s in part due to the intifada, which constituted an overt mass targeting of the Shia population and led to a fully-fledged diaspora.

During the Iran–Iraq War, sectarian identity had been repressed in public discourses and sometimes even subsumed into a narrative of national identity by the state to avoid fissures in the Iraqi army which was predominately Shia. The blackout on the word 'Shia' highlighted the state's wariness not to provoke sectarianism, using instead coded words like 'Persian', 'foreign' and 'extremist' to denote treacherous and dissident members of the sect. In turn, many Shia attempted to prove their nationalist credentials, which they saw as unrewarded given the huge sacrifices made during the war. The reluctance of Shia religious authors to use the word 'Shia' in their works, even in works directed at their own audiences, points to a wider understanding of religious revivalism and a desire to focus on the 'essence' of religion, rather to engage in highly charged debates in identity politics. Published in Beirut in 1991, expressions of a sect identity in *A Travel Ticket* are more pronounced than in earlier Islamic novels. Khalid's burgeoning religious sensibility is Shia in nature, specifically the political emphasis on revolting against injustice. After his arrest, Bahr prepares his sister for his death, asserting that pain and suffering are from God and are good for humans providing purification from sin. This view echoes a traditional Shia understanding of jihad which has centred on pain and physical suffering since the bloody martyrdom of Husayn, the grandson of the Prophet Mohammed in Karbala, Iraq. This scene also mirrors events recounted from Shia tradition, where Husayn had prepared his sister Zaynab for his death by encouraging her to have faith and accept the will of God. Bahr's arrest and death by torture at the end of the novel also foreshadows the fate of the Sadrs, who are explicitly mentioned in the text as a means of inspiring both readers and characters to be patient in the face of divine tribulation.

Pan-Shiism features in the text with the return of Khalid's brother Amir from Switzerland, having also experienced a spiritual epiphany and fallen in love with a devout Shia artist from Lebanon. The couple had met during several mixed-gender gatherings at exhibitions and other social events for those with a belief or none, and the Lebanese girl had stood out because she would not shake hands with men.[84] Here we find a radical view of the West as a space for spiritual growth, which allows for the connection with other Shia from the Arab world. This revised attitude towards the West was crucial for the new Iraqi diaspora, as the potential of host countries to become 'a home from home' is what makes *ghurba*, an emotive term that refers to the state of being away from one's homeland, bearable. The archetype of the devout woman being a catalyst for change features in the novel; so, too, is the idea that men are inherently imperfect individuals. Amir's Lebanese love interest dies from an incurable disease, and on her deathbed she implores him to remain devout and steadfast in his faith for her sake. Yet again, freak accidents, sudden deaths, suicides and illnesses appear in religious novels stemming from technical immaturity and their perspective on fate as fickle and capricious, and life as essentially a series of trials and tribulations. For example, Khalid's father reveals that in order to marry up, he bought tickets for all his family members and convinced them to leave Iraq so that he would not be shamed by being associated with them in front of his new wife and in-laws. His family does indeed agree to leave Iraq, however, their plane crashes and they all perish. Not having learnt his lesson, Khalid's father then does the same thing by offering Bahr and Hind tickets out of the country in order to prevent his son from marrying down; an offer that is wholeheartedly rejected by the couple. To exact his revenge on Hind, Khalid's father alerts the Baʿthist authorities about the political activities of Bahr, which leads to the latter's arrest and execution.

The 'conversion' of the secular Khalid by Hind and their subsequent marriage constitutes what the author calls a 'silent revolution',[85] which disrupts familial structures and even the emotional bonds between Khalid and his family who is disowned and ostracised for his new alliances. Khalid expresses his sense of loneliness and isolation to his new comrades in a genuine and believable way, and is subsequently initiated into a new family and a network of believers at the university who gather in religious circles 'as chicks gather around their mother'.[86] The novel ends with the news of the execution of the Sadrs which is more shattering for Khalid than the deaths of his parents,[87] highlighting a process of bond substitution in which affiliation centres on the brotherhood of faith, rather than kinship and blood. The rushed and sudden way in which Khalid's parents, who had been prejudiced against Hind for being religious and poor, are 'killed off' is symptomatic of artistic immaturity, as plot threads are brought together without much development to serve as a lesson for the reader.

The title of *A Travel Ticket* seems incongruous to its political content, as Khalid's attempt to bribe undesirables is the only direct reference to tickets. However, the travel motif features heavily in 1990s exilic texts, so the ticket could symbolise leaving one's country behind or even death as the ultimate journey. The cover (Appendix 2, Figure 6) is of the sea at sunset echoing the protagonist Bahr (meaning Sea) and Hind's seafaring heritage. The intense gaze of a woman's eyes pierces the sky as a symbol of the relatively strong depictions of the feminine in the text. The eyes, however, exist as an abstract symbol divorced from the face in the same way women function in abstract terms in the novel. Al-Ansārī attempts to balance the political, symbolic, moral and practical have produced a somewhat disjointed text that is very much reflective of its time of production; a more nuanced understanding of morality, exile and the financial pressures facing women in Iraq during the 1990s are transposed onto a backdrop of one of the most transformative movements in modern Shia history.

Concluding Remarks

Taken out of context, the Islamic novels discussed in this chapter seem to be of little interest beyond their status as extremely popular reading for teenage Shia girls and young adults across Iraq and the Gulf at a time of religious revivalism. At face value, they represent a conservative attempt to spread certain Islamic values and interpretations of religious dogma in order to uphold the status quo inherent in religious configurations of gender relations and identity and to resist the secular liberation of women. However, once contextualised, it becomes clear that the choice of theme (most often marriage) and narrative genre is part of a resistive counter-discourse which challenges the secular state's legitimacy and gives a voice to a religious community that was often the subaltern despite forming the majority of the country. It is not a coincidence that Iraqi Shia women authors were pioneers in producing the Islamic novel given the reverberations felt by the Iranian Revolution at a time when secular discourses were predominant across the Middle East. More importantly, however, as Iraqi women were the most literate of Shia Arabs, and as Iraq became metaphorically and literally inundated with texts under the Baʿth with book production rates soaring in the late 1970s and especially the 1980s, it seems inevitable that a counter-narrative challenging the secular values of Baʿthism would eventually emerge in fiction. Interestingly, religious fictional writing was adopted primarily by women, as novel reading, in the popular sense, was often construed as a female or feminine activity.

The popularity of religious novels was unprecedented in the history of Arab Shia literary culture and extended beyond the borders of Iraq to include young female readers in Shia communities in all the Gulf States as well as in

Lebanon. In many ways the novels represented vehicles through which Arab Shia women were able to bond together and established a common foundation of cultural references and moral values that went beyond geographic borders. A large part of the appeal of such novels was their familiarity and the resonance they had with a generation on the cusp of religious awareness, and on the threshold of an emerging supra-nationalist identity. It is important to remember that this was a time when Shia Arab girls as young as fifteen left their homes to join the ranks of religious students in the *hawzas*, or religious schools, in Iran immediately after the overthrow of the Shah in 1979. One cannot underestimate the sense of community forged and developed by discourses such as those in these novels in opening the eyes of young women, particularly in the Gulf, to go beyond a localised perspective, and many young women married from outside their countries whilst studying in religious seminaries after the Iranian Revolution. The emphasis on piety as the defining feature of a good person, rather than family, nationality or social class, constituted a kind of social revolution. However, this utopian ideal was short-lived, as after the initial zeal that came with the Iranian Revolution and its values of brotherhood and camaraderie, most students of religion returned to their countries, and fewer numbers ventured out during the war and beyond. We can see evidence of this change in Khawla al-Qazwinī's later work, for example, her novel *Memoirs of a Student Abroad* where societal approval and filial duty are privileged over personal happiness and the religious imperative to marry according to moral character and piety. Written in 1995 when it would have been difficult to give narratorial sanction to cross-cultural marriages (the protagonist from an unnamed Gulf country meets and falls in love with a Lebanese widower whilst a student in the United States) and to favour them over arranged marriages. This is due to both the inward-looking social and political climate in Kuwait at the time coupled with the author's conservative ideology, described by one critic of Kuwaiti women's literature as 'reactionary' and 'moderately right wing'.[88] It is important not to treat Islamic discourses as a totality, as ideological discourses are essentially pragmatic and responsive, and often do not reflect the theoretical 'core' values of Islam or in this case Shiism, but are instead dictated by political and social changes.

Dedications constitute the most important paratexual information towards understanding the function of bonds and social and religious bonding in Islamic literature written by women. Āmina al-Ṣadr's pseudonym Bint al-Hudā, whether genuinely desired or performed, seems to have paved the way for other conservative female writers to acceptably be acknowledged as writers on the front covers of their novels without recourse to pseudonyms. The debt to Bint al-Hudā was acknowledged by ʻAlyāʼ al-Anṣārī in *A Travel Ticket* and by Khawla al-Qazwīnī in her work *Zainab the Daughter of Men*. Al-Ansārī calls Bint al-Hudā 'the Guidance Counsellor of Generations', 'the Guider of Spirits', 'the Voice of the Truth in the face of Injustice and Oppression', 'a Sun in the sky of freedom'. Her text is the only one that refers explicitly to the execution of Bint al-Hudā and her brother the Ayatollah Mohammed Baqir Al-Ṣadr, and so this elaborate dedication is unsurprising. Interestingly, Bint al-Hudā herself does not dedicate her texts to anyone, signalling her isolation and the lack of a network of women to support her, on the one hand, and also the desire not to personalise or be acknowledged as an individual, on the other. The bonds between women and their desire to uplift and support one another through the act of storytelling and mentoring are evident in the dedications which are almost exclusively directly to different kinds of women; from mothers (ʻAlyāʼ al-Anṣārī's *A Woman's Anger*, May al-Ḥusaynī's *And the Trees Blossomed with Leaves* and Khawla al-Qazwinī's *Memoirs of a Student Abroad*) to sisters (al-Ḥusaynī's *And Darkness Dissipated*) and daughters (al-Ḥusaynī's *And the Sea Dried Up* and al-Qazwini's *Haifa*). These bonds between women elevate and inspire, but are ultimately at the service of God and the community of believers, which was at odds with the society envisioned by the secular Baʻth in the early years of Saddam's rule, but which posed little or no threat once religious and tribal discourses became ascendant and were integrated in Baʻthist discourses in the late 1980s and 1990s for strategic reasons. Knowing these not to be out of genuine conviction, religious writers continued to espouse conservative discourses well into the 1990s, often with the addition of explicit heritage elements as a way of validating Shia identity and the Shia experience in a post-intifada Iraq. This meant that texts were seen as potentially subversive for playing up heritage elements of Shiism in ways that did not exist before, thereby eliminating the possibility of publishing the books inside Iraq.

The texts in this chapter are important socio-historical documents, providing a wealth of information about the kind of political and religious climate experienced by Iraqi Shia women at the zenith of Shia revivalism. ʿAlyāʾ al-Anṣārī, May al-Ḥusaynī, Khawla al-Qazwīnī and Āmina al-Ṣadr produced large volumes of literary and non-literary works over a long span of time, and at a time of immense political and social upheaval. Theirs is a responsive corpus, which closely monitored the trajectory of state-sponsored political discourses and evolved in accordance with emerging social and political realities. For example, Khawla al-Qazwinī's works have shifted over the years from being politically engaged to acquiring a more social function in Kuwait, and in line with her interest in providing marriage consultation and advice. Differences within the individual works of an author's corpus can be attributed more to external factors, rather than artistic self-reflection or maturation. This is mainly because these works are didactic with an almost missionary quality about them, meaning that the artistic, aesthetic or stylistic element is ultimately at the service of the cause. It is the cause that dictates genre, plot and characterisation, and the 'literary' or artistic aspects of creative writing, including but not limited to, stylistic ingenuity and philosophical complexity, are blatantly and unashamedly secondary to what the authors see as a higher and nobler cause: that of political and social engagement through religion. All the authors discussed in this chapter consider themselves as fulfilling a religious duty by protecting new generations from the corrupting influences of alien ideologies on either side of the political spectrum. They also consider the potential corruption of women as symptomatic of the corruption of society on the whole. This means that women function as symbolic markers of piety–corruption, which strips them of their individuality and agency by placing the burden on them to be representatives of a utopian Islamic identity. Interestingly, secular propaganda writings have also attempted to do the same: to sacrifice individual characterisation for the sake of the symbolic cultural capital of women.

According to Rohde the use of the liberated woman to combat traditionalism and under-development in the war against the Islamic Republic became 'part and parcel of a war to defend the progress of women under the Baʿth'. The dichotomy between 'progressive' views on women by the state and 'regressive' traditional or Islamic views is a question of winning hearts and minds which is essentially a political question. The artistic necessities of allegorical works that have a didactic dimension at their heart, is that subtlety and nuance are sacrificed in order to ensure that the message is clear and not lost upon the reader. This message is that in the battle between good and evil, good will always triumph. The severing or reconfiguration of nationalist ties, social and even kinship bonds in favour of religious bonds is envisioned as a form resistance that is both narrow and wide, and the process of inclusion–exclusion implicates the reader who functions as a guest who is not permitted to penetrate the private realm of the novel. The re-privatisation of women's lives was used as a means of resisting Baʿthist state encroachment in women's affairs for the purposes of economic utilisation and nation-building. Islamic values and traditional female roles were thus emphasised in Islamic fiction by women as a bulwark to the secular processes of modernisation advocated by the state.

Notes

1. Nada Shabout, 'Images and Status: Visualising Iraqi Women', in Faegheh Shirazi (ed.), *Muslim Women in War and Crisis: Representation and Reality* (Austin, TX: University of Texas Press, 2010), pp. 150–1.
2. Khawla al-Qazwīnī, *Mudhakarāt mughtariba* (Bayrūt: Dār al-Ṣafwa, 2006), p. 20.
3. Rohde, *State–Society Relations in Baʿthist Iraq*, p. 76.
4. Ibid., pp. 77–9.
5. Samuel Helfont, *Compulsion in Religion: Saddam Hussein, Islam and the Roots of Insurgencies in Iraq* (New York: Oxford University Press, 2018), p. 60. The GFIW's intervention in the religious activities of women stemmed primarily from the idea that women were the most amenable to the effects of Islamisation.
6. *ʿAshura* refers to the tenth day of Muharram, the first month in the lunar calendar, and is a day of mourning for Shia Muslims. *ʿAshura* comes as part of an annual religious commemoration over the first ten days of the *hijri* new year and consists of a combination of processions, religious lectures and re-enactments of the martyrdom of the grandson of the Prophet Mohammed, Husayn ibn Ali in the year 680 at the hands of Umayyad forces in modern-day Karbala, Iraq. As for the *Arbaʿin* (lit. the fortieth), this is a day commemorating Husayn forty days after *ʿAshura*. The *Arbaʿin* used to be reserved exclusively for the

commemoration of Husayn, but is now practised more generally with the dead in Shia communities to give comfort to the relations of the deceased.

7. Zahra Al-Ali, *Women and Gender in Iraq*, p. 83.
8. Rizk Khoury, *Iraq in Wartime*, p. 63.
9. Hafez, 'Islam in Arabic Literature', p. 36.
10. Radwa Ashour, Ferial Ghazoul and Hasna Reda-Mekdashi (eds), *Arab Women Writers: a Critical Reference Guide 1873–1999* (New York: American University in Cairo, 2008).
11. Nadje Al-Ali, *Iraqi Women: Untold Stories*, p. 160.
12. Khalil Osman, *Sectarianism in Iraq: the Making of State and Nation since 1920* (New York: Oxford University Press, 2015), p. 80.
13. Salih J. Altoma, *Iraq's Modern Arabic Literature: a Guide to English Translations since 1950* (Lanham, MD: Scarecrow Press, 2010), p. xvii.
14. Bint al-Hudā, *Laytanī kuntu a'lam* (Bayrūt: Dār al-Ta'āruf, 1981), pp. 5–6.
15. Bint al-Hudā, *al-Bāḥitha 'an al-haqīqa* (Bayrūt: Dār al-Ta'āruf, 1980).
16. Bint al-Hudā, *al-Majmū'a al-qiṣaṣiya al-kamilā* (Bayrūt: Dar al-Ta'aruf, n.d.), pp. 125–205.
17. Bint al-Hudā, *al-Fadhīla tantaṣir* (Bayrūt: Dār al-Ta'āruf, 1980), p. 7.
18. Hafez, 'Islam in Arabic Literature', p. 32.
19. Bint al-Hudā, *al-Fadhīla tantaṣir*, p. 146.
20. Ibid., pp. 194, 196.
21. Ibid., p. 15.
22. Ibid., p. 29.
23. Ibid., p. 29.
24. Ibid., p. 43.
25. Ibid., pp. 80–1.
26. Ibid., pp. 90–1.
27. Ibid., p. 13.
28. Ibid., p. 16.
29. Ibid., p. 18.
30. Ibid., p. 10.
31. Ibid., p. 17.
32. Ibid., p. 213. The author adds that there are many female victims of corrupt secular society because women are easily affected and tempted by Western ideas.
33. Ibid., p. 36.
34. Ibid., p. 39.
35. Ibid., p. 45.

36. Ibid., pp. 140–2.
37. Ibid., p. 150.
38. Ibid., p. 151.
39. Joyce Wiley, 'Alima Bint al-Huda, Women's Advocate', in Linda S. Walbridge (ed.), *The Most Learned of the Shia: the Institution of Marja Taqlid* (New York: Oxford University Press), p. 154.
40. Bint al-Hudā, 'Kalima wa da'wa', pp. 154–5.
41. Wiley, 'Alima Bint al-Huda, Women's Advocate', p. 155.
42. In Shia Islam, lay members of the sect are required to choose a religious scholar, whose rulings they follow in everyday religious issues. This process is called *taqlid*, or emulation, and senior Shia clerics are labelled *marji*'s.
43. In a chapter titled 'Women and Work', Bint al-Hudā replies to a letter from a woman who asks her opinion on whether Islam approves of women working or not. Her response is interesting, especially as the type of work discussed was essentially skilled labour (she mentions doctors and engineers). According to Bint al-Hudā, individual women are not prohibited from working, but that work should not be considered a general goal for women who are financially comfortable. She laments the fact that such women would choose to work whilst employing nannies and other hired help to raise their children for them, and asserts that being a mother and wife is the most natural and important job for women. Bint al-Hudā, 'Kalima wa da'wa', pp. 204–5. Notably, Bint al-Hudā does not mention working-class women or those in financial difficulty, as one assumes that her response would have been different.
44. Khawla al-Qazwīnī, *'Indamā yufakkir al-rajul* (Bayrūt: Dār al-Ṣafwa, 1993).
45. Available at: http://www.khawlaalqazwini.com/JournalArticleDetail.aspx?aid=128, last accessed 10 December 2018.
46. Ibid.
47. Ibid.
48. Ibid.
49. In *Virtue Prevails*, Bint al-Hudā's twice mentions that her protagonist Naqa' reads Victor Hugo (Bint al-Hudā, *al-Fadhīla tantasir*, pp.123, 202).
50. Khawla al-Qazwīnī, *'Indamā yufakkir al-rajul*, pp. 21, 25.
51. Ibid., p. 43.
52. Ibid., p. 7.
53. Ibid., p. 53.
54. Ibid., p. 55.
55. Ibid., p. 67.

56. Ibid., pp. 69–70.
57. Ibid., p. 33.
58. Ibid., p. 123.
59. Ibid., p. 80.
60. Ibid., p. 236.
61. Ibid., p. 295.
62. Ibid., p. 296.
63. Ibid., p. 11.
64. Ibid., p. 18.
65. May al-Husaynī, *Wa inḥasar al-ẓalām* (Bayrūt: Dār al-Balāgha, 1993), p. 16.
66. Ibid., p. 18.
67. Ibid., pp. 162, 167.
68. Ibid., p. 193.
69. Pickthall, *The Meaning of the Glorious Quran*, 24: 32.
70. Al-Husaynī, *Wa inḥasar al-zalām*, pp. 130–1.
71. Ibid., pp. 210–11.
72. Ibid., p. 212.
73. ʿAlyāʾ al-Anṣārī, *Tathkirat Safar* (Bayrūt: Dār al-Hādi, 1999), p. 26.
74. Ibid., p. 19.
75. Ibid., p. 27.
76. Ibid., p. 45. The ideological texts in Part 1 often refer to 'human wolves' in order to dehumanise the enemy and justify violence against them.
77. Ibid., p. 44.
78. Ibid., p. 161.
79. Ibid., pp. 56–8.
80. Ibid., pp. 65, 81.
81. Ibid., pp. 56, 62.
82. Ibid., p. 66.
83. Ibid., p. 137. The historical context is only introduced two-thirds of the way into the novel, before that the plot seems to be just a parable.
84. Ibid., p. 92.
85. Ibid., p. 26.
86. Ibid., p. 70.
87. Ibid., p. 193.
88. Ishaq Tijani, *Male Domination, Female Revolt: Race, Class and Gender in Kuwaiti Women's Fiction* (Leiden: Brill, 2009), p. 35.

4

The National Gets Personal: Autobiographical Writings by Iraqi Women

This chapter discusses the various forms of life writing produced by Iraqi women in the shadow of the Ba'th Party, whether in exile or inside Iraq. It considers what is potentially subversive about the act of 'writing the self' at a time when the state was focused on forging a coherent national identity and encouraging collective solidarity in the face of its enemies. The chapter argues that the three texts by Dunya Mikhail, Haifa Zangana and Nuha al-Radi are resistive essentially due to the personalisation of individual struggle at times of war and difficulty, whilst simultaneously forgoing ego-centric understandings of the self or privileging an individual's identity over the plight of the group. The texts are distinguished by the way in which personal and political bonds are formed beyond state imperatives, as the authors situate themselves and their struggles as firmly embedded in the suffering and loss which have affected Iraqis of all backgrounds, and without a heightened sense of victimhood or vengefulness. Moreover, binaries such as personal–political, individual–community are deconstructed, and the texts posit instead the values of global citizenship, whilst validating the universal experiences of people suffering in wars and under tyranny. Rather than explicitly aligning themselves with regional and international feminist movements, the authors in this chapter are keen to express female experiences of war and tyranny in a way that includes victims of political oppression in the Arab world and beyond, be they male or female. Moreover, they have been very careful in their cultural critiques to avoid the pitfall of eurocentrism precisely because these are literary projects which resist both Ba'thist totalitarianism and American imperialism, and what they see as the duplicitous foreign policy of Western countries. Moreover, the texts challenge stereotypes about Arabs and Muslims through direct, often paratextual, political engagement, as well as significant artistic choices, such as choice of genre, and by complexifying issues of identity, which are often dealt with in simplistic terms by Western media and public discourses.

Literary discourses are in constant dialogue with political and social discourses and with each other, and resistive cultural movements in Iraq are not limited to gender, but in fact cut across gender boundaries, as the authors themselves stress. The chapter contextualises the literary works of Haifa Zangana, Dunya Mikhail and Nuha al-Radi by situating them alongside supplementary texts by Iraqi women and men, both literary and non-literary. It considers whether writings by women in general, and Iraqi women in particular, are inherently subversive as a 'subaltern' discourse, in the words of Spivak, and argues that this is not necessarily the case, despite the challenges to state narratives of nationhood which are often integral to gender discourses. Resistance, or 'writing back' functions on multiple layers, is not located solely in the content of literary texts. On one level, it functions in terms of context, language, audience and reception, which is a crucial consideration as all three works under discussion here were written and published in the 1990s and were then translated and/or republished in other countries many years after they were written.

The texts discussed in this chapter first emerged on the literary market at a time when Iraqi state publishing had ceased to swamp or inundate the market with propaganda, due, on the one hand, to the heavy toll caused by sanctions on the Iraqi economy, and on the other hand, to the ideological shift away from 'secular' processes of nation-building and their pertaining cultural manifestations, such as the novel and newspaper. At such a time, the newspaper was deemed more important and immediate, with the potential for far-reaching influence, and was therefore privileged with the limited funds that were available to the state. Also, the late 1990s and the beginning of the new millennium was a time of deep reflection; after two wars and long-lasting sanctions, Iraqis finally had time to absorb and digest the full implications of Baʿthist rule and the wars it had waged with its neighbours. All three texts were written over extended periods, endowing them with a reflective quality, which forms a sharp contrast to the hasty and careless propaganda works produced during the 1980s and the novels of Saddam Hussein produced in the new millennia.

In many ways the three texts represent a reaction against propagandistic literature, which was utilised in order to engineer shifts in public perception through language, and for maximum 'use-value'[1]; war novels in particular were produced at the peak of hostilities. These reactive, instantaneous material products actively shaped Iraq's cultural scene, but were essentially ephemeral; their high instrumental value deprived them of any symbolic value or 'staying power'. Conversely, artistic resistive texts were often published after the fall of Saddam Hussein in 2003. The belated, reflective and cathartic quality of the texts forms a marked contrast to the instantaneousness of literary production during the Iran–Iraq War. Ironically, although they participate in the unravelling of the propaganda discourses which maintained the regime, the pragmatism or 'use-value' of belated texts as cultural resistance against Ba'thist oppression is severely diminished when the time of production is considered. In fact, some of the texts have a distinctly post-modern feel that they could not have possibly been written before the late 1990s and the early 2000s. On the other hand, the texts also explicitly resist the US occupation and the sanctions which it had imposed on Iraq for over a decade, so their publication in or after 2003 is timely. Reflective rather than rushed, the texts lack the arrogance and self-assuredness of propaganda narratives and are written with a dignified simplicity and levity. Short, concentrated and emotionally intense, all the texts are undeniably poetic, and form a marked contrast to the lengthy and repetitive propaganda works discussed in Part 1 of the book, and yet seem to reference them paratextually. Moreover, the use of personalisation and fluid textual forms challenge structural rigidity and, by extension, the uncompromising and intolerant world view of state-sponsored literature.

Haifa Zangana's Nightmare in *Dreaming of Baghdad*

Written over eight years, Haifa Zangana's (1950–) original Arabic text *Fi Arwiqat al-dhakira* (1990), translated as *Through the Vast Halls of Memory* (1991), details the author's imprisonment and torture by the Ba'th as a result of her involvement with the then outlawed Iraqi Communist Party. The current text *Dreaming of Baghdad*, published in English in 2009, is a retelling of the author's original story; unlike traditional memoirs, it is notably brief, and is characterised by its non-linearity, lapses in memory and dramatic shifts in time and space. *Dreaming of Baghdad* is episodic, non-chronological and ambiguous in terms of genre, combining epistolary and diary forms whilst shifting action from Iraq to exile abroad in London. Writing from a distant place and time, the author describes mundane scenes from her childhood that have stayed with her, such as visiting her Kurdish father's relations in the north, and getting lost in the city souk at the age of five and being found by her mother. First imprisoned in Qasr al-Nihaya prison for political opponents and then in the now infamous Abu Ghraib prison for 'ordinary' crimes, Zangana was eventually moved to Zaʿfaraniya women's prison, primarily reserved for prostitutes and those with long or life sentences. In order to escape execution, she signed a document that she was not in fact political but was rather sexually involved with her comrades. Upon her release, Zangana continued her studies and graduated with a degree in pharmacy from Baghdad University, and then left Iraq in 1976 for political reasons and sought asylum in the United Kingdom.

Written in the first- and sometimes in the third-person to avoid the 'illusion of the self as the centre of events or history',[2] *Dreaming of Baghdad* is personal but not self-absorbed, and Zangana situates human beings as a self-destructive species, rather than herself, at the heart of the text. Furthermore, she immediately challenges our expectations of the memoir genre by avoiding the use of 'I' in the opening pages, immediately signalling that the text is not an autobiography. By locating the narratorial voice outside herself, there is a sense of an expansive perspective that is on the outside looking in, rather than from the self out towards the world. Indeed, according to the advice given to Zangana by a friend, the process of writing and remembering should 'always begin from the outside: get to the bottom of things, probe their depths, but always from the outside'.[3]

Dreaming of Baghdad begins at the end of the story: the author's exile in London, which prepares the reader for the text's non-linearity. The opening section 'Correspondence' adopts an epistolary form and consists of a series of letters sent to the author from a painter friend and former comrade, who is also in exile. The letters detail the plight of Iraqi refugees 'moving from country to country, endlessly choosing between submission and submission',[4] and carrying the burden of homesickness and grief: 'the wound inside you is your very existence'.[5] The author's comrade is tormented by nightmares of 'getting on the wrong plane',[6] symbolically indicating a sense of dislocation and wandering, as well as the fear and humiliation of border guards and immigration officers. Visa issues often appear in narratives from the Iraqi diaspora and feature more prominently in the other two texts in this chapter *Baghdad Diaries* and *Diary of a Wave Outside the Sea*.

Despite the hardships experienced in the homeland, exile does not provide the author with reprieve. In fact, 'Correspondence' is the part where the author 'dreams' of Baghdad, echoing the book's new title. The author's friend 'yearns for the sailor to settle and gaze happily at children's drawings empty of weapons and soldiers'.[7] As a painter, he is fixated on abstractions, and is unable to build himself a successful career because he resists being a token artist, painting 'heritage' paintings for the sake of Western audiences. The unnamed friend's comments seem to imply that dialogue with the West can be achieved through art, but that even with the freedoms accorded there, it is difficult to express oneself artistically without confirming Western generalisations about the East. Moreover, the West also carries its own burden of *ghurba* or *depaysement*; of feeling strange and out of place and is not a utopian haven. If there is any hope to be found, then it is to be found within Iraq itself, and not through a foreign 'saviour'. The section ends by looking forward to the future using its most emotionally poignant signifier: children. Young Iraqis are described as 'children of this country of soldiers and the dead',[8] a dystopian image which is balanced with the image of a girl at the end of a corridor talking to the sun about her fear of the darkness, and attempting to 'restore to hope some of its glory'.[9] The past, as a mirror image of the future, is evoked in history, roots and the individual and collective imaginary. In another letter, the friend asserts that the mind cannot be claimed like land, alluding to the invasion of Iraq which has been colonised, but the minds of its people have not: 'The mind is boundless and is the greater part of life. It is an area where no human can plant his country's flag and say, This is my land.'[10] The rootlessness of existence as a refugee is grounded in a pastoral metaphor linking 'home, garden, flowers', which also echoes the utopian rurality of the nation as the lost fatherland: 'Do you know I have fond memories of the *goulnaz* flower? My father used to like its transparent red colour, and when he died I tended the flowers in our garden.'[11]

In the second section of *Dreaming of Baghdad* titled 'Zino', the author provides a wonderful snapshot of a Kurdish border town with Iran, entirely dependent for its livelihood on the black market. Beautifully succinct and almost poetic, Zangana describes Zino as a melting pot of ethnicities and cultures: Arab, Persian and Kurdish, and vividly depicts the daily habits of the women of Zino, who are the first females that appear in the text, and the hustle and bustle of the market. The enduring image of Kurdish women is as busy, productive and creative individuals; strong-willed and industrious; these women mainly work in the production of handicrafts, as well as assisting men in farming. There is a strange idyllic aura about Zino, which emanates from the fact that it represents a place of origins despite the author's inability to speak Kurdish: her father's mother tongue. Zino is a significant point of reference because it evokes 'the rural' as a place of belonging, and where the author can connect with the man who 'was lost to her in the big city'[12]: her father.

In contrast, the third section 'Baghdad' begins with an image of Qasr al-Nihaya prison where the author was first incarcerated, as the city emerges as a suffocating and oppressive space. The torture and humiliation that the protagonist endures at the hands of her nefarious tormentors transforms the victim into 'an entity closed upon itself',[13] healed only through the act of writing and not through revenge. Although Zangana subscribes to the idea of history as cyclical, there is no meaningful sense of justice or relief that the head of the Iraqi secret intelligence Nazim Kazar, whom she names in the text, was executed only four years after her arrest. The tragic cycle of violence, which implicates even the author and her comrades themselves, signals a deeper sense of injustice that goes beyond individual grievances. Zangana is uncertain of the incorruptibility of humans: 'is there any guarantee that we too, will not wear the faces of the torturers in the future?'[14] The twist in the novel's epilogue about Haider, a fellow comrade released from prison after only three days (which immediately makes him a suspected collaborator with the government) is a case in point. Haider may have been executed by his comrades for fear that he was now an infiltrator, or maybe he was not; the author does not really remember. In fact, it is only when she sees his name on the list of missing persons in back issues of *al-Thawra*, the Ba'th's official newspaper in 1999, does she remember him at all.

Torture isolates the individual and pushes them to be preoccupied with their own personal needs, to inform on friends and loved ones in the hope of salvation and reprieve; in short, to do anything to survive as an individual. The author resists this idea of detachment from the community by remembering those who have died or disappeared, and who no longer have a voice. This signals the therapeutic quality of writing as a form of rehabilitation, which helps to open up the tortured individual so that he/she can return to the world by situating her experiences within a broader communal and global context. The cyclical nature of history, where 'the past is the present is the future'[15] is somewhat comforting because it does not relegate the author's experience with torture to the margins of exceptionalism. The text is expansive in terms of time and space, where wars and violence in Iraq throughout history are chapters in the same story. The author gives herself the 'advice' that, 'when at one with destiny, there is neither time nor space, life nor death'.[16] Here selfhood melts into eternity, and according to Hamid Dabashi in his chapter of *Stories of Torture*, Zangana uses a narrative distancing technique, which is not uncommon in accounts of torture and imprisonment.[17]

In a section titled 'Heart, What Have You Seen?', the narrative switches to diary form in Za'faraniya, the women's prison, with entries drawn and edited from Zangana's actual diaries whilst an inmate there. She highlights the cycles of violence which occur in the home and in the family as a reflection of political oppression and violence. Most of the women in Za'faraniya have been sentenced to death or life imprisonment for killing their husbands or other men; Um Wahid kills her abusive husband at the age of seventeen with the help of her brother, and prefers to stay in prison as she would probably be killed in revenge by her husband's family once released. Um Wahid's own mother is happy for her to die if that means saving the son whose life she had 'ruined'. Um Wahid is not a mother, yet she is given a *kunya*, or title, which evokes motherhood as the primary identity a woman should have. Here, being called a mother, an 'Um', highlights what the woman has lost as a result of her crime. Another character called Um Ali killed her husband's assassin with the help of her son in order to defend the honour of the family, and the mentally ill Um Jassim killed her husband in the most gruesome way after he took another wife. The Bedouin Um Athaba burnt her husband alive because he was abusive and imprisoned her in her home and is described as calmly knitting a jumper for her daughter, who was temporarily kept in an orphanage until her release from prison. This cosy image of motherhood is juxtaposed against graphic images of extreme female violence against each other and towards men who are unconventionally depicted as victims of honour killings, rather. Unfortunately for Um Athaba, she was the last woman to be sentenced to death by hanging before the abolishment of capital punishment for women in Iraq.[18]

Mothers are portrayed with kaleidoscopic variety in *Dreaming of Baghdad*, and unlike the mothers of state-sponsored literary propaganda, they are not evoked as symbolic ideals, but rather they are represented as individual humans with faults. Zangana highlights the maternal obsession to feed, as one of the only things mothers felt they could do to nurture rebellious children. She says that no one in the family replies to her mother when she asks for the millionth time what she should cook for them.[19] In Zino, a mother asks the author about her son who had joined the communists. Her first questions are 'Who cooks for him? Who washes his clothes?' The reply is ironic given that Zangana claims she never learned to cook herself: 'Nobody. He cooks for himself and for the others' she tells the doting mother. Moreover, the mother is indignant that her son's comrades tease her by saying that he bakes terrible bread, as in her eyes he can do no wrong.[20] The infantilisation of the communist fighter is highlighted in this scene, and exemplifies the emasculation of men in the text, which contains very few displays of male strength besides the tyranny of the state. This makes the contrast with female prisoners and other women in the text all the more stark. One poignant example of female strength is when the protagonist is lost at the age of five. Heavily pregnant and wary of entering the 'male world' of the souk, the author's mother summons her courage to frantically search for her child in an uncomfortable, and potentially threatening public space, and brings her home. Likewise, when Zangana is arrested, it is the admirable perseverance of her mother that forces the security personnel to admit that she had even been apprehended. Her daily visits to the prison for months on end, pestering the guards and insisting that they should pass on to her daughter a box of basic amenities despite their denials that she is even inside, sheds light on the impotence felt by the father.

On the other hand, it is the misogynistic societal views which ironically led to an under-estimation of the threat posed by women; Zangana's mother's mundane challenge to authority is not taken seriously, whereas it would have been a different matter altogether if her father had approached prison security. In fact, it is specifically the father who feels impotent about the deteriorating political conditions in Iraq and surrenders himself to an addiction to drinking and pills. Ultimately, images of male weakness and female strength, albeit violent manifestations of strength, rather than representations of victimisation, may be seen as 'anti-feminist' but serve Zangana's political project well.

In her chapter on Arab women's prison writing, Daphne Grace considers Nawal Saadawi's works as feminist 'proper', whereas due to its broader concerns, Zangana's original text *Through the Vast Halls of Memory*, on which *Dreaming of Baghdad* is based, is according to Grace not a feminist text, despite its author being an activist.[21] Set alongside Nawal el-Saadawi's volatile prison memoirs, Grace asserts that *Through the Vast Halls of Memory* discusses human issues that are non-gender specific, especially state brutality against political dissidents. It is true that Zangana's text does not revolve around women's issues, but the assumption that women's issues can and should be separated from broader issues such as political oppression and economic deprivation, highlights a narrow interpretation of what feminism means. Zangana does in fact highlight specifically female problems, such as menstruation, childbirth and domestic violence, which is committed by and against women. However, she seems to downplay the victimisation of women because that would not serve the political message of the text and the counter discourse it attempts to create, namely, that Iraqi women are not merely helpless victims to be saved. Ironically, *Through the Vast Halls of Memory*, the text Grace claimed was not feminist, was republished in 2009 as *Dreaming of Baghdad* by Feminist Press in the United States, which describes itself as 'an educational non-profit organization founded to advance women's rights and amplify feminist perspectives'.[22] It is also worth noting that a quotation from Saadawi, commending *Dreaming of Baghdad* appears on its front cover, and was probably chosen by Feminist Press as a marketing strategy to boost the book's sales and image. Referencing Saadawi as the undisputed authority on Arab women would have inevitably appealed to Western feminists, and explicitly marks Zangana's text as 'feminist' thereby widening the appeal of the text to a Western audience.

The hybridity of Zangana's position ethnically (her mother is Arab and her father is Kurdish) extends to the in between-ness of her position as the only female comrade in her group, something that could be understood only in sexual terms by her tormentors, and even by ordinary people of Zino. Even Zangana's comrades resented her presence with them, and feared that it would smear the reputation of opponents of the Baʿth and would make them an object of vicious rumours and speculation. As the author assumes her position on a mountain in Kurdistan alongside communist fighters, she wraps herself in male garb and looks 'like a little boy' in order to neuter her femininity, thereby transforming into an emasculated man.[23] Zangana does not romanticise opposition to the Baʿth in order to avoid conforming to the binaries of 'us' and 'them' or 'good' and 'evil' in spite of the moral urgency of her text. Ironically, misogynistic views of women ultimately saved Zangana's life, as her release from prison is predicated on the fact that she admitted to being a whore with no political beliefs. The state's insistence that only the loss of her reputation could save women like Zangana from death highlights the way in which 'dishonour' was used as a political tool, as well as the demeaning views held by the Baʿth vis-à-vis women (a sharp contrast to its so-called 'progressive' public discourse on women). As well as potentially leading to social ostracism and destroying women's chances of marriage, the use of dishonour also assumed that women were unable to conceive of political opposition and belittled their potential for resistance.

Following the trajectory of analysis in this book, close reading of primary texts must always bear in mind the paratextual information that surrounds them, such as titles or title change, cover illustrations and photographs, forewords and epilogues. This is particularly significant for the texts in this chapter, which have been 'repackaged' for publishing, often providing more telling information about how a text 'resists' than the content of the text itself. For example, *In the Vast Halls of Memory* was first published in English in 1990 to expose the horrors of the Baʿth to a Western audience 'which didn't know where Iraq was on the map', yet at the same time, this was an audience who during the Iran–Iraq War had perceived of Saddam Hussein as an ally of the West against post-revolutionary Iran. The book was then published in Arabic in 1995 after the invasion of Kuwait, when Saddam was isolated from the rest of the Arab world, having previously enjoyed the favour of Gulf States in particular, as the so-called 'defender of the eastern front'. Finally, Zangana's text was republished as *Dreaming of Baghdad* in 2009 in a neat synthesis of her political views which opposed both Saddam and the Americans as oppressors of the Iraqi people. In the words of the author herself, in the prologue of *Dreaming of Baghdad*: 'as we resist the occupation now, our message is clear: we did not struggle for decades to replace one torturer with another'.[24]

In *Dreaming of Baghdad*, the author made the decision to change the original title of her text *Through the Vast Halls of Memory*, directing the reader from a more universal understanding of political oppression, to a more specific narrative about the plight of political prisoners in Iraq. Why was there a need, either on the part of the author or the publisher, to mark the book as visibly Iraqi? This change in the title was arguably a marketing strategy as the text is not all set in Baghdad. In fact, Baghdad is not even posited as the centre of the book or events. If anything, the capital represents centralised state repression, whereas Zino, a Kurdish village on the Iranian border and therefore on the fringes of the state, represents childhood memories, paternal origins and ethnic roots. It is the smell of Persian carpets in Zino, mixed with coffee which sustained the author through times of deep despair and agony. Baghdad, a microcosm of the nation, can be said to represent Iraq, but the book is not nationalist in the traditional sense. However, using Baghdad as a buzzword, was more likely to have been included to make for a more grabbing title. In terms of the book's contribution to counter-public discourses and its opposition to media narratives on the invasion of Iraq, the accuracy of the title would have been a secondary consideration given the importance of disseminating the book, and its pertaining ideas.

To return to the title, the 'dreaming' part captures the continuous effort to remember, imagine and construct the nation. In this sense, it retains an aspect of the original title, but with the act of dreaming balanced with the concrete reality of Baghdad the city. Here, the creative attempt at imagining is grounded firmly in a context, whereas in the original title *Through the Vast Halls of Memory* only the unreliability of memory, its vastness and emptiness are captured and emphasised. Dreaming also encapsulates hope for a better future and inspires change, but it is also a dangerous endeavour. In the novel, the 'beautiful dreamer' Fouad, Zangana's comrade, lost his life, as did many other dreamers who dared to resist the Baʿth. Such is the cyclical nature of history, as Iraqis continue to dream for the impossible in the shadow of invasion and more war and civil strife. In many ways, the invasion of Iraq itself was born out of Western dreams of an 'easy' toppling of a crumbling regime; and one in which American soldiers would be welcomed with flowers like heroes.

Hamid Dabashi's foreword and Ferial Ghazoul's afterword frame *Dreaming of Baghdad* from different angles. Dabashi focuses on the political significance of the work, while Ghazoul emphasises its artistry and literary qualities, such as its structural complexity and thematic ingenuity. Both Dabashi and Ghazoul believe that the text will promote a better understanding of Iraq as a culture, and of Arab women as strong and fearless, thereby not conforming to Western stereotypes. The balance of art and politics in the text, almost as separate poles, nonetheless gives precedence to Dabashi's politicised interpretation of the text, by privileging it as the peritext which shapes the audience's interpretation of the text before it is received. The foreword frames *Dreaming of Baghdad* as a resistance narrative, not only against Saddam and the Baʿth, but also against the Americans. The mere mention of 'Abu Ghraib' by Dabashi is intended to strongly resonate with American readers of this edition of the book, as 'only one, among many symbols'[25] of the destruction caused by American imperialism in Iraq. Readers cannot help but think of the similarities between American torturers in Abu Ghraib and Zangana's Baʿthist tormentors.

The foreword immediately contextualises *Dreaming of Baghdad* by referring to current American foreign policy blunders in Iraq led by George W. Bush and Paul Bremer, and describes the text as 'politically punctilious'.[26] Dabashi adds that it is 'impossible to imagine a timelier context'[27] for Zangana's text in 2004. This is a significant statement which implies that the text is now more relevant than the actual time of publication fifteen years ago. Indeed, some texts can be more relevant for posterity if they are ahead of their time, but what Dabashi seems to miss in his impassioned piece is the power of the text to capture the cyclical quality of history. It may be a tragic coincidence that the text's critique of Baʿthist oppression was so apt as Iraq faces renewed Western violence and aggression, but it is the text's universal message on the plight of people struggling under oppression and the high human cost of resistance, which makes this appropriation possible in multiple contexts and not just the one highlighted by Dabashi. Having said that, the way in which the 'newness' of the text is emphasised, and the erasure of the first edition, points to a marketing strategy on the part of the publishers to highlight female responses to the 2003 Iraq war, and to contextualise these responses within a wider historical framework of Ba'thist brutality and western imperialism.

Dabashi attacks authors who attempt to ingratiate themselves with those in power by succumbing to Western narratives that support and perpetuate stereotypical and racist representations of the East and its people as an uncivilised and barbaric culture. As such, he critiques what he calls the 'self-promoting memoir industry',[28] pointing to the veritable explosion of memoirs in English by Eastern and African women. Dabashi describes some of these authors as 'self-sexualising'[29] opportunists who are self-absorbed and uncommitted to the anti-imperialist cause. He has in fact previously been at the centre of controversy by publicly criticising the Iranian author of *Reading Lolita in Tehran*, Azhar Nafisi, for in his words being 'a colonial agent and a native informer'.[30] Dabashi's irate essay on Nafisi's best-selling book centres on her depictions of Western culture as liberating and therefore superior to Persian culture, and on her fixation on the veil to titillate Western audiences. His critique of this dangerous cultural trend allows him to situate *Dreaming of Baghdad* text in an even wider literary and cultural battlefield and to endow it with moral superiority, as well as, in many ways, wresting it from any Western feminists who might want to appropriate Zangana for their own political agendas.

Taken against this background, Zangana's work is seen by Dabashi as ideal: it is politically engaged in the sense that resistance is expressed on many levels: first, it resists American aggression and imperialism: '[those] who have divided a deeply cultivated culture along sectarian lines to rule it better'. It also challenges the narrative perpetuated by what he calls 'embedded anthropologists'[31] serving the American colonial agenda and denying women the right to speak for themselves. There is a strong sense of cultural imperialism and collusion with the West, using the supposed oppression and disempowerment of women to justify the US invasion and the demonisation of an entire culture. This includes sensationalist memoirists who have achieved fame at a most opportune moment and at the expense of integrity and justice. If the intellectual's job is to 'speak truth to power', then, according to Dabashi, Zangana is an intellectual par excellence. In line with Dabashi's foreword, Zangana's prologue draws similarities between the Baʿth and the United States saying 'history has striven to repeat itself by rotating around a single axis, humans'.[32] I would argue that it is the work of Dabashi's foreword to politicise *Dreaming of Baghdad*, but the text remains unchanged as art in a way that is antithetical to the state-sponsored political texts discussed in previous chapters.

In Ferial Ghazoul's afterword, she points out that *Dreaming of Baghdad* is specific and global at the same time and can be located at the crossroads of various disciplines: literature, politics, history and human rights. For Ghazoul, the purpose of the text is, first and foremost, to bear witness, and she sees *Dreaming of Baghdad* as embodying 'literature from the witness stand'.[33] Interestingly, however, Zangana considers herself an unreliable witness, and the text is not written in a documentary style as survival accounts often are. Ghazoul seems to want to elevate the text as somehow 'above' literature because the events described are true, and because of the kind of suffering endured by its author. In *Writings of Consolation*, the author identifies three main reasons why political prisoners and victims of torture choose to write about their experiences. First, to defend their ideas and values, and to warn against the dangers of authoritarianism and injustice. Secondly, to bear witness, and, thirdly, to sustain comfort.[34] In her prologue, written specifically for the 2009 edition of her memoirs, and in line with Ghazoul's comments, Zangana asserts that through the act of writing, she felt that she was 'paying a debt, long overdue to my friends',[35] and that she broke her silence so as not to betray their memories. For the author, writing was a form of solace and healing, which liberated her from pain, and allowed her to escape the trauma of her past and to return to the present.

Although Zangana was arrested and tortured for her political activities, *Baghdad Diaries* is not didactic, and does not contain explicit critiques of the Baʿth as an ideology. The author does mourn the loss of her freedom, but does so in a way that validates the experiences of all Iraqis and people living under oppression. Globalising the experiences of a political prisoner frees the text and its author of egotism, or the imposition of certain stylistic conventions upon her, such as the necessity of 'documenting' history in the way the propaganda litterateurs were obligated to do. This highlights the two tensions inherent in Zangana's project: the imperative to bear witness to the horrors of Ba'thist oppression, on the one hand, and the decentring of the self and the use of memory lapses and its unreliability as a stylistic device, on the other. This brings us back to why the title of Zangana's text was changed from *Through the Vast Halls of Memory* to *Dreaming of Baghdad*: in an effort to retain the arguably more artistic dimension of memory, the act of dreaming is evoked alongside the city of Baghdad as concrete and knowable.

Haifa Zangana is the most politically active of the three writers discussed in this chapter, however, her *Dreaming of Baghdad* is ironically the least preoccupied with the minutiae of political events; she provides no dates and few names of political figures or organisations and almost no historical backdrop. Unbound by the specificities of region or national character, Zangana's text seems suspended in time, very much Iraqi, but extracted out of its context and transformed into an 'existential parable',[36] in the words of Ghazoul. It is important to bear in mind that Zangana writes in a variety of genres, both literary and non-literary: from journalistic articles to cultural histories. She therefore seems to detach her art from direct political engagement, which is kept for her articles and social and political critiques. This endows a universal and humanist quality to *Dreaming of Baghdad* which might otherwise have been localised and restricted to a specific time and place. Moreover, by shedding the 'excess' of context; by seeing it as superfluous, almost, and addressing the heart of the issue regarding her incarceration and torture: that of humans causing immense pain and suffering to other humans for power, Zangana ingeniously frees the text of potential interpretations of Arab exceptionalism. Ultimately, it is crucial to contextualise texts within the literary oeuvre and writings of authors themselves. Zangana does not delve into the political history of Iraq and its effect on women because she had already done this in her book *City of Widows* published three years earlier. Such a method of analysis makes it easier to begin to understand the author's literary philosophy; what she sees as the ultimate purpose of art, and whether its potential as resistance is stronger than pure activism.

A Different Kind of Realism: *Baghdad Diaries*

Written in English over the span of two decades, Nuha al-Radi's (1941–2004) *Baghdad Diaries* (2003) is a unique personal account of the effects of sanctions on an Iraqi family, written *sur place* in Baghdad. In the prologue to the text, and after stressing that all the characters in the book are real people, al-Radi says she is not a writer by profession, in a gesture of rhetorical uncertainty which forms a marked contrast to the over-confidence displayed by male writers of questionable merit who were catapulted to fame for participating in the state-sponsored propaganda initiative. The humility motif used here by al-Radi is not atypical in modern Arab literature. In fact, we have already encountered the trope in the previous chapters, including in the religious writings of Āmina al-Ṣadr and the novels of Saddam Hussein. However, whereas Saddam Hussein used anonymity together with other paratexts, such as supposedly donating all proceeds from book sales to charity in order to support his cult of personality, both Nuha al-Radi and Āmina al-Ṣadr (who says she is 'not a novelist or storywriter') seem to distance themselves from fictional writing as a means of lending more credibility to their works as truthful and honest; al-Ṣadr in particular presents herself as a truth-seeker, whereas al-Radi sees herself as a truth-teller. The humility motif is also present in the prologue to the last work to be analysed in this chapter: Dunya Mikhail's *Diary of a Wave Outside the Sea* (2009), where the author says that she did not intend to write the text as poetry, but that it was her English publisher who felt that her writings indeed fell within the conventions of that prestigious genre, and 'insisted that my book was poetry'. As a poetical memoir or 'memoirish' poetry, Mikhail's text 'drifted for a moment from the usual classifications'.[37] Despite not being a poet intentionally, however, Mikhail does see herself as one, when she thanks her husband 'for being able to live with a poet'.[38] The humility motif ultimately highlights conflicting views of creative writing as being both powerful but also a derivative activity that can imitate reality only in the way a shadow can capture just the form of an object rather than its true essence.

Born to a distinguished secular Shia family, painter, ceramist and diarist Nuha al-Radi spent a significant part of her childhood in India, where her father was stationed as a diplomat. Upon the family's return to Iraq after the revolution of 1958, al-Radi and her siblings were sent abroad to study, and she joined the Byam Shaw School of Art in London. Al-Radi's family left for Beirut in 1969, only to return to Iraq with the outbreak of the civil war in Lebanon in 1975 and stayed there for the next three decades. She died in 2004 in Beirut at the age of sixty-three from leukaemia, which she and her family blamed on the US use of depleted uranium.[39]An international sensibility permeates *Baghdad Diaries* owing in part to the author's privileged and intellectual family. However, the tone of *Baghdad Diaries* varies and is by no means monolithic in the views it expresses. Divided into four sections, the first two sections of the text titled 'Hotel Paradiso' and 'Embargo', perpetuate an 'us'/'them' polemic, as the author is preoccupied with the daily suffering caused by American sanctions and aligns herself with the actions of the Iraqi state: 'our big mistake was not to move out of Kuwait'.[40] However, in the final two sections, titled 'Exile' and 'Identity', which were added to the 2003 edition, al-Radi's perspective has expanded noticeably as she acquired a spatial distance from her home in Baghdad. The author is now endowed with a new philosophical perspective about man's propensity towards evil and the shared values and experiences of humankind.

Despite undergoing editing and re-editing since it was originally published in 1998, the text exhibits an emotional immediacy and the reactive quality of a memoir written at a time of great difficulty. Dedicated 'to the people of Iraq and to all others who have suffered the crippling effects of war and sanctions',[41] al-Radi's text ultimately contemplates broader issues outside the Arab world, including international women's issues. In the prologue to the second edition of her diaries, published in English in 2003, al-Radi states that she found it necessary to update the diary to cover the years since the first edition was published.[42] This explains the split in narratorial self-awareness midway through the diaries, as not only was the text extended to include all the years from 1998 to 2002, but also, crucially, the political context had changed. Al-Radi's extended and republished diaries aimed to bring to the fore a public counter-discourse against US state and media attempts to legitimise the invasion of Iraq. Ironically, like *Dreaming of Baghdad*, the extended version of *Baghdad Diaries* is timelier than the original English text of 1998, as it was published at a time when voices of outrage against the immense suffering caused by US sanctions were ignored. The author is aware of the political significance of the work in resisting American stereotypes of Arabs and Iraqis, which is given primacy over social critique or expressions of opposition to the Baʿth given the impending US invasion of the country.

Primarily by virtue of its genre, but also due to the historical moment in which it was produced, *Baghdad Diaries* is the most explicitly anti-American text out of the three works discussed in this chapter. It covers the second Gulf War, the bombing of Baghdad, and the 'thirty-strong aggression', as well as documenting life under the sanctions and the impending invasion of Iraq in 2003. Al-Radi is also critical of the Baʿthist regime, but not in an overtly political way as she does not belong to any political party. Instead, she complains about the Baʿth's mismanagement of crises in a resentful way due to the daily suffering caused by war and its civilian toll: 'we are paying the price while our leader is alive and well'.[43] The author regards Saddam's decision to invade Kuwait as irrational and describes propaganda attempts to disguise the catastrophic venture as pathetic: 'no one could understand our leader's intention', she says, adding that 'national radio claiming victory was disgusting'.[44] Al-Radi's sense of apathy is clear when she says: 'whoever we sent agreed to everything', not caring about the details of the ceasefire or interested in how it was managed.

According to al-Radi, history is one big cycle of oppression and violence and thus she asserts that George Bush Senior and Saddam Hussein are alike. Like Zangana, al-Radi subscribes to a cyclical view of history as 'nothing really changes, only the years'.[45] She stresses that often there is no point in even putting dates on the separate diary entries, as the days are just one miserable extension of time. On the very first page of part one of the diaries, ironically titled 'Hotel Paradiso', the narrator details how she remained certain until the very end that there would be no war in 1990, and how it became clear that her optimism was ill-founded. However, the work ends hopefully despite the impending invasion of Iraq: 'I hope and pray that war can be avoided.'[46] The reader is unsure as to whether this is an ironic rhetorical device used deliberately by the author or genuine wishful thinking, but is directed towards the former interpretation.

In her exasperated attempts to highlight the devastating effects of American sanctions on ordinary Iraqis, al-Radi often internalises and repeats the Baʿthist state sloganism. For example, she asserts that Iraq is being targeted because 'we stood up to the United States and said no'.[47] The author adds that she feels 'very bitter towards the West',[48] adding that enemies want 'to destroy our infrastructure to make more jobs for people in the West!'[49] Conspiracy theories like this appear repeatedly in the text due to the breakdown of coherent narratives to make sense of new political realities, as well as the dissolution of old political configurations and traditionally 'stable' nationalist identities. Al-Radi's incorporation of journalistic elements in the text, such as quoting political statements from the news and providing statistics of the dead and injured from the civil war in Lebanon or those arrested in Palestine, reaffirms the political salience of the text beyond exclusively Iraqi affairs, and locates the text firmly as a socio-historical document. Moreover, the use of a journalistic style often functions in a similar way to state-sponsored texts as evidence of the enemy's unscrupulous morals. Al-Radi's detailing of the mistreatment of Iraqi POWs in Iran is a case in point: 'They did all sorts of terrible things to him, including seven months solitary confinement in a loo – naked, with buckets of shit thrown on him.'[50] Al-Radi also uses a recurrent motif which is typical of the discourses found in the state-sponsored novels of the Iran–Iraq War, particularly those produced during its latter stages when the state was preparing the masses for peace. Al-Radi's exasperated rant against the cost of war which, she says, could have been used 'to feed the hungry of the world'[51] bears an eerie resemblance to expressions of pacifism, which had previously been censored during the early stages of the Iran–Iraq War, but were later not only tolerated, but even encouraged. However, unlike state-sponsored novels, the author does not absolve her own government from responsibility, and like Haifa Zangana, shares a humanistic viewpoint which validates the universal experiences of human beings suffering under war: 'one cannot blame individuals for what their governments do. Otherwise we would all have to answer for the mess we're in.'[52]

Al-Radi depicts a Baghdad that has been drastically altered demographically and geographically. Suleikh, the affluent district where the author resides, now only consists of a 'multitude of women'[53]; it is 'nothing but women',[54] with al-Radi's dog Salvi being the only sexually active male, alongside the male palm trees in her orchard, which are ever ready to pollinate. 'There are so few men in our lives',[55] the author says, and any remaining men are emasculated for not being able to do military service and spend their time away from the public sphere, often asleep at home. This crisis in masculinity has devastating consequences, as highlighted by the author: 'Rumour has it that one man poisoned a fish, fed it to his family and killed them all and himself.'[56] Conversely, women not only own and take charge of their own creative and personal space, they also encroach upon the public sphere despite the rise in conservative discourse adopted by the state in the 1990s. For example, in one episode, the author and her female relatives ride bikes down the hill in a carefree manner, much to the disdain of those around them.[57] Moreover, Um Imad, a mother, who is not identified by her real name, is described as 'the voice of the people' and 'the barometer of Iraq'.[58] In the absence of conscription-aged men, war seems to be the great leveller, which allows women more flexibility in defining and shaping gender roles. One effect of this is the way children are brought up during the war. Al-Radi notes that when told to play daddy, a young boy in the war imitates his father by doing nothing in the game and prefers to play the proactive maid.[59] The 'Embargo' section of *Baghdad Diaries* continues this egalitarian view of gender, as women shave their heads to be economical and only go once every four months to the hairdressers.[60]

However, there is price to pay for women's newfound power to appropriate personal and public spaces, as the increase in the mental load and responsibilities has meant that depression is the thing that has most increased since the war[61] and has disproportionately affects women. Al-Radi turns to writing as a means of maintaining her sanity and mental health, and the more extreme conditions become, the more creative and productive the author seems to get. According to one critic: 'the frenzy to survive is sublimated into a creative frenzy of expression that reveals the functional and cathartic power of art to symbolize discontent and resistance'.[62] Al-Radi thus attacks representations of Iraqi 'superwomen'[63] as perpetuated by the state during the Iran–Iraq War to encourage women to contribute to the economy through work and serve the cause of the nation by having more children.

The levelling effect of the war extends to creatures large and small. The author says even rats are hungry in this city, just like everyone else, but that the ruling Party are said to eat gazelle meat from a private farm.[64] In fact, all available produce is from government owned farms, whose sole aim, according to the author, was to derive maximum financial benefits. Animals remind the reader of the basics of existence: eating, sleeping, grooming, defecating, mating and reproducing. The text focuses on Salvi, the author's dog as a form of relief, and follows his life, particularly his 'lovers' and his litters. Despite being immensely attached to Salvi, al-Radi reports his death with no emotion, as it is juxtaposed with the deaths of human beings and would have been disrespectful. The encroachment of nature on the city signals the transformation of Baghdad from an urban metropolis, to 'pockets of little of villages'[65]; a regression to the pastoral origins that the Ba'th romanticised and found so admirable. According to Brinda Mehta, gardening in her orchard gives the author a 'sense of cultural wholeness', where cultivating the land is 'a political act of keeping memory alive in the earth's sediment as a primal archive for the future'.[66] On the other hand, the degeneration experienced by what was once the 'cradle of civilisation' is captured in all its poignance, as Iraq is driven back to the Stone Age and poverty, disease starvation are rife.

During the 'Embargo' section of *Baghdad Diaries*, the state becomes stricter, embarking on a nationwide piety campaign, and dealing out harsher punishments for crimes. Al-Radi is aware of being monitored and wonders what security thought of some of her private conversations with friends. Sarcastically, she claims that under the sanctions 'artists are given a free rein, otherwise I wouldn't have lasted this long'.[67] Perhaps, like Zangana, the misogyny of the Ba'th Party means that it does not conceive of a secular woman who is unaffiliated to any political party as threatening, despite, in al-Radi's case, being a Shia, and a sayyid. Amin Malak comments:

> The family whose difficulties, fears and frustrations the narrator ably articulates is an unusual case: they are privileged and seem to have certain cordial, working contacts with the regime: al-Radi's kiln is bought by the Palace (i.e. Saddam's); the family entertains ambassadors at its home for dinner; and she receives parcels from abroad through foreign journalists at a time when any contact with a foreigner would have led to questioning by the regime's ruthless secret services. Vodka and beer are served with their dinner, an unusual practice for an Iraqi Muslim family.[68]

The diplomatic status of Al-Radi's father and the family's secular lifestyle aligned her with an elite stratum of Iraqi society, and makes the reader question what life was like for the vast majority of Iraqis if the privileged were experiencing such hardships.

Another important consideration regarding how the state might have seen al-Radi was that she was not a writer by profession. Therefore, the potential of her memoirs as a propaganda tool against the West was high in use-value given that it was an eyewitness civilian account of suffering under Western sanctions written in English. Moreover, as a ceramist and sculptor, al-Radi is able to continue producing art under the Baʿth, as sculptures would be more difficult to decipher, let alone censor, than writing. Highlighting how certain modes of expression were underestimated, one state poet remarks at one of her exhibitions: 'You mean these stones and tin cans of yours are for sale?' She replies ironically that the poet lacks imagination.[69] In Nadje Al-Ali's *Iraqi Women: Untold Stories from 1948 to the Present*, she includes the testimony of a philosophy lecturer at Baghdad University who was left to her own devices throughout Baʿth rule, and without pressure even to join the Baʿth Party like almost all university lecturers were required to do. She laments the fact that she wasted her life studying Western culture, 'after all what they did to Iraq', but ironically, because as a discipline philosophy was regarded as unimportant, this probably saved her life and livelihood.[70] In addition, Hiyām Nāʾil al-Dawāf's study of book production under the Baʿth, philosophy publications were almost always at the bottom of all four periods studied. Abstract, unthreatening and not amenable to propagandistic usage, philosophy allowed this woman a rare opportunity to experience intellectual freedom, just as al-Radi's sculptures allowed her to experience artistic freedom.

Al-Radi's 'abstract' and 'neutral' ceramic art becomes politically engaged through interpretation, underscoring a kind of birth of the reader, envisioned by Barthes. However, to be politically engaged, to be effective as a device for political commentary, the meanings behind her sculptures must be spelled out to leave no doubt in the audience as to its meaning. The author must close her art, and by extension, her text, to multiple interpretations and artistic appropriation in order to attack American imperialism, its media, and with it the stereotypes it perpetuates about Iraqis, Arabs and Muslims. Ironically, this often leads to writing that borders on propaganda itself. Just as Zangana's anonymous friend at the beginning of *Dreaming of Baghdad* is entreated to paint something related to his own heritage as a 'token Iraqi', and can only produce abstractions, the narrator/protagonist of *Baghdad Diaries* refuses to be a token, and makes recycled sculptures as a way of criticising the sanctions:

> The CNN correspondent was totally uninterested in my art. She just wanted to know whether all Iraqis were rallying around Hussein Kamel.[71] 'What for?' I said. 'But I will explain some of my sculptures to you if you don't censor what I say. These particular sculptures are made of large coiled springs from lorries that I have painted to look like snakes; inside these coiled springs are a few stones painted to look like animals. The snakes symbolize dictatorship.' I told her they swallow people whole, not just our sort of dictatorship but all of them, yours included. 'In fact,' I added, 'yours is the biggest of all because it has swallowed up the whole world.'[72]

The heart of al-Radi's critique of the West revolves around the role of the media in legitimating the war by perpetuating ethnic and racial divisions and stereotypes. After a brief interview, the BBC edits and frames the author as a rant by 'an angry Iraqi woman',[73] spouting government propaganda by saying that Americans have no culture, which is why they want to destroy ours. According to al-Radi, this 'typical Iraqi' response was aired as opposed to the comments of al-Radi's quiet neighbour because it suited the purpose of the BBC to show Iraqis as aggressive and threatening in the wake of the invasion of Kuwait. However, it is often the case that in her attempt to construct a resistive narrative, al-Radi stereotypes the West as one monolithic block. She says, for example, that 'the only thing the West knows about us is the fable of the thief of Baghdad',[74] and her remarks to the BBC reporter about Americans not being cultured is also a generalisation which smacks of cultural arrogance.[75] Once life becomes increasingly difficult inside Iraq, and with no prospect but migration, al-Radi is adamant that she does not want to live in the West. In fact, in an interview, she begrudges having to visit the United States for treatment for leukaemia, as she had previously blamed her disease on the effects of uranium used by the Americans during Operation Desert Storm. Echoing views like Hamid Dabashi in his foreword to *Dreaming of Baghdad*, al-Radi highlights the unacceptable way in which the West categorises religious and ethnic identities; in the case of Iraq, Kurds and Iraqi Christians receiving preferential treatment when seeking asylum.

When asked at JFK Airport whether she was Kurdish or not, al-Radi's answer that she is mixed, as all Iraqis are, is met with the reply 'well you're not'.[76] The author's friend jokingly says she wants to write a book about sex in Islam so that she could get political asylum in Sweden.[77] This joke signals the West's obsession with and fetishisation of Eastern women and its view of Islam as opposed to the sexual liberation of women.

By part 3, titled 'Exile', the hitherto insular writing of al-Radi becomes more self-aware and in tune with her audience, as she takes on board her friend's advice that she cannot end the book with a mundane story of a spider in her room.[78] It is at this point where the beginning of the editing process becomes clear and broader reflections about national identity begin to emerge. Iraqi solidarity abroad proves that the nation exists in the bonds that people feel with one another, for example, the Iraqi baker in Beirut refuses to let al-Radi pay for her bread.[79] A central nationalist metaphor is the tanoor, the traditional bread oven, with tiles from Karbala, the Shia holy city and from the shrine of Abu Hanifa: 'a real cross-section of sects – a holy tanoor'.[80] Significantly, the tanoor breaks, as the text symbolically shifts emphasis to supra-nationalist bonds that go beyond even pan-Arabism or Islamism. Now that the author has left her orchard in Iraq, tree and fruit imagery is replaced by birds and bats as metaphors for freedom that are able to travel across borders without the need for IDs. Moreover, the inconvenience of the nation-state and its borders is highlighted by the issue of visas and bureaucratic issues pertaining to passports. The author's rootless existence gives her perspective about national characters: the Lebanese grumble; the Americans sue; Iraqis hoard things, are fooled by compliments and are easily flattered. Despite the fact that these observations were perhaps not intended to be taken seriously, nevertheless al-Radi perpetuates national stereotypes with such confidence that it makes it easier to express selfhood in a coherent and reliable manner. Issues of memory and doubts surrounding the question of selfhood would have compromised her political project which aims at resisting American neo-imperialism.

The penultimate section of the diaries 'Identity' is essentially a declaration of the author as a global citizen, as life in the diaspora endows the author with newfound wisdom and maturity. Al-Radi provides the reader with a glimpse into her travels at the end of *Baghdad Diaries*, first, in order to highlight her state of rootlessness as an Iraqi refugee, and, secondly, in order to experience a sense of community which is not bound by the confines of race, religion or ethnicity. In an English mass for Filipinos in Beirut, al-Radi remarks 'we all held hands and sang for peace in this world'.[81] By forming international bonds outside the conventional trajectory of communal identification dominated by language, race, sect or religion, al-Radi is subverting the nationalist narrative of the state. Moreover, her work is resistive on a microcosmic as well as macrocosmic level, as she provides intimate insights into life as a refugee, particularly the loss of dignity and 'out of place-ness' resultant from Western aggression on her country. There is a clear panning out in the perspective towards the end of *Baghdad Diaries*, and an awareness of issues beyond the borders of Iraq, which serves as an antidote for potential interpretations of Arab exceptionalism. In the prologue to the 2003 edition of *Baghdad Diaries*, the reader is made aware that Lebanon is now home despite its shortcomings, and throughout the book Eastern alternatives of escape are sought. In her quest for global citizenship (and a permanent visa), al-Radi resists both Arab stereotypes about the Indian subcontinent (she says she even considered a move to Pakistan at one point) and the image of the West as a beacon of freedom, safe haven or default destination for Iraqi refugees. She notes that the allure of the West often involves abuse of women's rights, as young Iraqi girls marry men they have not met to escape Iraq. This means that they in fact escape one patriarchy for another in the American houses of future husbands.

Women's issues are more explicitly expressed in the latter parts of the text. Al-Radi discusses the lack of representation of women in the Arab League which compares unfavourably with Pakistani women, who make up half of Pakistan's national assembly: 'I don't mean that women are the answer, but as we consist of half the world surely we should be working together'[82] she says. Like Zangana's *Dreaming of Baghdad*, *Baghdad Diaries* is women-centred, but it is not ideologically feminist as is clear from al-Radi's attitude to female political activism. She situates her diaries alongside similar works produced outside the Arab world, such as *The Diary of a Political Idiot: Normal Life in Belgrade*. This latter text was written from the Serbian capital during the NATO bombing of the former Yugoslavia in 1999, and its author, Jasmina Tešanović, made contact with al-Radi with the intention of forming an international feminist anti-war group. Al-Radi was doubtful, however, and says she had 'never been inclined towards segregation': 'it exists in such a large sphere in our society socially that I don't think it's the answer, after all it's the men who make war – so what's the point of a bunch of women being pacifists?'[83] According to al-Radi, this new anti-war group must not be limited by gender, colour or creed, and this inevitably distances her from the feminist cause.

The previous chapter discussed the exclusion of the female voice and representations of women from the vast corpus of state-sponsored works during the Iran–Iraq War, and questioned why there were no memoirs published by women at a time when the state had the ideological and financial impetus for the production of culture, and a significant number of memoirs by soldiers from the frontline were publicised in and through Iraqi media outlets. The chapter deduced that allowing feminine voices to be expressed would have potentially threatened the state's endeavour to construct an aggressive masculine identity, forged by necessity in order to boost the morale of military combatants. Moreover, as the shift towards more conservative discourses developed during the war, and with it a strict demarcation between private and public spheres, the female act of writing about their personal lives inside the home would have been seen as a violation of privacy, good taste and the feminine 'ideal' characterised by chastity and stoicism, as the day-to-day hardships and suffering encountered by women would have had to be recounted. On the other hand, male memoirs from the frontline often included some very frank discussions of sex which were never deemed too offensive to Iraqi audiences, as they seemed to reaffirm the healthy virility of Iraqi soldiers.

It is against this backdrop that *Baghdad Diaries* emerges as singular. By recording the everyday banality of living as a woman in Iraq during the sanctions period, and, significantly, doing so in English, al-Radi is resisting the erasure and disempowerment of Iraq as a culture and as a people due to the imposition of a brutal and unjust Western sanctions system. Brinda Mehta refers to this process as 'Memoryspeak' and explains that 'memory encodes itself in popular forms of cultural expression, such as music, art, food and communal identification'. She adds that 'politicizing the art of remembering in a subjective script provides popular opposition to military infractions, colonization and exilic dislocations'. According to Mehta, these are 'insurrectional modes of popular cultural resistance to war, trade embargoes and military occupation'.[84] Al-Radi's text is subversive due to its personalisation of the effects of wars on Iraqi civilians, who almost always remain anonymous, or are treated as an anonymous block of victims by Western media outlets. Moreover, it is the intimacy of the text that adds another subversive layer by challenging Iraqi cultural expectations of private and public identities. Al-Radi is frank in her discussion of bodily functions, in particular sex and defecation, and her text eschews rigid standards of female decency and propriety. Furthermore, her documentation of her personal life and that of her family and friends implies an identity that is confident and assured, and she does not shy away from expressing controversial political and religious views.

Politics and Poetics in Dunya Mikhail's *Diary of a Wave Outside the Sea*

Dunya Mikhail (1965–) is an Iraqi poet who currently resides in the United States. She left Iraq after being questioned about her first book *Yawmiyat mawja kharij al-bahr* (*Diary of a Wave Outside the Sea*) published in 1995 by Iraq's Ministry of Culture and Information while its author was working as a translator and journalist for the government's premier English-language publication, *the Baghdad Observer*. The text was translated as *Diary of a Wave Outside the Sea*, expanded and republished in a bilingual English–Arabic edition in 2009, at the height of media interest in Iraq before the Arab Spring and war in Syria. The text uses a combination of diary, fable, lyric, reportage and myth, and has won the Arab American Book Award, as well as the prestigious UN Human Rights Award for Freedom of Writing in 2001. *Diary of a Wave Outside the Sea* is an intensely personal account, and immediately draws the reader's eye to black-and-white photographs of the author and her family from her childhood in Iraq to her exile abroad. The stark rhetorical division between part one of *Diary of a Wave Outside the Sea*, written inside Iraq during the sanctions period, and part two written in exile provides a neat synthesis of the dynamic between the dilemmas of exile and psychological and cultural repression felt by writers in Iraq under the Baʿth. Taken together, the text represents a culmination of all the competing discourses in this project and is fitting to end to this book.

The first part of *Diary of a Wave Outside the Sea* covers the years 1991–4 and comprises a series of prose poems about the Second Gulf War and the effects of sanctions on the Iraqi people. Miriam Cooke describes the text as 'episodic, fantastic, sometimes mythic, and generally macabre'; a 'postmodern' mishmash, as according to Cooke, the Second Gulf War was 'a postmodern war'.[85] Perhaps due to the use-value perceived in the anti-American rhetoric that necessarily comes with any anti-war accounts from the Second Gulf War, the author managed to get the work published inside Iraq at a time of national crisis and economic austerity which had all but devastated the publishing industry. In the foreword to the 2009 bilingual edition, Mikhail claims she left Iraq because it became unsafe for her after the book was published. How then did it get published? Is it possible that it escaped state censorship? Part two of the text, present only in the 2009 edition, provides some explanation as to how a text can simultaneously be approved for publication by the state, and yet be deemed dangerous or subversive. Mikhail writes in the prologue that 'in the first part I could not say everything I remembered and in the second I could not remember everything I wanted to say'.[86] She details how a censorship committee questioned her about the character of Zeus in her poem; an absolute ruler depicted as revelling in torturing and subjugating others. She says that she was advised by a fellow writer Lutfiyya al-Dulaimi not to submit the Zeus poem for publication, and sent her the code 'the flowers are withering' as a sign that she should leave Iraq.[87] Writers in Iraq under the Baʿth often mediated the boundaries of freedom of speech, and journalists were often able to 'get away' with subtle criticisms while working for government newspapers because their articles and reportage assured the government of their loyalty. This might explain why the censorship committee allowed Mikhail's poetry collection to be published in spite of the troublesome poem. On the other hand, perhaps the book was published in order to implicate its author in anti-government sentiment, thereby settling some personal scores, which was not at all uncommon in elite circles. The text itself contains contradictory elements and messages designed to confuse readers; its anti-Americanism is clear, but there are also subtle criticisms of the government, albeit masked in symbolism and mythology.

The title of the text is significant, as it implies something that is of place, an entity that belongs to something greater as it were, and yet miraculously exists outside it. In other words, it has left the force that brought it into being.

This can apply to the poet's state of exile, of losing one's sense of belonging in one's own country, of feeling out of place in Iraq. However, there is also the inability to escape *depaysement*: cultural isolation and loneliness once in exile. The vastness of the sea removes the individual wave as the centre of history, yet the wave insists on marking itself as different and as individual. The sea can also be said to stand for human experience, rather than merely being an unconventional nationalist metaphor, if indeed it is one. Ultimately, the sea metaphor does not convey solidity, but fluidity, as it is difficult to determine where the wave begins and where it ends. This is precisely why being outside the sea is so revolutionary and subversive. Separating the wave from the sea implies movement rather than stagnation; it is brazen and non-conformist. In the blurb of *Diary of a Wave Outside the Sea*, Iraqi novelist Fadhil al-Azzawi describes the work as 'a long poem about wars in Iraq and their impact on the soul', 'a spiritual document about the impact of war on Iraq'. Framed as resistance, and not just personal memoir, war (*harb*) becomes sea (*bahr*), as the plight of the Iraqi people melts into the sea of human experience and a history of suffering.

The book's cover is split into two parts: one in Arabic and the other in English. A wave divides them visually into black and white. The hybridity of language signals the in-between-ness of the author and her text; of being neither here nor there. However, the cover also foreshadows the stark contrast between the two parts of the text: one written inside Iraq, the other in exile. The black-and-white duality of Arabic and English, Iraq and the United States, home and exile are reflected in the chessboard bought for the poet by her father who said, 'this is life. Black and white.'[88] As a chess master herself, the author uses the game as a subtext for attacking absolute rule. She says she abandoned the game because it seemed unfair to her that all the pieces would have to sacrifice themselves for the king: 'when the wars came, I quit chess: it was pointless to sacrifice all those pawns only to protect one king'.[89] This view directly challenges the symbolic relationship between the ruler and the ruled in Saddam Hussein's *Zabiba and the King*, where Zabiba sacrifices herself for the king, exclaiming: 'I die and King Arab lives!'

The colours of the chessboard are transposed onto the walls of a hospital and a symbolic shroud of death. Black signifies the author's mourning for her father, a longing which transfers into yearning for the absent lover. Here also, as with texts by Zangana and al-Radi, there is no critique of Iraqi patriarchy, and no sense that the protagonist's father was an exception to other Iraqi men. Only the human dimension of the father–daughter relationship is highlighted, rather than using the father as a tool for social commentary. This is another example of the 'non-feminist' aspect of the texts in this chapter, as understood (or misunderstood) by Western feminists. Simawe sees the fact that Mikhail's writing is not 'woman centred' as an achievement in itself. She asserts that 'the capability of the poet to step out of her culture and language evidently endows her with a divine perspective that is both cruelly objective and immensely compassionate'.[90]

Dunya Mikhail's 'poems' are not divided by titles or any other divisions besides line spacing. This allows her to blur the boundaries between verse and prose, as the text flows as a narrative. The poem that begins with 'Through your eye' is a passionate attack on sanctions, where the personal is violated by the political, leading to violence:

> Through your eye
> history enters
> and punctured helmets pour out.

The female child's submission to the will of the United Nations, with eyes and mouth closed, is a haunting image of surrender and fragility which is balanced with the defiance of the vertical tombs: 'because we will die standing'. Iraqis resist by turning 'fences into gardens'; by pretending to be sheep, grass and flowers[91]; all images of pastoral utopianism signifying growth, intuition and beauty. The vertical growth of vegetation, upright and stoic, symbolises Iraqi resistance to being flattened by the enemy's bombardments and cultural imperialism. Even children's mouths open ever so slightly, 'like a bud', indicating that the future of Iraq has not died, despite disease and starvation. Pastoral imagery was normalised by this point in Iraq's cultural history and had been appropriated by the state in almost all public discourses. It was common practice to equate 'rurality' with the cultural authenticity of the nation, and in the 1990s particularly, idealisation of the land was one way for the government to appease tribal sensitivities, as an important power base for Saddam. Here, the transformation of Iraqis into natural phenomena signifies the authenticity of a nation that will always rise from the dead. As an Iraqi

Christian, Mikhail also infuses pastoral imagery with a sanctified religious significance. She asks: 'shouldn't the bee be able to fly over the fence-tops?'[92] echoing the freedom of flying creatures to cross borders unconstrained, just like in *Baghdad Diaries* where bats and birds are able to experience freedom in ways that Iraqi refugees cannot. Bees represent community and productivity, as well as being significant symbols of the immortality of the soul and resurrection in Christianity. On the other hand, the blockade is depicted as so harsh and unnatural that it divides oxygen from hydrogen atoms in water, thereby interfering with the laws of nature at the most basic level. This poem is one of the more linear poems, and there is significantly less ambivalence compared with the rest of part one. It has a 'vertical' quality, like an arrow targeting the UN and the West, and adopts an accusatory tone that all but disappears in part two of the text, which celebrates horizontality.

The first part of *Diary of a Wave Outside the Sea* is characterised by its ambiguity; rhetorical questions fill the lines with open-ended statements, allowing the writer to avoid giving an opinion or adopting a fixed position that can potentially be used against her by government censors. For example, 'What will we do now without enemies?'[93] and 'I wonder how the critics who linked the theory of aesthetics with that of explosions felt when they saw the bombs fall over the building of the Iraqi Writers Union, and the Academy of Fine Arts?'[94] Here, Mikhail takes a dig at war theorising, as those who glorified violence through art now get their comeuppances. However, this interpretation is not present in the text in a way that could indict its author. Likewise, 'Is the war over?'[95], a constant refrain, signals a disbelief in the possibility of being at peace after being in a constant state of war, where 'the war merchants sell the air and glorify medals made of tin'.[96] Does this refer to Iranian war merchants, American war mongers or Baʿthist state literary critics and publicists? Deliberate ambiguity was a classic method used by Iraqi writers inside Iraq to critique and resist, as well as a means of escaping accountability. This is precisely why clarity was extolled and encouraged by state literary critics, to better serve the purposes of mobilisation and to make monitoring easier. However, the loophole of mythology, which was espoused by the Baʿth in the form of Mesopotamianism to bolster Iraqi national identity, allowed writers to use mythological symbols without being chastised.

The nation is so implicated in violence that it can be defined only through its enemies, aggression and the act of war-making. For Mikhail, rather than the nation containing the individual, the individual makes the nation insignificant by carrying it in his/her hand: 'I hold my homeland in my palm. / There is nothing but gasping.'[97] The nation is 'a crushed dream',[98] where the subject is implied and unclear, whereas Iraq as a victim of aggression is stressed. Mikhail's criticism of American aggression must have been attractive to Iraqi censors, and an 'us/them' polemic is often expressed, for example, 'every day they fill jars with words or wars; every day we shatter the jars'.[99] However, this is undercut by critiques of official war apparatus, from the infrastructure, like war merchants, to the superstructure, such as art critics and state commemorative activities for the dead. Designed to confuse censors, excessive pronoun use makes the subject of sentences difficult for the reader to decipher; 'they' could mean anyone. Mikhail observed:

> In Iraq, there was a department of censorship with actual employees whose job was to watch 'public morals' and decide what you should read and write. Every writer needed approval first before publishing. That's why I used a lot of metaphors and layers of meanings. This was probably good for my poetry but, still, you do not want to use such figures of speech just to hide meanings.[100]

Although the state advised writers specifically against obscurantism, mythical and symbolic works were often tolerated if the state could find use in them. Mikhail's spelling out of the letters making up the word freedom is a case in point, as this could refer to freedom from sanctions, or one of the core Ba'thist beliefs according to Michel Aflaq. In another part of the text, one state literary critic asks, 'why would someone talk about a turtle when he means to talk about war?'[101] signalling the state's impatience with symbolism and metaphor, and the ways in which writers were urged to just 'get to the point' and make their stances on the war as clear as possible.

The heart of part one of *Diary of a Wave Outside the Sea* is a poem about Zeus, depicted as an absolute ruler who 'cuts stars from the sky and sticks them onto chests and shoulders until the whole world is dark'. He gives his ferocious pet tigers 'lessons on the art of domestication before a portrait of Zeus holding a whip in one hand and gold in the other'.[102] In part two of *Diary of a Wave*, Mikhail describes how she sat before a panel of censors who asked: 'who is this god, Zeus, in your poem?', to which she replies: 'it is not the writer's job to explain. It is the reader's task to understand.'[103] Despite passing government censorship and being published inside Iraq, the author claims that she had to leave Iraq because of the danger to her life caused by publishing the poem. It may seem unusual that the Ba'thist censorship bureau would agree to publish a text that disapproved of Ba'thist rule, but it was not uncommon for the state to lull writers into a false sense of security by accepting their manuscripts, only then to use the texts as evidence to indict them. Part two of a *Diary of a Wave Outside the Sea*, written in exile, is more prose-like and less symbolic than part one; the author's defiance of state hegemony is clearer, and the tone of the text is more reflective and less urgent, compared with part one. A fellow poet of Mikhail compares prose poetry to 'marrying a foreign woman'[104]: exotic, subversive and anti-nationalist. The poet eventually does marry a foreign woman, at a time when the state explicitly discouraged this, and leaves Iraq. Here, artistic choice represents the making of connections between disparate elements, like marriage.

Deconstructing the discourses of nation from inside Iraq was central to the resistive function of part one of *Diary of a Wave Outside the Sea*. For example, the author calls out to the nation: 'O my homeland, you possess an idea like a needle',[105] emphasising how insignificant, yet potentially lethal, the nation can be. She adds that 'the earth had become bloated from swallowing too many martyrs',[106] an unsettling image of the nation choking on the dead who return to her after making the ultimate sacrifice. On the other hand, critical views of the nation metamorphose into nostalgia, as the poet leaves her homeland with nothing but a copy of *The Little Prince*: 'great friends', she says 'like homelands, are never compensated'.[107] For Mikhail, the act of remembering the homeland becomes a way of resisting the erasure of Iraqi identity in exile, as well as the actual physical flattening of Iraq and its cultural heritage and historical identity by the 2003 American bombardment and invasion. Seemingly contradictory views of the nation result from the dual purpose of Mikhail's text, as symbolised by its bilingual edition. According to the author, the solidarity felt by Iraqis points to nationalist sentiments that are not contrived or artificially enforced. For example, when a wall between their homes collapses, the author's neighbours did not bother to rebuild it as they decide to share the land.[108] Taken in the context of part two of *Diary of a Wave Outside the Sea*, this moment of solidarity challenges Western narratives about the different components of Iraqi society as being essentially fractious. It also emphasises the integrity of the Iraqi state without undermining the intimately personal account of the author. Interestingly, however, Mikhail signals her departure into the world as a global citizen based on her decision to take *The Little Prince* with her, rather than an Iraqi novel which would have symbolised her cultural ties to the nation. The Little Prince leaves his planet and his beloved rose and is unable to return except through the release of his soul through death. The inability to return home is emphasised by Mikhail towards the end of the text, when the rise of religious extremism affects her husband's family in Iraq and leads to the kidnap of his niece by masked men. Mikhail's fellow writer and friend Lutfiyya al-Dulaimi tells her: 'our city has been eaten by the wolf'.[109] Mikhail's last words express a death-like finality, disconnecting her from her homeland forever, whilst echoing the Little Prince's quest for his planet. She evokes the smell of rose in her garden in Iraq which she says she will 'never smell again'.[110]

Diary of a Wave Outside the Sea encapsulates three decades of Baʿthist rule with intensity and dignified brevity. Mikhail captures the cultural environment of Iraq in the 1980s in lucid strokes; a cultural milieu which saw the expansion of opportunities for new writers to emerge and limited opportunities for women, a time of opportunism, as poetry is sold for a high price to 'poets who had money, but lacked inspiration',[111] in order to establish their names quickly and to catapult themselves into fame. It captures the 'excess' in the production and consumption of state-sponsored works highlighted in other chapters in this book, the swamping of female voices, considered a relatively benign and non-threatening alterity, as well as more explicitly resistive voices. It discusses the theoritisation of violence, the intellectualisation of war through literary criticism, artistic restrictions on writers through the imposition of certain forms and literary styles, and the disdain for symbolism as of low use-value for mobilisation purposes. Mikhail also paints a vivid picture of civilian life during the war, particularly the encroachment of state media into the private lives of Iraqis: from special propaganda classes at university, to state propaganda publications on display during a national book fair and propaganda on television. The author asserts that Iraqi channels aired 'exactly the same programs every day'. One programme called 'scenes from the battlefield' showed gory pictures of the dead who could not be distinguished as they were 'covered with blood that was the same colour'.[112] These macabre scenes are then juxtaposed with episodes from Tom and Jerry, signalling the trivialisation of death and the dead and the normalisation of violence in Iraqi society.

The poet's sweetheart Mazin tells her personal stories from the battlefield that are excluded from the state war narrative, such as the fear of emasculation by one soldier who lost both his legs, when he asks the nurse if his penis is intact.[113] Mazin's fellow soldiers are deep in reflection, asking questions about the universe, about God, happiness and pain, the individual and the community, 'what is more important, your homeland or your freedom?' they ask each other. In many ways this question captures the dilemma of resistance: by protecting the homeland against its enemies, the soldier is doing his patriotic duty, but is also supporting dictatorship in the process. On the other hand, desertion and exile signify a betrayal of the homeland at a time of need, just like exposé books which align themselves with Western narratives about the East and its oppression of women. Hassan, a mutual friend of Mazin and Mikhail says he does not want to be 'part of a chorus, part of the herd or even part of the march'.[114] Hassan intellectualises the war in ways that state intellectuals and writers never did by using philosophy, that abhorred subject which always featured at the bottom of the number of books produced under the Ba'th. He questions what it means to be human and yearns for a future dystopia/utopia where machines would replace humans:

> It will be a life completely pure, without governments, enemies,
> hatred, hurts, disappointments, pain,
> without religion, victory, or loss.

Hassan's sweetheart Arwa objects: 'what about emotions and sensual pleasures? / This is a world without art', for 'there can be no art in such nothingness'.[115] For Hassan, however, there is freedom in emptiness; a serene calm which transforms individuals into beings that are at one with nature and with a bird's-eye view on the world. Humans would melt back into nature, just as they do in death when returning to the earth to be buried. Nihilism becomes a philosophical choice, necessary to make sense of the war and to transform it into an intellectual conundrum. Hassan writes odes in praise of 'the horizontal', the levelling of differences, the circularity and non-linearity of perception. He praises sleep precisely because it is horizontal; an instinctual state where all human beings are equal. This contrasts to the poem from the first part of *Diary of a Wave Outside the Sea* which centres on vertical images of resistance, and where the dead are laid to rest in vertical tombs. For Hassan, the individual has precedence over the community, and although the reason is not made explicit, he is imprisoned, either due to suspicions surrounding his Kurdish roots or his expressions of dissent and desire to desert. Upon release, Hassan is emotionally and mentally traumatised by his ordeal.

Whereas Hassan turns to philosophical reflection to make sense of the war, the supernatural is legitimated in the text, as fortune-telling and reading coffee cups become a means of acquiring knowledge in an unpredictable modern world. In the same way, conspiracy theories in *Baghdad Diaries* and other forms of understanding the world have the precedent over traditional modes of knowledge and forms of thought, signalling the failure of secular socialism, as well as other parochial identities like tribal affiliation and religion. Superstitious rituals and beliefs are observed in the text, reminiscent of an episode in Nadje Al-Ali's *Iraqi Women: Untold Stories* where superstitious explanations abound about how her elderly aunt became blind, specifically citing the 'evil eye' as a cause.[116] However, it is only after the sanctions that tolerance for superstition and witchcraft became a phenomena in Iraq, rather than just an expression of Arab cultural heritage, due to 'stress, anxiety, depression and various neuroses'.[117]

Mikhail also remembers another dissenting fellow student Jan, who would laugh mockingly at state-sponsored poetry:

> He was known for his satirical laughter in response to any traditional or mobilizing poem. We all saw the practices of the party and revolution as a joke. But only Jan actually laughed at the joke. The rest of us never laughed at the government except in private with friends that we trusted, those that wouldn't write secret reports about you, sending you to hell.[118]

Sadly, Jan was found dead and homeless on a street in Australia, thereby shattering the illusion of exile in the West as a safe haven. This is in contrast to the author's desperation to leave Iraq and her fear of being arrested after watching two editors at her workplace being taken by Iraqi intelligence: 'I returned to work, waiving my intention to protest, waiving my entire homeland. I was in false exile and I longed to be in a real one.'[119] By remembering her friends, 'eternalising' them in photographs and poems, Mikhail resists the state's erasure of the personal stories of individual suffering caused by its oppression and senseless wars.

In Saadi Simawe's introduction to Dunya Mikhail's other poetry collection *The War Works Hard*, published after *Diary of a Wave Outside the Sea*, a Sufi dictum is used to characterise Mikhail's work: 'the wider the vision, the smaller the sentence becomes'.[120] The condensed quality of *Diary of a Wave*; its poetisation of the mundane and the emotional intensity and brevity of its lines challenges an entire corpus of propaganda writings characterised by their emotional apathy, robotism and excess language or 'wordiness'. What makes Mikhail's work singular is the vastness of its scope, spanning three decades and capturing all the conflicting discourses present in Iraqi public and cultural life; it is in many ways a pertinent end to this book as it represents a culmination of discursive elements which are appropriate to understanding and shedding light on all previous chapters. The use of brevity as a stylistic technique and political choice has emerged as a defining feature of other resistance works by Iraqi authors, including Haifa Zangana, and is also significant considering the wider issue of representing reality, and the relationship between art and the state in Iraq under the Ba'th.

Concluding Remarks

It is significant that the three works discussed in this chapter by Haifa Zangana, Dunya Mikhail and Nuha al-Radi do not directly attack or critique Iraqi patriarchy, which is why feminist literary critics have considered some of the texts 'not feminist'. Indeed, the works are by and large preoccupied with more universal concerns, rather than purely female ones. However, the ways in which they have been excluded critically from the corpus of 'feminist writings' sheds light on the eurocentric nature of Western feminism, which privileges resistance that is expressed explicitly through the (often sexualised) female body, and in art, through negative characterisations (and often stereotypes) of Eastern men. According to Fedwa Malti-Douglas, the body will always necessarily be 'the most privileged category of analysis in Arab women writers' work'. Is it inevitable that the body and 'liberated' sexual activity would be the sole means of female resistance given how taboo the topic of sex is in Arab culture? Crucially, there is no fixation on the body in the works in question; no self-absorption or self-obsession about sexuality; and no penchant towards locating the individual human being, whether male or female at the centre of events or configuring the subject as the locus of history. Moreover, the texts do not always privilege all-female bonding and identification, and more universal human bonds are favoured instead.

The lack of a consensus on what feminism actually means in the West is often transposed onto arguments surrounding cultural products produced by women from a non-Western cultural heritage. This is indicative of certain forms of cultural hegemony and imperialism which assume that there is a limited or ideal way of resisting, most likely according to the standards of sexual liberation. The assumption that agency can be established and expressed only through the female body, by uncovering or covering, by resisting sexual relations outside marriage or by embracing them, are binaries problematised by these authors. Why is it deemed necessary to label texts and their authors in such a manner? What are we doing when we deny a text a figurative medal for being feminist, and what are we taking away from the text otherwise? It seems that feminism is sometimes used as a yardstick to measure Western approval of texts by Eastern women and also a way of undermining texts that do not fit in with this world view. Voices that are not deemed 'feminist enough' are not allowed to 'speak' for the women of their country or represent them in the same way that a feminist text is privileged as the true voice of resistance in non-white women. Language is essentially a voice, but it is a voice that is expressed through a filter of perception which dictates what it is possible to say and not say. The authors in this chapter attempt to direct their dissenting voices in and through English towards the West in order to critique Western intervention and military action in Iraq, whilst refusing to be apologetic about the crimes committed by the Ba'th Party.

Despite their strong political salience, these texts by Iraqi women writers reveal a philosophical complexity that is rarely polemical. They are meditative artistic pieces which seldom express the immediacy or urgency of the didactic or overtly political texts analysed in previous chapters of this book. The texts consider the processes of remembering, writing and representing; of the unfolding of history and the passage of time. This forms a stark contrast to propaganda art which is rarely self-reflective, as ideological texts cannot afford to betray self-doubt, and texts are merely transparent containers of political messages. By virtue of its genre, Nuha al-Radi's *Baghdad Diaries* is the most politically engaged of the three works discussed in this chapter and often adopts a journalistic style as part of its resistive discourse; the relatively stable form and linear chronological manner in which the text unfolds allow for strong anti-Western sentiments to be expressed. Moreover, as it is an 'of the moment text', documenting the trials and tribulations of everyday life under American sanctions, the tone of *Baghdad Diaries* is one of increasing outrage and exasperation, where issues of identity become secondary to the instinct for survival. There is a change in both tone and perspective in the latter parts of al-Radi's text, written in exile, as the author's detachment from the everyday preoccupations with survival allows her to contemplate issues of gender and identity in a broader manner. Dunya Mikhail's book of poetry *Diary of a Wave Outside the Sea*, particularly its first part, is the most abstract of the works, again perhaps, by virtue of its genre. First published in Arabic, the text is steeped in the mythology of ancient Iraqi cultures and Mikhail's own Christian Arab heritage, making political messages ambiguous and often difficult to decipher. This is understandable given the precariousness of Mikhail's situation as a writer under surveillance inside Iraq. In the second part of the text, written in exile in the United States, Mikhail's poetry becomes more overtly political and less symbolic, although it retains the unique quality of Mikhail's free verse.

According to Bakhtin, genre should be privileged as the central prism through which texts should be interpreted. In the case of Mikhail and Zangana, genre boundaries, and by extension individual identities, are deconstructed, leaving a flexible space in which to reflect on difficult experiences without the 'us'–'them' polemic which we sometimes find in al-Radi's *Baghdad Diaries*, a text that possesses the most stable/traditional format out of the three works. Robin Ostle identifies 'autobiographical tendencies' in modern Arabic literature, rather than embodying a fixed genre precisely because an egotistical understanding of the self as central and somehow detached from social and political contexts has not yet developed.[121] Indeed, it seems that the concept of selfhood is utilised only inasfar as it contributes to the humanising counter-narratives of the three authors, who do not propagate their stories as exceptional 'survival' stories in the way that some populist memoirs written by some Middle Eastern women have. According to Ostle, autobiographies are instruments of the powerless and writing is an empowering act on behalf of the individual and the community. Likewise, *In the House of Silence*, Fadia Faqir argues that it is through writing that Arab women can gain this empowerment.[122]

The texts in this chapter exhibit many genre-bending characteristics to varying degrees; some blur the lines between fact and fiction using the motif of the unreliability of memory to reflect on the place of personal narratives in history. Others resort to the poeticisation of individual experiences as a means of contemplating on traumatic experiences and making sense of them. Dunya Mikhail's *Diary of a Wave* is undeniably poetic, but she claims it was not intended as poetry[123]; Haifa Zangana's *Dreaming of Baghdad* is an artistic memoir characterised by its poeticism, which incorporates epistolary elements and the author's own diary entries from prison. The use of multiple genres and lapses and omissions in memory is not just a post-modern device, but is used as a means of challenging grand narratives on identity, history and the family perpetuated by the state; structures which are deemed to stifle the liberties of groups as well as individuals. This seems to have been a necessary response to extreme conditions of torture and the psychological trauma of sanctions and exile on the Iraqi collective memory. Also, the use of hybridity in form, as well as content, is to resist categorisation and ethnic and religious stereotypes; is to resist both Baʿthist authoritarianism and American imperialism. The kind of resistance envisioned by these authors exists at the very level of perception through genre-bending and the fluidity of form amalgamation. This is why we find poetry that is not exactly poetry and memoirs which are dramatised through memory lapses, with the unreliability of the self as a central motif, and without compromising the urgency and emotional intensity or the authenticity of traumatic experiences.

What can be termed 'resistance at the level of perception', be it through the adoption of hybrid forms and the use poeticisation as a means of reflecting on traumatic personal and collective experiences is not limited to Iraqi women writers. This is an important point, as it addresses the issue of whether women's writing is inherently resistive, an accepted view in Western feminist literary criticism, especially regarding writings by non-Western women writers. The question of whether women resist differently in an artistic sense implies that the female world view is somehow radically different than the male one. I would argue, however, that narrative non-linearity as well as other artistic choices seem to have been the creative response of Iraqi writers regardless of their gender. For example, Sinan Antoon's debut novel *I'jaam*, the story of a Christian student of literature at Baghdad University in the 1980s, who is imprisoned for writing subversive poetry about the Ba'th, combines fragments of dreams, 'hallucinations' and the memories of the protagonist written in the first-person, all framed as a manuscript found in prison, and made intelligible by the security forces who 'translate' the text by adding dots and diacritics for the purposes of surveillance. Antoon describes the non-linearity of the novel as 'a political and philosophical choice. It is an attempt to disrupt what I take to be the hegemonic discourse and the truth of the regime and of Big Brother.'[124] Non-linearity, often posited as a hallmark of the female world view and artistic endeavour, is used by Antoon to challenge grand narratives of war, nationalism and minority identities in Iraq.

Phenomenologist Maurice Merleau-Ponty argues that thought and language are simultaneously constituted, 'such that there is no thought apart from its expression in the flesh'.[125] In the context of totalitarianism, this often means that rigid literary form represents an uncompromising view of the world. For example, Dunya Mikhail and Sinan Antoon offer similar views on the state's disdain of the free verse movement. The police chief interrogating Furat, the hapless protagonist of Antoon's novel, attacks free verse as a twisted Western 'innovation', or *bid'a*, designed to ruin Arabic culture, and adds that he writes traditional Arabic poetry in rhyming couplets.[126] Dunya Mikhail provides detailed descriptions of cultural life in Iraq under Saddam, where she and other writers were obligated to attend official poetry readings, with 'exits guarded by policemen'. The poems, she says 'glorified Saddam and the army and had traditional rhyming patterns'.[127] Here, form reflects political restriction, with the guards functioning as a visual signifier of physical and cultural suffocation. On a rare trip to America, the writer was able to freely express to her friends certain criticisms of state-sponsored cultural production: 'I had filled her notebooks with criticisms of Iraqi war literature, of writing filled with disgusting heroism and Iraqi soldiers as supermen, of "medals of courage" given daily to generals and killers, of awards given to writers who praise the killing.'[128] There is an awareness of and direct references to 'trashy propaganda literature', which as a corpus represented an important paratext for resistance, both in form and content.

Iraqi writers and academics have found innovative ways to give an authentic voice to Iraqi women, and even research has sometimes challenged the conventions of academic writing. Nadje Al-Ali's *Iraqi Women: Untold Stories*, embodies the hybridity of genre that characterises much of the corpus of writing on Iraqi experiences during the war. Al-Ali combines anecdotes from her own childhood in Iraq with excerpts from first-person accounts by women of various ethnic and religious backgrounds, alongside a historical overview of women in Iraq. On one level, it contains autobiographical elements, including photographs of the author's family. On the other hand, Al-Ali attempts to be as representative as possible of the variety of female Iraqi experiences in ways that are not possible in the literary texts discussed in this chapter because they resist through personalisation and localisation. Al-Ali resists through a different kind of personalisation; hers is a book where multiple voices, including her own, are contextualised in their social and political milieu. However, as she makes clear in the introduction to *Iraqi Women: Untold Stories*, middle-class women form the majority of women's views presented, despite their ethnic and religious diversity. This is because the middle class formed the bulk of the Iraqi diaspora and the stories in Al-Ali's text were recorded in exile. Al-Ali is aware that new paradigms have emerged, prompting the use of labels such as 'Kurdish', 'Shia' and 'Sunni' when politically opportune, when they are in fact religious and ethnic categorisations that are historically contingent. Her oral history project expresses 'multiple and contesting truths',[129] which nonetheless highlight the 'significance' of memory alongside academic history. As such, personal narratives are placed alongside historical 'truths' without embracing full post-modernism, in which all opinions are all equally valuable, regardless of their truthfulness.

Al-Ali makes it clear what the book is not about, and these are all topics that have thus far been dictated by Western political and media interests: she immediately shifts attention away from the personality of Saddam Hussein, decentring the former dictator and his family as the primary way to access information about Iraq. She also adds that the book is not about the wars endured by Iraq at the hands of its dictator, nor is it about Islam and the plight of Muslim women. Al-Ali notes how she at first rejected her publisher's invitation to write a book about Iraqi women as a way of resisting Western stereotypes of Arabs which often revolve around the status of women. In line with the female writers discussed in this chapter, she is careful not to paint a picture of Iraqi patriarchy that reinforces orientalist stereotypes of Muslim women as victimised or oppressed, especially given that she is writing in English to a Western audience. In fact, most of the stories contained in the volume are of strong, brave Iraqi women who have resisted political oppression and kept families together, sustaining them in desperate times. The book is in many ways a celebration of the strength and resilience of Iraqi women; a counter-narrative to 'passive' representations of Arab/Muslim women. There is a constant fear expressed by the author that a book about Iraqi women after the 2003 invasion would be misconstrued in terms of culture, religion, tradition and Eastern despotism. One important way in which Al-Ali overcomes this dilemma is her interdisciplinary and innovative use of genre which combines oral history, social anthropology and political history, whilst validating a wide range of textual data as worthy of analysis, including fiction, such as excerpts from Betool Khedairi's seminal novel about the war with Iran: *A Sky so Close*. Al-Ali sees Iraq as a nation that is alive in migrant and exiled communities, in their hearts and imaginations, and has founded a charity called 'Act Together: Women's Action for Iraq'. Unlike the three creative writers discussed in this chapter, the author self-identifies as a feminist activist, yet she is eager to publicise the plight of women and to highlight injustices against them in a way that does not indict Muslim men. Personalisation remains an important way of continuing the struggle against injustice, and Al-Ali starts her 'On Living with the Baʿth' section by invoking images of matriarchy: 'my earliest childhood memories of Iraq revolve around my grandmother, Omi Baghdad, sitting cross-legged on the patio leading from the kitchen to the garden'.[130]

According to Pascal, we are torn as humans between the infinitely large and the infinitely small. I would argue that the authors discussed in this chapter have succeeded in striking a balance between what is individual and personal, and broader political and philosophical issues which have at their heart the potential of human beings to do evil and the plausibility of resistance in a corrupt world. They use genre and genre-bending to maximise resistance on the level of content and perception. In the case of Dunya Mikhail and Haifa Zangana, poeticisation in its symbolic economy and concentrated power provides a space for reflection on philosophical, mythical or artistic questions, complexifying communal identities and challenging stereotypes. Poeticism, and by extension poetry itself, has the potential for subversion, first, due to its opacity, noted by Sartre, and, secondly, due to poetry's strong link with politics in Arabic culture. It is no coincidence, then, that in Sinan Antoon's *I'jaam*, Furat and his Shia lover Areej listen to the smuggled poetry readings of al-Jawahiri as a form of resistance. Likewise, whilst imprisoned by the Ba'th, Zangana consoles herself with the poetry of Mudhaffar al-Nawab, a veritable giant of modern Iraqi literature, but also a revolutionary who was imprisoned and repeatedly tortured for his affiliation with the Communist Party. Like autobiography, poetry also subjectivises experiences in a way that is at odds with the homogenising effects of state culture. This is particularly true of Dunya Mikhail's text, which is surrounded by 'personalising' paratexts such as family photographs and letters. As for Nuha al-Radi, the least poetic text of the three, her stable diary format allows for more direct and scathing attacks on US foreign policy, and the expression of an assured transnational identity rooted in the East. Whereas the unreliability of memory as a marker of selfhood is central to Zangana's *Dreaming of Baghdad*, it does not serve al-Radi's project to think of identity as unstable or fluid, and there is an emphasis that her testimonials are truthful and reliable. However, al-Radi's text also serves to humanise and personalise Iraqi individuals as innocent victims of internal oppression and foreign aggression in order to resist Western media narratives which deliberately avoid humanising Iraqis as part of their political agendas to downplay the suffering caused by their government's military intervention.

Sophisticated resistance works on multiple levels and does not have to be ideological or evolve around clear-cut issues, as is the case in the novels of the Islamic writers in Chapter 3. In their refusal to conform to neat and tidy categorisations of meaning or black-and-white dichotomies, of oppressor–oppressed, for example, or male violence vs. female subjugation, resistive texts use ambiguity as a form of resistance. Ambiguity is provocative in the face of the state's arrogant certainty and emphasis on transparency of meaning and undisputed obedience. Moreover, resistance through form, such as the use of genre-bending and the complexification of identity issues is crucial in distinguishing didactic from artistic resistance. Notably, all of the authors discussed in this chapter possess a hybrid and/or minority identity: Sinan Antoon's mother is American, Nadje Al-Ali's is German, Haifa Zangana's father is Kurdish, and Dunya Mikhail and Nuha Al-Radi are affiliated to religious minority groups, the former being an Iraqi Christian, and the latter a Shia Muslim. The Shia, of course, form the majority of Arab Muslims in Iraq, but their disempowerment under Saddam aligns them politically and discursively with marginalised groups. As previous chapters have shown, state anxiety surrounding racial purity was manifested in uncompromising narratives about identity. Therefore, the very existence of hybrid ethnic or racial identities or religious 'others' had the potential to be subversive in its challenge to the homogenisation of nationalist discourses, which privileged the voice of male Arab Sunnis.

The reconfiguration of nationalist, ethnic and even the artificial political bonds enforced by the Ba'th Party are replaced by various human bonds which often cut across cultures. In the texts by women in this chapter, this often includes female family bonds, connections with nature, friendship and camaraderie, mother–daughter relations and, finally, heterosexual love, which is present in Dunya Mikhail's text but not in the works of the other two authors, who never married. Nonetheless, it is significant that heterosexual love is downplayed, as the body has too often been a privileged loci of feminist attention. There is a sense that the authors do not want to trivialise wider issues of justice and belonging for the sake of personal gratification, or by a fixation on the body. This is exactly what Hamid Dabashi was referring to in the foreword of *Baghdad Diaries* when he critiqued the 'self-sexualisation' of some Middle Eastern female authors who have gained popularity in the West. Personal sexual desire is not discussed, nor are direct sexual acts ever described in the works by Zangana, Mikhail and al-Radi, although they do not shy away from the topic itself. This is significant, as many Arab feminist writers have sought to deliberately break taboos on sex and female desire as a way of resisting patriarchal discourses on women and femininity. In so doing, such writings exhibit a preoccupation with the body as the centre of knowledge, resistance and pleasure, whereas these authors challenge this assumption leading to their exclusion from the label 'feminist'.

In Saddam Hussein and Āmina al-Ṣadr's works, unity in marriage represented the nationalist ideal, and a utopian manifestation of the author's secular/religious ideologies, respectively. In the narratives of the authors in this chapter, the marriage trope is marginal and holds little symbolic value. Resistance exists through networks; a multiplicity of varied social bonds, not the linearity of the marriage (or any other) metaphor of kinship. This is essentially the difference between the didactic and the artistic. Whereas religious authors resisted explicitly through ideology, these authors do so through form, attempting to affect modes of thought, artistic formation and by extension, social and political processes.

Notes

1. According to Thomas O'Beebee: 'the 'reality' of a text lies in its use-value', that is to say, its 'instrumentality in a certain type of action'. O'Beebee, *The Ideology of Genre*, p. 278. O'Beebee's configuration of a 'pragmatics of genre' theory applies to all speech acts, and not just written texts or other cultural products.
2. Haifa Zangana, *Dreaming of Baghdad* (New York: Feminist Press, 2009), p. 3.
3. Ibid., p. 35.
4. Ibid., p. 12.
5. Ibid., p. 14.
6. Ibid., p. 13.
7. Ibid., p. 15.
8. Ibid., p. 10.
9. Ibid., p. 16.
10. Ibid., p. 11.
11. Ibid., p. 12.
12. Ibid., p. 22.
13. Ibid., p. 32.
14. Ibid., p. 53.
15. Ibid., p. 43.
16. Ibid., p. 34.
17. Hamid Dabashi, 'Damnatio Memoriae', in Julie A. Carlson and Elisabeth Weber (eds), *Speaking of Torture* (New York: Fordham University Press, 2012), pp. 140–61.
18. Zangana, *Dreaming of Baghdad*, p. 122.
19. Ibid., p. 71.
20. Ibid., p. 62.

21. Nawar Al-Hassan Golley (ed.), *Arab Women's Lives Retold: Exploring Identity through Writing* (Syracuse, NY: Syracuse University Press, 2007), p. 192.
22. See at: http://www.feministpress.org/mission.
23. Zangana, *Dreaming of Baghdad*, p. 72.
24. Ibid., p. xi.
25. Ibid., p. 5.
26. Ibid., p. vii.
27. Ibid., p. ix.
28. Ibid., p. ix.
29. Ibid., p. viii.
30. Sanaz Fotouhi, *The Literature of the Iranian Diaspora: Meaning and Identity since the Iranian Revolution* (London: I. B. Tauris, 2015), p. 129.
31. Zangana, *Dreaming of Baghdad*, p. ix.
32. Ibid., p. 53.
33. Ibid., p. 167.
34. Rivkah Zim, *The Consolations of Writing: Literary Strategies of Resistance from Boethius to Primo Levi* (Princeton, NJ: Princeton University Press, 2014), p. 16.
35. Zangana, *Dreaming of Baghdad*, p. 5.
36. Ibid., p. 160.
37. Dunya Mikhail, *Diary of a Wave Outside the Sea* (New York: New Directions, 2009), p. vii.
38. Ibid., p. viii.
39. Available at: https://www.theguardian.com/news/2004/sep/07/guardianobituaries.iraq, last accessed 3 November 2019.
40. Nuha Al-Radi, *Baghdad Diaries: a Woman's Chronicle of War and Exile* (New York: First Vintage Books, 2003), p. 38.
41. Ibid., p. 4.
42. Ibid., p. 7.
43. Ibid., p. 47.
44. Ibid., p. 48
45. Ibid., p. 7.
46. Ibid., p. 211.
47. Ibid., p. 25.
48. Ibid., p. 32.
49. Ibid., p. 29.
50. Ibid., p. 120.

51. Ibid, p.34.
52. Ibid., p. 40.
53. Ibid., p. 26.
54. Ibid., p. 70.
55. Ibid., p. 50.
56. Ibid., p. 94.
57. Ibid., p. 19.
58. Ibid., p. 103.
59. Ibid., p. 196.
60. Ibid., p. 96.
61. Ibid., p. 93.
62. Brinda Mehta, *Rituals of Memory in Contemporary Arab Women's Writing* (Syracuse, NY: Syracuse University Press, 2007), p. 219.
63. Nadje Al-Ali, *Iraqi Women: Untold Stories*, p. 152.
64. Ibid., p. 99.
65. Ibid., p. 30.
66. Brenda Mehta, 'Dissidence, Creativity, and Embargo Art in Nuha al-Radi's Baghdad Diaries', *Meridians: Feminism, Race, Transnationalism* 6(2) (2006): 229.
67. Al-Radi, *Baghdad Diaries*, p. 130.
68. Amin Malak, 'Between the Artist and the General: War Memories of Baghdad', *Life Writing* 9(4) (2012): 407–420, DOI: 10.1080/14484528.2012.712894.
69. Al-Radi, *Baghdad Diaries*, p. 134. It is important to note here that the plastic arts were also appropriated by the state as part of its propaganda war against Iran. See Al-Khalil, *The Monument*. However, the embargo on Iraq and the heavy toll of economic sanctions led to diminished funds to the all arts, but especially the plastic arts as their low use-value and high cost of production compared with written works was not deemed worthy of investment. Moreover, texts could be disseminated more easily and faster and could reach Western audiences in ways in which the plastic arts could not, which was an important consideration from a government propaganda perspective.
70. Nadje Al-Ali, *Iraqi Women: Untold Stories*, p. 121.
71. Saddam's cousin and husband to his daughter Raghad who broke with the state and deflected to Jordan in 1995. He was given assurances that all would be forgiven if he returned to Iraq with his family. Upon his return in February 1996, however, he was forced to divorce Raghad and was denounced as a traitor and executed.

72. Al-Radi, *Baghdad Diaries*, p. 135.
73. Ibid., p. 43.
74. Ibid., p. 199.
75. Ibid., p. 44.
76. Ibid., p. 155.
77. Ibid., p. 71.
78. Ibid., p. 150.
79. Ibid., p. 137.
80. Ibid., p. 53.
81. Ibid., p. 138.
82. Ibid., p. 203.
83. Ibid., p. 178.
84. Mehta, *Rituals of Memory*, p. 26.
85. Cooke, *Women and the War Story*, p. 266.
86. Mikhail, *Diary of a Wave Outside the Sea*, p. vii.
87. Ibid., p. 66.
88. Ibid., p. 4.
89. Ibid., p. 71.
90. Dunya Mikhail, *The War Works Hard* (New York: New Directions, 2005), p. xi.
91. Mikhail, *Diary of a Wave Outside the Sea*, p. 27.
92. Ibid.
93. Ibid., p. 76.
94. Ibid., p. 17.
95. Ibid., p. 18.
96. Ibid., p. 28.
97. Ibid., p. 11.
98. Ibid., p. 12.
99. Ibid., p. 28.
100. See at: https://ndpublishing.wordpress.com/tag/diary-of-a-wave-outside-the-sea.
101. Mikhail, *Diary of a Wave Outside the Sea*, p. 79.
102. Ibid., p. 49.
103. Ibid., p. 91.
104. Ibid., p. 79.
105. , Ibid,, p. 26.
106. Ibid., p. 22.

107. Ibid., p. 68.
108. Ibid., p. 84.
109. Ibid., p. 123.
110. Ibid., p. 124.
111. Ibid., p. 81.
112. Ibid., p. 73.
113. Ibid.
114. Ibid., p. 74.
115. Ibid., p. 76.
116. Nadje Al-Ali, *Iraqi Women: Untold Stories*, p. 2.
117. Ibid., pp. 204–5.
118. Mikhail, *Diary of a Wave Outside the Sea*, p. 81.
119. Ibid., p. 110.
120. Mikhail, *The War Works Hard*, p. xiii.
121. Dalya Abudi, *Mothers and Daughters in Arab Women's Literature: the Final Frontier* (Leiden: Brill, 2011), p. 88.
122. Fadia Faqir and Shirley Eber (eds), *The House of Silence: Autobiographical Essays by Arab Women Writers* (Reading: Garnet, 1999).
123. Mikhail, *Diary of a Wave Outside the Sea*, p. vii.
124. See at: http://electronicintifada.net/content/sinan-antoon-i-think-myself-global-citizen/8760, last accessed 26 March 2020.
125. Ann V. Murphy, 'Sexuality', in Hubert L. Dreyfus and Mark A. Wrathall (eds), *A Companion to Phenomenology and Existentialism* (Chichester: Blackwell, 2009), p. 497.
126. Sinan Antoon, *I'jaam: an Iraqi Rhapsody* (San Francisco, CA: City Lights Books, 2007), p. 30
127. Mikhail, *Diary of a Wave Outside the Sea*, p. 84.
128. Ibid., p. 95.
129. Nadje Al-Ali, *Iraqi Women: Untold Stories*, pp. 3–4.
130. Ibid., p. 109.

Conclusion: Binaries, Bonds and Moving beyond the Ba'th

In her 2004 novel *'Ali and 'Aisha: an Iraqi Symphony of Love*, Islamic novelist 'Alyā' al-Anṣārī depicts a fictive Sunni–Shia love story to represent the potential for peaceful religious coexistence in a unified Iraqi nation emerging from the trauma of authoritarianism and occupation. Inter-sect marriage is a well-established phenomenon in Iraq, and is hardly unprecedented. However, al-Ansārī's text draws on a literary trope that bears the hallmark of didactic nationalist writings, which is that a Shia man and a Sunni woman are brought together, rather than the opposite. This specific gender configuration signals the unease with which ethnic and religious collectivities 'give away' their women to the 'Other', whereas the idea of subsuming a Sunni woman within a Shia family where the children of the union will remain Shia, seems less radical and thus more comfortable. Moreover, the narrative's tragic, pessimistic ending and failed alliance almost seems to be an extension of unconsummated marriages in state-sponsored texts, where national harmony is desirable metaphorically but ultimately unrealistic. That being said, in the context of the Islamic novel this expansive nationalist perspective beyond pan-Shiism or the insularity of the Iraqi Shia community in *'Ali and 'Aisha* is a huge development, as the beginnings of an inclusive universalist sensibility begins to emerge, in part due to the advent of the age of technology and globalisation, where cosmopolitanism is not necessarily limited to secular feminism. At the centre of the issue of establishing nationalist or religious bonds is voice and identity, that is to say, that once bonds are symbolically formed between disparate elements in Iraqi society, a power negotiation begins to establish whether the relationship is one of equals or, as in Saddam's *Zabiba and the King*, a dynamic where power is skewed in favour of one side.

Iraq was the first modern Arab nation-state to appropriate and fund the wide-scale production of novels in an unprecedented attempt to create a selective and coherent national identity steeped in a mythical and glorious history to boost national pride as part of its nation-building endeavours ranging from the economy to education. Richard Lowenthal asks 'what impels us to tamper with history . . . We alter the past to become part of it as well as to make it our own . . . Most of all we alter the past to "improve it" – exaggerating aspects we find successful, virtuous, or beautiful, celebrating what we take pride in, playing down the ignoble, the ugly, the shameful.'[1] The homogenisation of voice in the historical experience in the process of 'making history' in Baʿthist Iraq necessitated acts of exclusion, marginalisation and discursive violence designed to transform art into propaganda and history into politics. By using sheer bulk to swamp dissenting voices and to write 'over' history as I term it, the Baʿthist state attempted to shape the contours of an Iraqi national identity by creating a canon based on war literature which necessarily excluded women due to the consolidation of the public–private spheres dichotomy. In the case of canon formation in Iraq, panegyrics and over-zealous nationalist novels were allocated a canonical status in accordance with the state's need to mobilise during its military endeavours, and for this reason, these novels often fell short artistically and rarely circulated beyond Iraq to other parts of the Arab world.

Transformative moments in history under the Baʿth brought notable changes in state discourses on women; the 1970s represented the height of pan-Arab secularism, where women's empowerment emerged as a defining feature of Baʿthist discourses. The country also witnessed an explosion in the number of female readers due to intensive literacy campaigns, as well as a pertaining boom in secular state publications directed at women. The 1980s, on the other hand, represented a setback in the gains made by Iraqi women and a regression in progressive discourses which led to a shift towards a more conservative view of women, with literary representations centring on women as victims of war or mourning the loss of their male kin. Moreover, the vivid but rare depictions of female combatants in state literature were designed to emasculate 'disloyal' elements in Iraqi society, thus perpetuating conservative views on gender by 'shaming' men into action. In 1982, the war was blamed by the head of the General Federation of Iraqi Women (GFIW), Manal Yunus, for the lack of commitment to gender equality by state institutions. Furthermore, Saddam's speech to the GFIW in May 1986 prioritising nationalist struggle over gender rights is generally considered to have signalled the end of state discourses on the 'liberation of women' which he had publicised as being a Party priority in 1980. The 1990s and the sanctions period witnessed an ascendency of conservative moral discourses with the state's 'Faith Campaign' reaching its peak, and parochial tribal values extolled in Iraqi cultural production. This came hand in hand with the passing of conservative laws regarding women; for example, 1990 saw the reintroduction of a law that made so-called 'honour killings' legal, and although the law was abrogated two months later, the practice remained unofficially tolerated throughout the 1990s and beyond. This era also witnessed a literary 'drought' in works that were reliant on state funding, due to the harsh economic conditions of the sanctions period.

The growth in book production and the expansion of the press was a process that began when the second Baʿth seized power in 1968, so one could argue that Saddam's subsequent policies were merely an extension of these, or that further growth under the second Baʿth was proportionate to the rising numbers of readers and new schoolchildren. However, as al-Dawāf notes in the concluding remarks to his study, book production numbers fluctuated dramatically from year to year, particularly during the war, meaning that (in the words of Eric Davis) there was 'no long-term strategy for cultural production, which was dictated instead by individual political agendas'.[2] Indeed, the second half of the Iran–Iraq War witnessed a sudden boom in book production, as the necessity for the appearance of normalcy and strength provided impetus for the material production of texts. This not only coincided with Iraqi military setbacks on the battlefields, but also setbacks for Iraqi women on the home front. The rise of the state-sponsored novel seemed at times inversely to correlate with the fate of Iraqi women in terms of legislative rights, as it came to embody a militant and masculine identity which excluded women as potential 'history makers'. However, at times it actually mirrored the fate of women, such as in the 1990s when there was a symbolic decline in the status of both women and the novel.

In many ways, both the novel and women were subjected to similar processes of appropriation and marginalisation due to their status as 'symbolic capital for the construction of such an apparently contradictory rhetorical space'.[3] The state's contradictory views not only stemmed from the exploitation of Iraqi women as symbolic signifiers of either progress and liberalism or of national honour and traditional identity, but also the proxification of the 'Woman Question' as an accessible and subtle representation of sensitive issues such as religion and race. In his novels, for example, Saddam Hussein extols purity and chastity in women and this translates on a wider scale into an idealisation of the purity of the nation's origins, which are to be found in the rural, rather than 'contaminated' urban areas. Stated in this way, the state-sponsored Iraqi novel seems typical of more mainstream nationalist literature in the Arab world; its obsession with roots expresses an anxiety about the identity of the nation, which in many ways is determined by women as the bearers of children: the nation's future. However, the valorisation of male perspectives in dictator literature often leads to the conflation of chivalry, jealousy and cruelty, and make for a nationalist narrative that seems to deliberately exclude women as active participants in making history. Instead, women exist as the 'honour' of men, which like Iraq, must violently be protected from the violation of strangers. Saddam also delivers a scathing critique of the sexual promiscuity of non-Arab women in his novels in order to highlight the treacherousness of the Baʿth's enemies abroad. Narratives of purity and the control of bloodlines feature heavily in state-sponsored discourses as a means of maintaining the pure source of Arab roots, where women become a medium through which a nation's future is readied, and where they are expected to transmit but not really produce culture, as was the case during the Iran–Iraq War when women were marginalised as producers of literature.

The discursive preoccupation with the female body highlights an anxiety about Iraq's national identity, and the proxification of women's issues is equally evident in the works of female Islamic writers who use female piety and modest dress in their novels as a means of extolling the virtues of Islamism as a political ideology over that of secular Baʿthism. Literary texts do not exist in isolation from other texts and discourses and are inextricably tied to the material practices that bring them into being. For example, the novels of Āmina al-Ṣadr and others must be analysed in the context of a growing secular print culture, with an increasing number of state publications directed at women, which led to a battle between secular and religious forces vying for the influence of the economic and potentially political power of the emerging female reader. As a result, we find explicitly moralistic titles and other paratexts (such as the pseudonym of Āmina al-Ṣadr herself: 'Bint al-Hudā' or 'daughter of righteous guidance') designed to entice the reader as an ideological marketing strategy. According to Haddad, 'the problem faced by successive Iraqi regimes has been the multiplicity of Iraqi nationalisms and the clashing visions of Iraq'.[4] This is reflected in the competing visions of women, not only between Baʿth and anti-Baʿth, but also within Baʿthist state discourse itself, as representations of women under the 'progressive Baʿth' which had stressed the equality of men and women, and had established GFIW as its female arm, differed dramatically from more conservative approaches to women, aimed at bucking the Islamic tide and appeasing tribal sensitivities after the war.

The devastating cultural legacy of the Iran–Iraq War continues to cast its shadow on the Iraqi literary scene and Arab intellectual history. In many ways, the war represented a watershed for Iraqi literature, dividing literary production into two distinct groups: exiled 'resistance' writing against the war and the state, and extreme nationalist pro-war literature from within Iraq.[5] Ironically, the latter also framed itself as 'resistance' writing in the face of a joint Zionist/Persian/Western plot, called the Baʿth's 'unholy trinity' by Ofra Bengio.[6] Exiled literature was also preoccupied with nationalist themes, and it is this struggle between 'competing nationalisms' rather than 'nationalist' and 'anti-nationalist' which still characterises modern Iraqi political and cultural discourses. Those who stayed in Iraq under Saddam were often seen as collaborators, and those who left were often painted as self-entitled or as treacherous cowards who had abandoned their homeland and preferred to align themselves with imperialist invaders. Salām 'Abbūd's scathing indictment of *adab al-dakhil* ('literature of the inside'), in which he accuses all but very few writers who stayed in Iraq of collaborating with the government, epitomises the polemical nature of cultural debates in Iraq. 'Abbūd bears much resentment for those who broke with Saddam only after the Iran–Iraq War, instead of speaking out against Baʿthist crimes from the very beginning. He believes that these intellectuals were instrumental in sustaining the regime and improving its image abroad, which gained Western support and prolonged the suffering of Iraqis and Iranians during the war. 'Abbūd's book *The Culture of Violence in Iraq* aimed at documenting all involvement with the state by litterateurs, artists and writers, including some big Arab as well as Iraqi names. In order to highlight the impossibility of resistance, he provides anecdotes about Iraqi writers who pretended to be sick when contacted by the Ministry of Culture regarding why they had not produced any pro-war pieces and their attempts to buy time using a variety of excuses, including promises of large works in progress. 'Abbūd does not consider abstract literature as a challenge to the state narrative, as only those texts that told the truth through direct political engagement could be deemed properly resistive.

Hannah Arendt's seminal work *The Origins of Totalitarianism* alludes to the shallow and almost trance-like momentary persuasion which propaganda induces:

> The members of totalitarian movements, utterly fanatical as long as the movement exists, will not follow the example of religious fanatics and die the death of martyrs (even though they were all too willing to die the death of robots). Rather they will quietly give up the movement as a bad bet and look around for another promising fiction or wait until the former fiction regains enough strength to establish another mass movement.[7]

Genuine conviction, though often absent, is nevertheless deemed by individuals to be unwavering at the time, as loyalty to the state is maintained only by its physical existence, and the fear of state violence. Fear, self-delusion and genuine conviction are not as easily distinguishable as it first may seem, and the success (and danger) of propaganda lies in its ability to blur these boundaries. According to Lisa Wedeen, the hegemonic power of the state lies in its ability to make its subjects dissimulate, rehearse and perform its discourse, even without personal conviction.[8] In Iraq, many of those who had defended the regime, praised and wrote for it during the Iran–Iraq War in particular, were to leave the country to seek asylum in the West as political refugees after Saddam's invasion of Kuwait, claiming they had been persecuted for exercising their freedom of speech. According to one state literary critic: 'the writer must express a clear position on the war in his fiction, and the literary critic has the right to link the writer's beliefs to the text's narratorial voice as they are part of the same consciousness, and should thus parallel each other exactly. Ambiguity signifies either a problem in the writer's commitment, weak artistic capabilities or an attempt at evasion.'[9] 'Abbūd quotes Muhsin Jasim al-Musawi during the war saying that 'there is no other choice but life and the nation in the face of death and the enemy'. He then recounts anecdotally the interesting example of writer Rushdī al-'Āmil who was ill for long periods during the war, and when interviewed by the press in 1987, he was asked to explain why he had been silent all this time.[10] 'Abbūd adds that 'due to the length of the war, all tricks to avoid writing on it were exhausted'. Moreover, state literary critics were keen to make it clear to writers that they understood what was behind excessive symbolism and wordplay.[11]

This book has attempted to highlight the close relationship between culture, ideology and the state through the prism of women, whilst avoiding simplistic notions of hegemony and resistance under totalitarianism. State discourses on women fluctuated in their adoption of and disregard for women's rights, mirroring the novel's fate in gaining or losing state favour. Likewise, the Ba'th was not even in the way it exercised power vis-à-vis acts of subversion, and its exercises in power through censorship should not be treated as a totality. If the state was satisfied with authors' loyalty or 'nationalist credentials' due to any of the following factors – ethnic or religious background, gender, or previous publications and public stances – they were often accorded more freedom. Censorship was also directed by the historical moment which determined whether certain discourses were deemed threatening or not and when, particularly anti-war/pacifist voices and expressions of religiosity. The corpus of ambiguous texts, which used mythology and symbol to allow writers inside Iraq some respite from the intensely polemical and embattled discursive plane, challenges the idea of a top-down effect of power, even in the most dangerous and uncompromising political contexts. The history of Ba'thist Iraq was certainly not the resistive playground envisioned by Foucault in his theories of power and resistance, but was nevertheless characterised by moments of tension and release resulting from ideological ambiguity in practice and dictated by socio-economic and political opportunism, rather than uniform censorship and oppression. Paratexts, fringe material and information surrounding the main text, thus become important signifiers of the negotiation, or in the case of women, ideological 'bargaining' between author and state, and often constituted a means through which authors indicated their loyalty and ideological affiliation in order to ingratiate themselves with the state or, conversely, to escape its wrath. More can be done to study the bargaining aspects of grey area texts vis-à-vis state censorship, particularly artistic works. These kinds of texts are beyond the scope of this book as they do not fall into the realm of explicitly ideological or political texts or do not feature women prominently.

State censorship, even under authoritarianism, is often not applied equally and privileges certain genres and discourses which it regards as threatening its hegemony. Moreover, state censors often interpret texts according to who wrote them and may read subversive meanings into texts written by minority authors for example, whilst according more freedom to authors known to be pro-government. One wonders whether if a Shia writer who was not as high-profile as Āmina al-Ṣadr had written her novels, or if she had written them in the 1990s instead of the 1970s, would she have been met with the same hostility; and whether her call encouraging women to dress modestly, for example, a line which the state itself promoted in the 1990s, would have been a cause for state concern? If Sartre declared the death of the author as the key to unravelling meaning in the text, the writer in Iraq is held responsible not only for every word she/he produces, but also for every potential interpretation of that word. These are crucial considerations if we are to understand why few literary giants of modern Iraqi fiction were able to stay and continue producing works inside Iraq that were not exclusively state-sponsored or propaganda. It is also crucial to our understanding of what resistance is and how it functions. Often a work is accepted by censors if it is untimely, that is to say, that it is released to an audience in a specific historic and social context in which its effect would be blunted. A good example of this would be religious discourses in literary works, deemed almost unpatriotic, foreign and extreme during the 1970s, and were then embraced by the state itself in the 1980s, and formed a legitimate part of public discourse.

The paratexts approach utilised allows for the expansion of the scope of scholarly enquiry to include non-canonical texts that provide a broader understanding of Iraq's cultural history and its turbulent relationship with totalitarianism. It also allows us to move away from simplistic notions of superstructure/base or the hegemonic aspects of the Baʿth's ideological state apparatus. It seems more useful to see the corpus of texts produced under the Baʿth broadly, both collaborative and resistive, as an integral part of the trajectory of the Arab Iraqi novel which shaped and continues to shape responses to occupation, extremism and other emerging political realities in Iraq. While the history of the Iraqi novel is a long and rich one, this book notably excludes many of the better-known literary figures in Iraq in order to shed light on a wider variety of written responses to political upheaval, including the voices of propagandists who shaped the cultural landscape of the country for decades. Indeed, it seems unusual that the unprecedented involvement of the Baʿthist state in literary production, producing an immense number of novels in a cultural and nationalist endeavour which was and still is unmatched by any other Arab state, should go almost completely unnoticed critically. The ambiguous status in Iraqi literary tradition and the convoluted nature of state-sponsored war novels has led to their inevitable exclusion from 'high literary' debates. Likewise, interest in Saddam's novels predictably waned very soon after his execution in 2006, and the very rare discussions of his novels are subsumed within more general analyses of Iraqi state political discourses. However, the study of dictator literature as something other than a hegemonic exercise stemming from an insidious cult of personality can reveal something about the status of the author in Arabic literature and the symbolic value of writing as an intellectual activity, in particular the writing of narratives for nationalist purposes.

The book looks forward to new studies in Arabic literature which incorporate a more extensive range of cultural phenomena, thereby contributing to a better understanding of the role of the literati and cultural practitioners in authoritarian contexts. Religious writings, especially populist writings, should also be studied further given the immense interest in religion and the expression of sectarian identities that had hitherto been suppressed in Iraq. The potency of religion in imbuing narratives of sexual purity with an aggrandised ethical dimension, for example, is used as a weapon to demonise the women of competing ideological affiliations who are described as depraved and dishonourable. Indeed, the term for honour in Arabic *sharaf* and its adjective *sharif* carries the connotation of sexual purity. Religious discourses define women in terms of their sexual activity as the female body allows for the procreation and preservation of a religious identity through marriage, essentially a vessel for allowing religious identities to extend, persist and gain the upper hand politically and socially through a larger demographic. Once this dominance is achieved and established, the conciliatory discourses of the state are then adopted by formerly marginalised expressions of religiosity, as is evident in a novel like *ʿAli and ʿAisha*, which performs national unity and religious harmony through allegory.

Iraqi writers are constantly revisiting Saddam's wars and will continue to do so, responding with personalised and heterogeneous voices to the unrelenting uniformity of the state narrative. In a pivotal scene in Antoon's *Iʿjaam*, the protagonist Furat is summoned to the police chief's office 'to discuss literature', as the chief says he is also a writer. After showing Furat his notebook, he explains his literary preferences, saying that he is a traditionalist who writes 'mobilising literature' (*adab taʿbawi*). He adds that, 'culture cannot be separated from reality. We are now in a state of war; our very existence is being threatened; our borders are being threatened. Every creative endeavour must ultimately aim at mobilisation.'[12] The chief is particularly unimpressed by the free verse espoused by the new generation, as for him it is essentially a Western importation. Modern free verse poetry is, of course, not constrained structurally, as in the case of the classic *qasida* which is strict in its use of a mono-rhyme and half lines. According to the Iraqi poet and pioneer of Arabic free verse, Nāzik al-Malāʿika, the traditional *qasida* form narrows and constrains the range of meanings possible in a poem, which is why it must be discarded for the sake of individual poetic freedom.[13] Configured in such a way, poetry (in particular free verse) represents individuality and subjectivity, whereas the novel represents the collective and the nationalist. The self-indulgence of poetry, described by Sartre as a stained-glass window which alters vision, was essentially dismissed as being too personalised and subjective for the purposes of propaganda and history-writing, and the same can be said of writings by women, which were deemed overly self-reflective and emotional and were therefore excluded from the war narrative in both its early and late stages. The parodic elements of *Iʿjaam* with its caricatures of government propagandists cannot be properly understood in isolation from the media and literary discourses of the 1980s, and highlight the intense transtextual dialogue between literary and non-literary texts which directly or indirectly speak to each other in spite of a political ambiance that was antagonistic towards dialogue and difference.

According to Baccolini and Moylan, 'the dystopian genre has always worked along a contested continuum between utopian and anti-utopian positions (that is, between texts which are emancipatory, militant, open, indeed critical; and those which are compensatory, resigned and anti-critical)'.[14] It is the perceived dystopia of the colonial period in the Arab world which first fuelled the utopian discourses of Arab nationalism, which in turn have bred a dystopian authoritarian reality. This configuration highlights utopia's potential for social change and transformation, which appears in the form of a socialist utopia in Saddam's *Men and a City*, for example. However, the projection of this kind of a utopia presumably after it has been achieved, and at a time of neo-tribal conservative agendas results in a paralysis of action and resistance. By concealing inequalities and smoothing over contradictions, the utopia establishes its hegemony through compensation, which is a feature of almost all the literary production of the period. Moreover, the cyclical nature of the utopia–dystopia dichotomy has led to a new wave of dystopian literature and literary criticism, which has emerged with renewed energy and urgency in the light of Iraq's descent into sectarian violence in 2006. This dilemma is highlighted in 'Abd al-Laṭīf al-Ḥirz's *al-Mustahil fi al adab al 'iraqi* where he contends that:

> Iraqi intellectual discourse today is very sensitive, and is either overly optimistic without any real reason for being so given the present situation, or conversely, is very pessimistic about the future of culture . . . Both approaches: baseless optimism and extreme hopelessness do not provide adequate solutions to the problem in Iraq as a whole, including the cultural issue. This is a dilemma that extends throughout decades of totalitarian rule, the colonial period and the parasitic features which have accumulated in this sick body since its first epic experience as recounted in the Epic of Gilgamesh, to the sad elegies of Karbala's tragedy . . .[15]

Works like Sinan Antoon's *I'jaam*, Iraq's *1984* and a veritable Orwellian nightmare is a prime example of the dystopian genre in Iraqi fiction. The novel ends with the prisoner escaping prison onto empty streets as the dictator falls, without the reader knowing whether the eerie silence (not euphoria) is a delirium in the mind of the narrator or actually takes place. Likewise, albeit in a more jingoistic tone, Jāsim al-Raṣīf's 2007 novel *Ru'ūs al-ḥurrīyya al-mukayasa* (*The Stifled Heads of Freedom*) ends with a depressive scene at a cemetery:

> While everyone was praying for the dead, their prayers were interspersed by the howls of sad women and the hopeful claims by those 'whose heads had been bagged' *dhawi al-ru'us al-mukayasa* [by the Americans] about a breakthrough which would come soon, the incessant buzz of American helicopters could be heard around the mourners and the cemetery. Some children threw stones at the sky, which they had picked up from the new graves, before they disappeared in the wide horizon of the city of Ramadi. At this time a large group of men arrived, faces covered, with their weapons, ready to perform prayers for the dead.[16]

Although dystopia might seem like a way of resisting the utopia projected by totalitarianism, it in fact also paralyses the potential for change in a similar way: by positing the impossibility of change rather than its real possibility or desirability: 'the Iraqi text, which was haunted by the question of exile is now plagued by the question of impossibility'.[17] This 'excess' in pessimism, in the hopeless and nihilistic possibility of finding a way out of the current political/cultural crisis has ultimately been bred by an excess in the belief in Iraq's ability to recreate the 'miracles' to which Saddam refers at the beginning of *Zabiba and the King*. Rhetorical and discursive 'excess' invariably produce excessive reactions. In Iraq, alternate identities which could not be expressed or enacted publicly under Saddam, have since his fall experienced a huge cathartic release. In some cases, this has led to an exaggerated expression of cultural and religious differences, which had previously been suppressed under the pretext of Iraqi nationalism and pan-Arabism. Likewise, there has been an explosion in texts written by Iraqi women after the collapse of the Baʿthist state with its pertaining ideological structures and discourses which had previously swamped dissenting voices.

The seeds of dystopia, then, are in fact inherent in utopia itself and vice versa. In the novel by al-Raṣīf to which I refer to above, the author indulges in pre-dystopian nostalgia under Saddam, through the figure of the female character *al-ʿadba'* (the name of the Prophet Mohammed's she-camel):

> She sighed and whispered to herself reproachfully as she gazed for long into the eyes of Mr. President: 'what have we done to you?' 'What have you done to us?' 'What have we done to you and what have you done to us?' However, she turned the page of the newspaper quickly when an American helicopter passed. They say their satellites can see 'the black ant in the darkest of nights' to spy on Iraqis. She turned the page back to the picture and stared at Mr. President's beautiful eyes and his long forefinger which he was using to point or to threaten someone. 'We are lost Abu Uday! We are lost!'[18]

The woman in this passage represents the nation's vulnerability and regret at welcoming an American invasion, and her appeal to Saddam as a saviour of Iraq. Baccolini and Moylan are correct in observing that 'the struggle for the future is always a struggle between competing utopias'.[19] Utopias are indeed forward-looking, but they are drawn from the collective memory of the past and 'only those who choose to remember are capable of taking responsibility for their actions and being accountable. Choosing to ignore or forget what was or what we did ultimately means avoiding responsibility and may lead to political paralysis.'[20] The role of memory is particularly important here, as remembering becomes a form of resistance, echoing Mahmoud Darwish's *Memory for Forgetfulness*; an exercise in catharsis in order for trauma to eventually be forgotten, and for reconciliation to be ultimately possible. Al-Ḥirz describes his work as a 'necessary process of archiving',[21] a 'fever' to use Derrida's term, which inadvertently contributes to the vicious circle of 'archiving and counter-archiving, and this means that the battle will continue'.[22] Paraphrasing Milan Kundera, Baccolini adds that 'in order to fabricate a single, true, hegemonic discourse, which citizens will unquestioningly follow, it is necessary to erase memory'.[23]

The centrality of remembering differently may serve to explain why writers in the resistance part of this book, such as Dunya Mikhail, 'Alyā' al-Anṣārī and Haifa Zangana chose to focus on the past as a way of challenging the monologic discourse of the state. On the other hand, an apologetic writer like Jāsim al-Raṣīf focuses on the present–future, thereby 'over-writing' history in the same way novels of the Iran–Iraq War aimed to rewrite the history of the conflict as it was being made:

> where memory functions in the present, but derives its *raison d'être* from past experience, propaganda – though frequently drawing on pre-existing rhetoric, myth or expectation – looks forward: its success depends on a correct reading of hopes and fears, and is measured by the extent to which its concrete form affects beliefs and actions yet to come.[24]

Baccolini also contends that 'the conditions of dystopian citizens are not so different from those of a prisoner, who, having no control over space nor over the present and the future, can reside only in the past'.[25] These citizens live in the symbolic past, rather than trying to achieve an instrumental purpose by looking forward to the future. The importance in recognising utopia as a potential form of authoritarian propaganda should not blind us to the fact that it exists in almost all political discourse, and can impart hope and courage to those resisting established power. Furthermore, the transformative power of any utopia should be coupled with a critical awareness of what is 'smoothed' over or ignored, and its potential to silence debate as a 'dead' language.

The set of cultural discourses on women – political, social and literary – perpetuated by the state highlight the ultimately subaltern nature and status of women. Despite the oft-repeated phrase in Arab social and political discourses that 'women are half of society', women in Iraq were often dealt with as a minority discursively. At times of national crisis, for example, women were expected to stop campaigning for equal rights and to focus on supporting the national cause which often meant supporting the state's war propaganda. Although not treated as an identity that could potentially lead to split loyalties in the way ethnic or religious identities were perceived, nevertheless minority discourses informed fears of the possible disloyalty of women. The link between women and 'foreignness', for example, manifested itself in the state-sponsored texts examined in this book, underlying anxiety regarding the nation's purity from racial contamination through marriage. Moreover, the state' ability to curb female discontent and to prevent the formation of a unified feminist opposition stemmed from the exacerbation of tensions pertaining to identity markers which were deemed more threatening than gender, such as religious, sectarian, ethnic and political identities.

As a 'minority' discourse, Baʿthist attitudes towards women can be used to shed light on other minority discourses, such as the representation of the Kurds or Iraqi Christians. In many ways the treatment of women, whether merely publicised or actual, provides a gauge for other minorities in Iraq in terms of the tokenistic inclusion and exploitation of minorities as symbols of national unity whilst simultaneously eroding their legal and religious rights. However, interestingly, although deemed less threatening, the symbolic significance of women was much stronger than minority groups in Iraq, as woman could be the embodiment of the nation, whereas at best ethnic and religious minorities are perceived as partners. Kurds, for example, feature as spouses but reluctantly so; the eagerness to include them symbolically, to pretend that the Kurds were loyal to the state was, in the words of Fāṭima al-Muḥsin, to replace fantasy with reality, which became a more urgent undertaking as the Kurds were breaking away from the state. Interestingly, although the rhetoric of women's rights and liberation was undoubtedly deemed a less threatening discourse than that pertaining to the religious or ethnic rights of non-Sunni Arab groups in Iraq, subversive activities by women from those groups was often dealt with in the same ferocious and violent manner as challenges to the state by men. The brutal murder of Āmina al-Ṣadr and the withholding of her body by Baʿthist authorities is a case in point.

The book argues against over-simplifying or homogenising female voices or adhering to a traditional vs. a modern paradigm, whereby Islamic is read as resistive and secular as collaborationist. Instead, it has attempted to delineate a trajectory where various discourses are ascendant at different times, leading to micro-resistances that are inextricable from their historical context. The strong conservative tone of the novels of al-Ṣadr, often at odds with the authors stated position elsewhere, came in direct response to what she perceived as the corrupting influence of secular government publications directed at women. Al-Ṣadr's self-effacement using a pseudonym, her desire to deliver God's message as a vessel rather than as a creator of dialogue, predictably never narrativised her own life in line with social and religious codes on propriety and modesty. The privacy and secrecy of her personal life was maintained as an example of public engagement within the boundaries of morality and Islamic ethics which enabled a generation of religious women the precedent to follow suit. On the other hand, personalisation was used by non-religious authors to resist the archetypes of women perpetuated by both the state and orientalist stereotypes of Eastern women, be it the fertile and all-sacrificing Iraqi woman during the Iran–Iraq War, or the militant revolutionary type encouraged with the impending invasion of Iraq. According to al-Hassan Golley, the process of 'Writing Back' assigns 'historical significance to women's daily experiences as a cultural activity'.[26] It seems appropriate then to expand the scope of materials to include types of writing that are not elite in order to explore how power speaks about women and why it uses stories about women to do so or not.

Notes

1. Richard Lowenthal, *The Past is a Foreign Country* (Cambridge: Cambridge University Press, 1985), pp. 331–2.
2. Davis, *Memories of State*, p. 25.
3. Miriam Cooke, *Women Claim Islam: Creating Islamic Feminism Through Literature* (New York: Routledge, 2001), p. xx
4. Fanar Haddad, *Sectarianism in Iraq: Antagonistic Visions of Unity* (Oxford: Oxford University Press, 2011), p. 34.
5. Salām Ibrāhīm includes a third group of writers (including Mohammed Khudair) inside Iraq who used 'the mask of history and poeticism' to avoid explicitly supporting the state or incurring its wrath. Salām Ibrāhīm, 'Adab 'irāqī lā adab khārij wa dākhil', *Nuṣūṣ 'Irāqīya* 23 (July 2005).
6. Bengio, *Saddam's Word*, p. 14.
7. Hannah Arendt, *The Origins of Totalitarianism* (Cleveland, OH: Meridian Books, 1958), p. 363.
8. Lisa Wedeen, *Ambiguities of Domination: Politics, Rhetoric and Symbols in Contemporary Syria* (Chicago, IL: Chicago University Press, 1999), p. 12.
9. Umar Ṭālib, *Fī qiṣṣat al-ḥarb: dirāsa naqdīya*, pp. 13–14.
10. 'Abbūd, *Thaqāfat al-'unf fī al-'Irāq*, p. 24.
11. Ibid., p. 26.
12. Antoon, *I'jaam*, p. 49.
13. She adds that the best poets are those who are able to create new words and meanings. Nāzik al-Malāʾika, Shaẓāyā *wa Ramād* (Beirut: Dār al-ʿawda, 1971), p. 16.
14. Raffaella Baccolini and Tom Moylan (eds), *Dark Horizons: Science Fiction and the Dystopian Imagination* (New York: Routledge, 2003), p. 8.
15. Al-Ḥirz, *al-Mustaḥīl fī al-adab al-'irāqī*, p. 67.

16. Al-Raṣīf, *Ru'ūs al-ḥurriya al-mukayasa*, p. 317.
17. Al-Ḥirz, *al-Mustaḥīl fī al-adab al-'irāqī*, p. 29.
18. Al-Raṣīf, *Ru'ūs al-ḥurrīya al-mukayasa*, p. 199.
19. Baccolini and Moylan, *Dark Horizons*, p. 26.
20. Ibid., p. 119.
21. Al-Ḥirz, *al-Mustaḥīl fī al-adab al-'irāqī*, p. 21.
22. Ibid., p. 270.
23. Baccolini and Moylan, *Dark Horizons*, p. 125.
24. Valerie Holman and Debra Kelly (eds), *France at War in the Twentieth Century: Propaganda, Myth and Metaphor* (New York: Berghahn, 2000), p. 4.
25. Baccolini and Moylan, *Dark Horizons*, p. 125.
26. Al-Hassan Golley, *Reading Arab Women's Autobiographies*, p. xiv.

Appendix 1: Novel Summaries

***Al-Fadila tantasir* (1969)**: *Virtue Prevails* by Bint al-Hudā tells the story of sixteen-year-old Naqa' who is engaged to be married to Ibrahim, an upright man from a devout family. Naqa''s blissful happiness at the match is interrupted by her maternal cousin Su'ad, who is irreligious and jealous of Naqa' as she had hoped to marry Ibrahim herself. Su'ad's husband Mahmud is rich and spoiled, and the couple lead a disreputable life of parties and affairs. Out of vengefulness, Su'ad attempts to ruin Naqa''s reputation by directing her unsuspecting husband to woo her. She tells him that Naqa' is merely dressed as a saint but is in fact a woman of ill-repute. However, once Mahmud approaches Naqa' at a public park, he realises that she is not the woman his wife painted her to be. Mahmud is gradually influenced by his conversations with Naqa' and learns to change his ways to lead a more religious life. The novel's end thus echoes its title, with virtue, represented by Naqa', prevailing over sinfulness, as embodied by Su'ad, who is threatened with divorce.

***Al Raqs 'ala aktaf al mawt* (1981)**: 'Ādil 'Abd al-Jabbār's *Dancing on the Shoulders of Death* claims to be the first novel of the war, and tells the story of a group of young patriotic men at war and their feats of bravery and camaraderie. Action shifts from the war front to the home front, where two members of the group Khidr and Shihab compete for the love of a young girl called Shayma. The novel ends with the death of Khidr on the battlefield, who gives his friend his blessing to marry Shayma. Shihab honours his friend by refusing to marry Shayma despite her advances and chooses instead to devote himself to Khidr's widowed mother.

***Al Fasil al thalith* (1983)**: Jāsim al-Raṣīf's debut novel (in two parts) *alAl Fasil al thalith* (*The Third Troupe*) won first prize in the *Qadisiyat Saddam* competition for the novel in 1983. The events of the novel revolve around the tragic love story of an Arab soldier Fa'iz (meaning 'Victor', a significant name choice), deployed in the Kurdish areas north of Iraq, and the beautiful and daring Prishnak, a Kurdish girl from a nearby village. The menace of the Iranian enemy is easily countered by a superior army on the frontline, but the Popular Army's (*al-jaysh al-sha'bi*) ability to 'protect' Kurdish villages from '*al-mukharribin*' (vandals), the word used by the author to describe Kurdish rebels allied to Iran, is often in doubt. The couple are abruptly killed by the Iranians soon after announcing their engagement: Fa'iz in what is described as 'a suicide mission' to avenge his close friend and comrade Khalid, and Prishnak on her way up the mountains to deliver food to her fiancé and his comrades.

***Khatt ahmar* (1987)**: *Red Line* by Jāsim al-Raṣīf is a four-part novel set in Basra and recounted from the perspective of different characters in the first-person: Hamid 'Ubaid, a gardener and old widower with two children: Basma and Hassan; 'Abdullah 'Ali a young air pilot; 'Adil Hassan a young marine officer, who competes with 'Abdullah for the love of a girl named Shadha; and, finally, Zuhair Talib, Shadha's father, the drunk head of a dysfunctional family. The protagonist's son Hassan reported 'missing' on the battlefield, and also his daughter Basma is killed in a raid on their house just before the 'victory' at Huwaiza, and the half-hearted public parades of joy on the street which ensue.

***Wa inhasar al zalam* (1987)**: *And Darkness Dissipated* by May al-Husaynī narrates the story of a devout young woman called Raja' whose parents Ayda and Hameed die suddenly, leaving her in sole charge of supporting her younger brother. Her eldest brother 'Isam is depicted as wayward and irresponsible and prefers to settle in Switzerland where he was studying, rather than returning to Iraq to help his siblings. Raja' is wise and intelligent and is approached by her rich neighbours to tutor their daughter Nada, who is struggling in her studies. Raja' is able to help Nada pass her exams, but more importantly serves as a religious mentor, persuading Nada to adopt a more religious lifestyle, to the dismay of Nada's family. Nada's brother Sami is particularly upset about his sister's new religious views and fears that she has been brainwashed. However, he too comes to be inspired by Raja''s piety and commitment and changes his liberal lifestyle. Raja' and Sami marry, thus relieving Raja' of the burden of providing for her family. As for Raja''s brother ʻIsam, he is unable to reconcile himself with his new Western lifestyle and and commits suicide leaving behind a wife and two children.

***ʻIndamā yufakkir al-rajul* (1993)**: *When a Man Thinks* by Khawla al-Qazwīnī tells the story of Muhammad, a devout young political science university student in an unidentified Arab country. Muhammad marries his incompatible cousin Manal to please his mother, and in return for her allowing his sister Fatima to marry the revolutionary poet Ali, Muhammad's best friend and comrade. Muhammad is politically active in the Islamic youth movement and finds a job as a journalist at a local newspaper, where a plot against him is concocted by a combination of Arab and Western intelligence services. Muhammad is sent to Russia on a conference with Suzanne, a secretary at the newspaper who is assigned the task of seducing him in order to tarnish his reputation and that of the Islamic youth movement. However, Muhammad refuses Suzanne's advances and harshly admonishes her for allowing herself to be objectified as a sexual object for men. Upon their return, Suzanne commits suicide in mysterious circumstances and Muhammad is publicly accused of being implicated in her death. 's wife Manal does not stand by him and believes the rumours surrounding his involvement with Suzanne. She subsequently divorces him and does not allow him to see their son. Broken-hearted, and subsequently imprisoned and tortured, Muhammad's citizenship is revoked and he is banished to Turkey. The novel ends with Muhammad leaving the country to continue his postgraduate studies at Oxford University, whilst continuing to work as a journalist for an Islamic newspaper based in London. At the end of the novel, Muhammad falls in love with the committed Kawthar, a student and researcher and marries her. However, his newfound happiness is cut short on a trip to France for a conference, where he is assassinated by unknown gunmen at his Paris hotel.

***Tadhkirat Safar* (1999)**: *A Travel Ticket* by 'Alyā' al-Anṣārī is a text set in the late 1960s and 1970s. The novel tells the story of Bahr and Hind, a brother and sister forced to leave their small fishing village for the city to escape a tyrannical uncle who has terrorised their community and monopolised its wealth. Despite the hardships faced by the siblings, Bahr works hard to support his sister financially and also manages to continue his studies. His sister Hind also attends university and meets the rich and liberal Khalid, whom she 'converts' and eventually marries. He also joins a group of political youths committed to the Islamic cause, but this ultimately leads to his imprisonment and execution.

***Zabiba wa al-malik* (2000)**: *Zabiba and the King* is a fictional historical allegory set in ancient Iraq and attributed to Saddam Hussein. The novel tells the story of a love affair between a married peasant girl named Zabiba and a fictional King Arab. Zabiba, who represents the people of Iraq, is raped by her abusive husband on 17 January (the date US-led forces were deployed to force Saddam out of Kuwait) and dies defending King Arab and his country. The novel features a parliamentary debate after Zabiba's death, during which characters that represent 'undesirable' ethnic or social groups are symbolically purged by being thrown out of the assembly.

***Al-Qal'a al-ḥaṣīna* (2001)**: *The Fortified Castle* is a novel by Saddam Hussein set at the University of Baghdad during Iraq's invasion of Kuwait and the ensuing Operation Desert Storm. It tells the story of a burgeoning romance between a Sunni Arab student from a village in the north named Sabah and his classmate the Kurdish Shatrin from Sulaymaniya. The couple receive training in combat together at the university and are then deployed in Mosul for their compulsory military service. Despite being surrounded by death and destruction, the atmosphere is jovial and both Shatrin and Sabah are unharmed. However, the novel ends abruptly with tension between the protagonists, although their engagement is still intact. The onus is on Shatrin due to her dubious nationalist credentials and her Kurdish background; on a visit to Sabah's village, Shatrin's greed is revealed when she expresses the desire to see the family estate divided amongst the heirs so that she can have a share when she marries Sabah.

***Rijal wa madina* (2002)**: *Men and a City* is a fictionalised autobiography by Saddam Hussein which uses pseudonyms to recount the story of Saddam Hussein's childhood up until his involvement in the failed assassination attempt on Abd al-Karim Qasim. It focuses on the physical hardships faced by Salih (the character who represents Saddam in the novel) and his role in the rise of the Baʿth Party with the support of his Tikriti clan.

***Baghdad Diaries* (2003)**: Written in English over the span of two decades, Nuha al-Radi's *Baghdad Diaries* is a unique personal account of the effects of sanctions on an Iraqi family, written *sur place* in Baghdad. It was originally published in 1998 in English, and a second part was added to the 2003 edition after the author had left the country. The text recounts the day-to-day struggles of al-Radi and her family with the increasing degeneration of the quality of life and services in Iraq, such as the collapse of water, electricity and sewage services. Due to the privileged class status of the author owing to her diplomatic connections and relative economic prosperity, there are also anecdotes of embassy visits, art exhibitions and visits abroad. Al-Radi's perspective expands noticeably once in exile, as she has now acquired a spatial distance from her home in Baghdad and the immediate survival needs that preoccupied her in the first part of the text, and she seems to be endowed with a higher philosophical perspective about man's propensity towards evil and the shared values and experiences of humankind.

***Ukhruj minha ya malʿun* (2003)**: *Get Out, Damned One!* is Saddam's last novel, and thus the most scrutinised in Arab and Western media. Like *Zabiba and the King*, it is an allegorical novel set in an unspecified and confused ancient past, although presumably after the advent of Islam. It begins with the story of a man named Ibrahim who has three sons who represent the monotheistic faiths of Judaism, Christianity and Islam. Hasqil, who represents the Jewish tradition, is disowned and exiled by his father and seeks refuge with the 'desperate tribe', only to repay their hospitality by overthrowing their leader and bedding his foreign wife. The leader's daughter organises a rebellion against Hasqil and the powerful foreign allies he has made to secure his power.

***Diary of a Wave Outside the Sea* (2009)**: an intensely personal and poetic account of life under the Ba'th in Iraq, *Diary of a Wave Outside the Sea* by Dunya Mikhail is a bilingual text that is divided into two parts: part one covers the years 1991–4 and comprises a series of prose poems about the Second Gulf War and the effects of sanctions on the Iraqi people. This part was first written in Arabic and was published in Iraq in 1995 by Iraq's Ministry of Culture and Information. On the other hand, part two was written in exile and provides a neat synthesis of the dynamic between the dilemmas of exile and psychological and cultural repression felt by writers in Iraq under the Ba'th. It also details how the author was interrogated about a specific poem from her original Arabic text, in which she depicts Zeus as an absolute ruler, ultimately leading her to leave Iraq for fear of arrest. The text is also the personal story of the author as she is reunited in the United States with her college sweetheart Mazin after years of separation, her subsequent marriage and the birth of her daughter Larsa. In her new home in exile, the author's final reflections are on the loss of artistic freedom in Iraq, as well as the rise of the menace of Islamic extremism in the country after the fall of Saddam Hussein.

***Dreaming of Baghdad* (2009)**: Written over eight years, Haifa Zangana's (1950–) original Arabic text *Fi Arwiqat al-dhakira* (1990), translated as *Through the Vast Halls of Memory* (1991) details the author's imprisonment and torture by the Ba'th as a result of her involvement with the then outlawed Iraqi Communist Party. The current text *Dreaming of Baghdad* published in English in 2009, is a retelling of the author's original story and shifts action from Iraq to exile abroad in London. Writing from a distant place and time, the author describes mundane scenes from her childhood that have stayed with her, such as visiting her Kurdish father's relations in the north, and getting lost in the city souk at the age of five and being found by her mother. First imprisoned in Qasr al-Nihaya prison for political opponents and then to the now infamous Abu Ghraib prison for 'ordinary' crimes, Zangana was eventually moved to Za'faraniya women's prison, primarily reserved for prostitutes and those with long or life sentences. In order to escape execution, she signed a document stating that she was not in fact political but was rather sexually involved with her comrades. The text is in many ways a tribute to comrades lost to Ba'thist violence and oppression, but is also a warning that history repeated itself with the American invasion of Iraq in 2003.

Appendix 2

Figure 1 Taken without permission from Canadian artist Jonathon Earl Bowser, the cover of Saddam's first novel *Zabiba and the King* (2001)

Figure 2 The cover of *Get Out, Damned One!* for the post-fall of Saddam edition. Markedly different from his other novels which use artwork, this edition uses cartoon-style drawings instead

Figure 3 The original cover of *Get Out, Damned One!* (2002 or 2003) produced in a similar style to *The Fortified Castle*

Figure 4 The cover of the only edition of *The Fortified Castle* (2001)

Figure 5 Saddam's quasi-autobiography *Men and a City* (2002)

Figure 6 *A Travel Ticket* (1999) by ʻAlyāʼ al-Anṣārī

Figure 7 *When a Man Thinks* (1993) by Khawla al-Qazwīnī

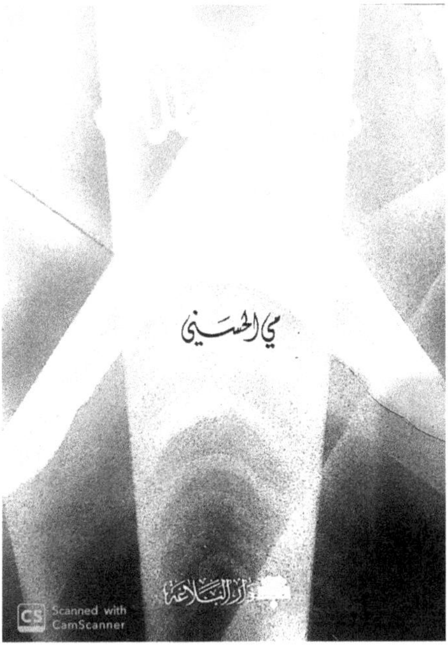

Figure 8 *And Darkness Dissipated* (1993) by May al-Ḥusaynī

Figure 9 *Memoirs of a Student Abroad* (1995) by Khawla al-Qazwīnī

Figure 10 *The Seeker of Truth* (1980) by Bint al-Hudā

Figure 11 *Virtue Prevails* (1980) by Bint al-Hudā

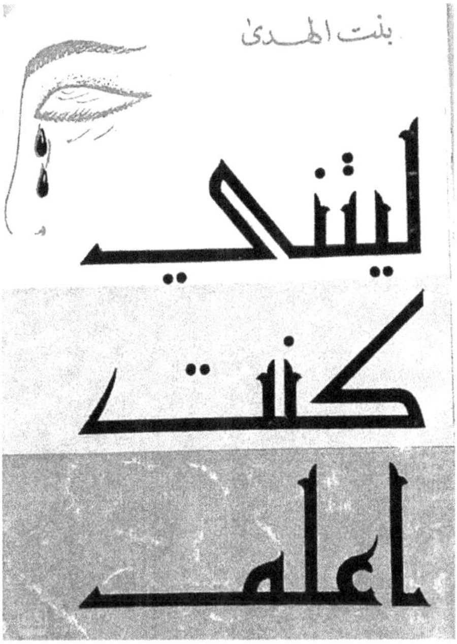

Figure 12 *I Wish I Had Known* (1981) by Bint al-Hudā

Bibliography

Works Cited in Arabic

'Abbūd, Salām, *Thaqāfat al-'unf fi al-'Irāq* (kulūniya: Manshūrat al-Jamal, 2002).

'Abbūd, Salām, 'Man kataba riwāyāt ṣaddām ḥusayn? ṣaddām yulqi khiṭāban 'ala nafsih wa al-dhākira tu'lin ḥarbahā 'alā al-ra'īs', al-Hiwār al-Mutamaddin, 1309, 6 September 2005.

'Abbūd, Salām, 'Qirā'a fī adab ṣaddām ḥusayn al-riwā'ī', al-Hiwār al-Mutamaddin, 1307, 4 September 2005.

'Abbūd, Salām, 'al-Diktatūr yarwī sīratahu: mukhaiyilat al-'unf bi'athar raj'ī', 9 January 2006, available at: http://www.iraqmemory.org/INP/view.asp?ID=68.

'Abd al-Ilāh, Lu'ay, '"Ukhruj minhā yā mal'ūn": Naṣṣun aqal min ḥikāya wa akthar min khuṭba: istibdād al-rāwi', *al-Sharq al-Awsaṭ*, 13 September 2004.

'Abd al-Jabbār, 'Ādil, *al-Raqṣ 'alā aktāf al-mawt* (Baghdād: Dār al-Thawrah, 1981).

'Aflaq, Michel, *Fī sabīl al-ba'th* (Bayrūt: Dār al-Ṭalī'ah lil-Ṭibā'a wa-al-Nashr, al-Ṭab'a 7, 1972).

Al-'Alawī, Ḥasan, *al-Shī'a wa al-dawla al-qawmīya fī al-'Irāq: 1914–1990*, 2nd edn (London: Dār al-Zawrā', 1990).

Al-'Āmil, 'Ādil, 'Fu'ād al-takirlī fī ḥaḍrat al-kātib al-kabīr Ṣaddām Ḥussein', *al-Madā*, 26 September 2004.

Al-Anṣārī, 'Alyā', *Tadhkirat Safar* (Bayrūt: Dār al-Hādi, 1999).

Al-'Azzawī, Fāḍil, '"Zabība wa al-malik" riwāya li-kātibihā: al-'irāqī bayn al-kūkh wa al-qaṣr hal kataba ṣaddām ḥusayn hādhihi alriwāya?', available at: http://aslimnet.free.fr/ress/em_ghi/fadel.htm, last accessed 29 March 2019.

Al-Barrāk, Fādil, *al-Madāris al-yahūdiya wa al-īrānīya fī al-'irāq* (Baghdād: n.p., 1985).

Al-Dawāf, Hiyām Nā'il, *Ḥarakat nashr al-kutub al-'irāqīya: dirāsa maydānīya li-al-kutub al-manshūra wa al-nāshirīn li-al-fatra 1975–1994* (Baghdād: Wizārat al-Thaqāfa wa-al-I'lām, Dār al-Shu'ūn al- Thaqāfīya al-'Āmma 'Āfāq 'Arabīya', 2000).

Al-Dūrī, 'Abd al-'Azīz, *al-Judhūr al-tārīkhīya li-al-shu'ūbīya* (Bayrūt: Dār al-Ṭalī'a, 1988).

Al-Ḥusaynī, May, *Wa inḥasar al-ẓalām* (Bayrūt: Dār al-Balāgha, 1993).

Al-Ḥirz, 'Abd al-Laṭīf, *al-Mustaḥīl fi al-adab al-'irāqī: istinbāṭāt al-naṣṣ al-jadīd wa rāhin al-mashhad al-thaqāfī fi zaman al-iḥtilāl*, silsilat gharīb 'ala al-ṭarīq (Bayrūt: Dār al-Fārābi, 2008).

Al-Jubūrī, 'Adnān Rashīd (ed.), and 'Adnān Aḥmad al-Rabī'ī, Ghanīya 'Abd al-Wāhid; al-mushrif al-'āmm Ḥamīd Sa'īd, *al-Munāzala al-sha'bīya: umm al-ma'ārik, ru'ya sha'bīya, 'arabīya, 'ālamīya* (Baghdād: Dār al-Ḥurrīya, 1999).

Al-Malā'ika, Nāzik, Shaẓāyā *wa Ramād* (Beirut: Dār al-'awda, 1971).

Al-Muḥsin, Fāṭima, 'al-ra'īs wa tajalīh al-riwā'ī', *al-Thaqāfa al-Jadīda*, available at: http://www. althakafaaljadeda.com/fatma_almu7sen.htm, last accessed 4 October 2009.

Al-Qadhdhāfi, Mu'ammar, *al-Qarya al-qarya, al-arḍ al-arḍ, wa-intiḥār rā'id al-faḍā' wa-qiṣaṣ ukhrā* (London: Riad El-Rayyes, 1995).

Al-Qal'a al-ḥaṣīna: riwāya li-kātibihā (Baghdād: Dār al-Ḥurrīyya, 2001).

Al-Qazwīnī, Khawla, *'Indamā yufakkir al-rajul* (Bayrūt: Dār al-Ṣafwa, 1993).

Al-Qazwīnī, Khawla, *Mudhakarāt mughtariba* (Bayrūt: Dār al-Ṣafwa, 2006).

Al-Raṣīf, Jāsim, *al-Faṣīl al-thālith* (Baghdād: Wizārat al-Thaqāfah wa al-I'lām, 1983).

Al-Raṣīf, Jāsim, *Khaṭṭ aḥmar*, al-Ṭab'a 2 (Bayrūt: al-Mu'assasa al-'Arabīya li-al-dirāsāt wa al-Nashr; 'Ammān: Dār al-Fāris, 2000).

Al-Raṣīf, Jāsim, *Ru'ūs al-ḥurriya al-mukayasa* (Bayrūt: al-Mu'assasa al-'Arabiyya li-al-dirāsāt wa al-Nashr, 2007).

Al-Sa'd, Muslim 'Alāwī Shiblī, *al-Ḥiqd al-fārisī wa Qādisīyat Ṣaddām: dirāsa taḥlīlīya li-judhūr al-ḥiqd al-fārisī 'ala al-umma al-'arabīya* (Basra: al-Amāna al-'Āmma li-al-Marākiz wa al-Hay'āt al-'Ilmīya al-muhtamma bi Dirāsāt al-Khalīj al-'Arabī wa al-Jazīra al-'Arabīya, 1982).

Al-Sharīf, Hindī Muḥammad, *Shuyūkh al-nafṭ?* (n.p.: Maṭābi' Dār al-Sha'b, 1991).

Al-Takirlī, Fu'ād, 'Qirā'a fi riwāyat ṣaddām ḥusayn "ukhruj minhā yā mal'ūn" (1–2): khalṭa 'ashwā'iya bayna al-tārīkh wa al-siyāsa bi ramziya fajja', *al-Sharq al-Awsaṭ*, 13 September 2004.

Bint al-Hudā, *al-Bāḥitha 'an al-haqīqa* (Bayrūt: Dār al-Ta'āruf, 1980).

Bint al-Hudā, *al-Fadhīla tantaṣir* (Bayrūt: Dār al-Ta'āruf, 1980).

Bint al-Hudā, *Laytanī kuntu a'lam* (Bayrūt: Dār al-Ta'āruf, 1981).

Bint al-Hudā, 'Kalima wa da'wa', in *al-Majmū'a al-qiṣaṣiya al-kamilā* (Bayrūt: Dār al-Ta'āruf, n.d.).

Birjāwī, Ibrāhīm, *Mushāhadāt ṣaḥāfi 'arabī 'alā al-jabhah: min zākhū ilā al-fāw* (Baghdād: Dār Wāsiṭ, 1987).

Fawzī, Fāruq 'Umar, *al-'Irāq wa-al-taḥaddī al-fārisī* (Baghdād: Dār al-Shu'ūn al-Thaqāfīya al-'Āmma, 1987).

Fawzī, Farūq 'Umar, *al-Fīkr al-'arabī fī mujābahat al-shu'ūbīya: 'asr al-khilāfa al-'arabīya al-islāmīya*, silsilat al-mawsu'a al-tārikhīya al-muyasara (Baghdād: Wizārat al-Thaqāfa wa al-I'lām 'Dār al-Shu'ūn al-Thaqāfīya al-'Āmma, 1988).

Fawzī, Farūq'Umar, *al-Khumainīya wa ṣilātuhā bi-ḥarakāt al-ghulūww al-fārisīya wa bi-al-irth al-bāṭinī* (Baghdād: Māṭba'at Munazzamat al-Mu'tamar al-Islāmī al-Sha'bī, 1988).

Fukaykī, 'Abd al-Hādī, *al-Shu'ūbīya wa al-qawmīya al-'arabīya* (Bayrūt: n.d.).

Ghīṭānī, Jamāl, *Ḥurrās al-bawwābah al-sharqīya: al-jaysh al-'irāqī, min ḥarb tishrīn awwal (uktūbar) ilā ḥarb al-shamāl,* (Cairo: Maktabat Madbūlī, 1975).

Ḥadīdī, Ṣubḥī, 'Zabība wa al-malik wa al-mukhābarāt al-markazīya', in *al-Quds al-'Arabī* (n.d.).

Ḥammādī, Sa'dūn, *Dawr al-adab fī al-wa'y al-qawmī al-'arabī: buḥūth wa munāqashāt al-nadwa al-fikrīyya allatī a'addahā wa naẓẓamahā markaz dirāsāt al-wiḥda al-'arabīya*, al-ṭab'a al-thālitha (Bayrūt: Markaz Dirāsāt al-Wiḥda al-'Arabīya, 1984).

Ḥizb al-Ba'th al-'Arabī al-Ishtirākī: al-Qiyāda al-Qawmīya, *al-Minhāj al-thaqāfī al-markazī*, vol. 2 (Baghdād, 1977).

Ibrāhīm, Salām, 'Adab 'irāqī lā adab khārij wa dākhil', *Nuṣūṣ 'Irāqīya* 23 (July 2005).

Ibrāhīm, Salām, *al-Wajh al-nāṣi' li-al-naṣ al-'irāqī: al-kitāba laysat nuzha wa lā la'iban bi al-kalimāt*, Nuṣūṣ 'Irāqiya: 27, January 2006.

Ja'far, Muḥammad Rāḍi, *Uslūb al-ra'īs al-qā'id: al-binā' al-khārijī wal maḍāmīn al-balāghīya*, silsalat al-fikr al-riyādi: 16 (A'ẓamīyya, Baghdād: Wizārat al-Thaqāfa wa-al-I'lān, Dār al-Shu'ūn al-Thaqāfīya al-'Āmma 'Āfāq 'Arabīya', 1991).

Khiḍr, 'Abbās, *al-Khākīya: Min awrāq al-jarīma al-thaqāfīya fī al-'irāq* (Kūlūniyā: Manshūrāt al-Jamal, 2005).

Lādhiqāni, Muḥyī al-Dīn, 'Tāriq wa zabība', *al-Sharq al-Awsaṭ*, 19 February 2004.

Mukhīf, 'Alī 'Abd al-Ḥusayn, *Fī qiṣṣat al-ḥarb: dirāsa naqdīya* (Baghdād: al-Jumhūrīya al-'Irāqīya, Wizārat al-Thaqāfa wa-al-I'lām, Dā'irat al-Shu'ūn al-Thaqāfīya wa al-Nashr, 1984).

Naḥnū mutawāḍi'ūn bi-dūn du'f wa-aqwiyā' bi-dūni ghurūr, al-Silsila al-Wathā'iqīya: 49 (Baghdād: Wizārat al-I'lām: 1976).
Nāṣir, 'Abd al-Sattār, *al- Shahīd 1777* (Baghdād: Wizārat al-Thaqāfah wa-al-I'lām, 1981).
Nāṣir, 'Abd al-Sattār, 'Bihudū': qāmūs al-kawārith', jarīdat al-Zamān (1542), 28 June 2003.
Nizār, Ja'far Ḥusayn, *'Athrā al-'aqīda wa al-mabda': al-shahīda bint al-hudā* (mawqi' al-masādir al-islamiya, 1985).
Qabbānī, Aḥmad, *al-Sab' yaḍḥak* (Wizārat al-Thaqāfah wa-al-I'lām, 1985).
Rijāl wa madīna: riwāya li-kātibihā (Baghdād: Dār al-Ḥurrīyya li-al-Ṭibā'a, 2002).
Ṣafadī, Dalāl Khalīl, Ḥawādith wa 'ibar: yashtamil 'ala ḥawādith wa-qi'īya wa-qiṣaṣ tahdhībīya (Marji'yūn (Lebanon): [s.n.], 1935).
Ṭālib, 'Umar, *al-Ḥarb fī al-qiṣṣa al-'irāqīyya* (Baghdād: Wizārat al-Thaqāfa wa-al-I'lām, Dā'irat al-Shu'ūn al-Thaqāfiya wa-al-Nashr, 1983).
Ṭālib, 'Umar, *Malāmiḥ al-masraḥīya al-'arabīyya al-islāmīya* (al-Maghrib: Dār al-Āfāq al-Jadīda, 1987).
Ukhruj minhā yā mal'ūn: riwāya li-kātibihā (Baghdād: Dār al-Ḥurrīyya li-al-Ṭibā'a wa al-Nashr, 2003).
'Zabība wa al-malik fī al-idhā'a wa al-talafizyūn wa al-masraḥ al-'irāqī', *Saḥīfat al-Mu'tamar al-'Irāqī*, 29 September 2001.
Zabība wa al-malik: riwāya li-kātibihā (Iraq: s.n., 2001).

Works Cited in Other Languages

Abudi, Dalya, *Mothers and Daughters in Arab Women's Literature: the Final Frontier* (Leiden: Brill, 2011).
Aburish, Said K., *Saddam Hussein: the Politics of Revenge* (London: Bloomsbury, 2001).
Adam, Heribert (ed.), *Hushed Voices: Unacknowledged Atrocities of the Twentieth Century* (Highclere: Berkshire Academic Press, 2011).
Al-Ali, Nadje Sadig, *Secularism, Gender and the State in the Middle East: the Egyptian Women's Movements* (Cambridge: Cambridge University Press, 2000).
Al-Ali, Nadje Sadig, 'Reconstructing Gender: Iraqi Women between Dictatorship, War, Sanctions and Occupation', *Third World Quarterly* 26(4/5) (2005): 739–58.
Al-Ali, Nadje Sadig, *Iraqi Women: Untold Stories from 1948 to the Present* (London: Zed Books, 2007).
Al-Ali, Zahra, *Women and Gender in Iraq: Between Nation-building and Fragmentation* (Cambridge: Cambridge University Press, 2018).

Al-Hassan Golley, Nawar, *Reading Arab Women's Autobiographies: Shahrazad Tells Her Story* (Austin, TX: University of Texas Press, 2003).

Al-Hassan Golley, Nawar (ed.), *Arab Women's Lives Retold: Exploring Identity through Writing* (Syracuse, NY: Syracuse University Press, 2007).

Al-Khalil, Samir, *The Monument: Art, Vulgarity, and Responsibility in Iraq* (Berkeley: University of California Press, 1991).

Allen, Roger, *An Introduction to Arabic Literature* (Cambridge: Cambridge University Press, 2000).

Allen, Roger, *The Modern Arabic Novel: An Historical and Critical Introduction*, 2nd edn (Syracuse, NY: Syracuse University Press: 1995).

Al-Muʿalla Abdul Ameer, *The Long Days* (Pt 1), trans. Mohieddin Ismail (London: Ithaca Press, 1979).

Al-Musawi, Muhsin Jassim, *The Post-Colonial Arabic Novel: Debating Ambivalence* (Leiden: Brill, 2003).

Al-Musawi, Muhsin Jassim, *Reading Iraq: Culture and Power in Conflict* (New York: I. B. Tauris, 2006).

Al-Radi, Nuha, *Baghdad Diaries: a Woman's Chronicle of War and Exile* (New York: First Vintage Books, 2003).

Althusser, Louis, *Positions* (Paris: Éditions Sociales, 1976).

Altoma, Salih J., *Iraq's Modern Arabic Literature: a Guide to English Translations since 1950* (Lanham, MD: Scarecrow Press, 2010).

Amatzia, Baram, *Culture, History and Ideology in the Formation of Baʿthist Iraq, 1968–1989* (London: Macmillan, with St Antony's College, Oxford, 1991).

Anderson, Benedict, *Imagined Communities: Reflections on the Origins and Spread of Nationalism* (London: Verso, 1991).

Antoon, Sinan, *I'jaam: an Iraqi Rhapsody* (San Francisco, CA: City Lights Books, 2007).

Arendt, Hannah, *The Origins of Totalitarianism* (Cleveland, OH: Meridian Books, 1958).

Ashour, Radwa, Ferial Ghazoul and Hasna Reda-Mekdashi (eds), *Arab Women Writers: a Critical Reference Guide 1873–1999* (New York: American University in Cairo, 2008).

Baccolini, Raffaella and Tom Moylan (eds), *Dark Horizons: Science Fiction and the Dystopian Imagination* (New York: Routledge, 2003).

Bakhtin, Mikhail, *Discourse in the Novel*, in *The Dialogic Imagination: Four Essays by M. M. Bakhtin*, ed. Michael Holquist, trans. Caryl Emerson and Michael Holquist (Austin, TX: University of Texas Press, 1981).

Baram, Amatzia, 'Neo-Tribalism in Iraq: Saddam Hussein's Tribal Policies, 1991–1996', *International Journal of Middle East Studies* 29(1) (1997): 1–31.

Baron, Beth, *Egypt as a Woman: Nationalism, Gender, and Politics* (London: University of California Press, 2005).

Barthes, Roland, 'The Death of the Author', in *Image, Music, Text* (New York: Hill & Wang, 1977), pp. 142–8.

Barthes, Roland, 'From Work to Text', in Josué V. Harari (ed.), *Textual Strategies: Perspectives in Post-Structuralist Criticism* (Ithaca, NY: Cornell University Press, 1979), pp. 72–83.

Bengio, Ofra, *Saddam's Word: Political Discourse in Iraq* (New York: Oxford University Press, 1998).

Bengio, Ofra, 'Saddam Husayn's Novel of Fear', *Middle East Quarterly* 11(1) (2002): 9–18.

Bottomley, Gill, 'Post-multiculturalism? The Theory and Practice of Heterogeneity', paper presented at the conference *Post-colonial Formations: Nations, Culture, Policy*, Griffith University, Brisbane, Queensland, July 1993.

Brennan, Timothy, 'The National Longing for Form', in Homi K. Bhabha (ed.), *Nation and Narration* (New York: Routledge, 2006).

Cassirer, Ernst, *The Myth of the State* (New York: Doubleday, 1955).

Carey, James W., *Communication as Culture* (London: Unwin Hyman, 1989).

Carlson, Julie A. and Elisabeth Weber (eds), *Speaking of Torture* (New York: Fordham University Press, 2012).

Carter, Cynthia, Gill Branston and Stuart Allan (eds), *News, Gender and Power* (London: Routledge, 1998).

Chatterjee, Partha, *Nationalist Thought and the Colonial World: a Derivative Discourse* (Minneapolis: University of Minnesota, 1986).

Chubin, Shahram and Charles Tripp, *Iran and Iraq at War* (London: I. B. Tauris, 1988).

Cockburn, Patrick, *Muqtada al-Sadr and the Fall of Iraq* (London: Faber and Faber, 2008).

Cooke, Miriam, *Women and the War Story* (Berkeley: University of California Press, 1996).

Cooke, Miriam, *Women Claim Islam: Creating Islamic Feminism Through Literature* (New York: Routledge, 2001), p. xx

Cottle, Simon, *Mediatized Conflicts*, (Maidenhead: Open University Press, 2006).

Dabashi, Hamid, 'Damnatio Memoriae', in Julie A. Carlson and Elisabeth Weber (eds), *Speaking of Torture* (New York: Fordham University Press, 2012).

Davis, Eric, *Memories of State: Politics, History and Collective Identity in Modern Iraq* (Berkeley: University of California Press, 2005).

Davis, Lennard, *Resisting Novels: Ideology and Fiction* (New York: Methuen, 1987).

Dawisha, Adid, *Iraq: a Political History from Independence to Occupation* (Princeton, NJ: Princeton University Press, 2009).

Dines, Gail and Jean M. Humez, *Gender, Race and Class in Media: a Text-Reader* (London: Sage, 2002).

Easterlin, Nancy and Barbara Riebling (eds), *After Poststructuralism: Interdisciplinarity and Literary Theory* (Evanston, IL: Northwestern University Press, 1993).

Efrati, Noga 'Productive or Reproductive? The Roles of Women during the Iraq–Iran War', *Middle Eastern Studies* 35(2) (1999): 27–44.

Fandi, Mamoun, *(Un)Civil War of Words: Media and Politics in the Arab World* (Westport, CT: Praeger Security International, 2007).

Fotouhi, Sanaz, *The Literature of the Iranian Diaspora: Meaning and Identity since the Iranian Revolution* (London: I. B. Tauris, 2015).

Enloe, Cynthia, *Does Khaki Become You? The Militarization of Women's Lives* (San Francisco, CA: Pandora Press, 1988).

Enloe, Cynthia, 'Womenandchildren: Making Feminist Sense of the Persian Gulf Crisis', *The Village Voice*, 25 September 1990.

Faqir, Fadia and Shirley Eber (eds), *The House of Silence: Autobiographical Essays by Arab Women Writers* (Reading: Garnet, 1999).

Fish, Stanley, *Is there a Text in this Class? The Authority of Interpretive Communities* (Cambridge, MA: Harvard University Press, 1980).

Forgacs, David (ed.), 'Hegemony, Relations of Force, Historical Bloc', in *A Gramsci Reader: Selected Writings 1916–1935* (London: Lawrence & Wishart, 1999), pp. 189–222.

Foucault, Michel, *l'Histoire de la Sexualité I: la Volonté de Savoir* (Paris: Éditions Gallimard, 2005).

Foucault, Michel, 'What is an Author?', in Josué V. Harari (ed.), *Textual Strategies: Perspectives in Post-Structuralist Criticism* (Ithaca, NY: Cornell University Press, 1979), pp. 141–61.

Genette, Gérard, *Paratexts: Thresholds of Interpretation* (Cambridge: Cambridge University Press, 1997).

Geoghegan, Vincent, 'Remembering the Future', *Utopian Studies* 1(2) (1990): 52–68.

Ghanim, David, *Gender and Violence in the Middle East* (Westport, CT: Praeger, 2009).

Gray, Matthew, *Conspiracy Theories the Arab World* (London: Routledge, 2010).

Guth, Stephen, 'Why Novels not Autobiographies', in Robin Ostle, Ed de Moor and Stefan wild (eds), *Writing the Self: Autobiographical Writing in Modern Arabic Literature* (London: Saqi Books, 1998), pp. 139–47.

Haddad, Fanar, *Sectarianism in Iraq: Antagonistic Visions of Unity* (Oxford: Oxford University Press, 2011).

Hafez, Sabry, 'The Modern Arabic Short Story', in M. M. Badawi (ed.), *Modern Arabic Literature* (Cambridge: Cambridge University Press, 1997), pp. 270–328.

Hafez, Sabry, 'Islam in Arabic Literature: the Struggle for Symbolic Power', in Abir Hamdar and Lindsey Moore (eds), *Islamism and Cultural Expression in the Arab World* (London: Routledge, 2015).

Haikal, Mohammed Ḥussein, *Zainab*, trans. John Mohammed Grinsted (London: Darf Publishers, 1989).

Hamdar, Abir and Lindsey Moore (eds), *Islamism and Cultural Expression in the Arab World* (London: Routledge, 2015).

Hanna, Sami A. and George H. Gardner, *Arab Socialism: a Documentary Survey* (Leiden: Brill, 1969).

Helfont, Samuel, *Compulsion in Religion: Saddam Hussein, Islam and the Roots of Insurgencies in Iraq* (New York: Oxford University Press, 2018).

Helms, Christine, *Iraq: Eastern Flank of the Arab World* (Washington, D.C.: Brookings Institution, 1984).

Holman, Valerie and Debra Kelly (eds), *France at War in the Twentieth Century: Propaganda, Myth and Metaphor* (New York: Berghahn, 2000).

Jameson, Frederic, *The Political Unconscious* (Ithaca, NY: Cornell University Press, 1981).

Joseph, Souad, 'Gendering Citizenship in the Middle East', in Souad Joseph (ed.), *Gender and Citizenship in the Middle East* (Syracuse, NY: Syracuse University Press, 2000), pp. 3–33.

Khalil, Samir, *Republic of Fear* (London: Hutchinson Radius, 1991).

Khoury, Dina Rizk, *Iraq in Wartime: Soldiering, Martyrdom and Remembrance* (Cambridge: Cambridge University Press, 2013).

Köroğlu, Erol, *Ottoman Propaganda and Turkish Identity: Literature in Turkey during World War I* (London: Tauris Academic Studies, 2007).

Lawrence, Robert (ed.), *Zabiba and the King: by its Author Saddam Hussein* (College Station, TX: Virtualbookworm, 2004).

Levitas, Ruth, *The Concept of Utopia* (Syracuse, NY: Syracuse University Press, 1990).

Liechty, Joseph and Cecelia Clegg, *Moving Beyond Sectarianism: Religion, Conflict and Reconciliation* (Dublin: Columba Press, 2001).

Long, Jerry, *Saddam's War of Words: Politics, Religion and the Iraqi Invasion of Kuwait* (Austin, TX: University of Texas Press, 2004).

Lowenthal, Richard, *The Past is a Foreign Country* (Cambridge: Cambridge University Press, 1985).

Makdisi, Usama, *The Culture of Sectarianism: Community, History and Violence in Nineteenth-Century Ottoman Lebanon* (Berkeley, CA: University of California Press, 2000).

Makiya, Kanan, *Republic of Fear: the Politics of Modern Iraq* (Berkeley: University of California Press, 1989).

Malak, Amin, 'Between the Artist and the General: War Memories of Baghdad', *Life Writing* 9(4) (2012): 407–420, DOI: 10.1080/14484528.2012.712894.

Malti-Douglas, Fedwa, *Men, Women, and Gods: Nawal El Saadawi and Arab Feminist Poetics* (London: University of California Press, 1995).

Majaj, Lisa Suhair, Paula Sunderman and Therese Saliba, *Intersections: Gender, Nation and Community in Arab Women's Novels* (Syracuse, NY: Syracuse University Press, 2002).

Matar, Dina, 'Rethinking the Arab State and Culture: Preliminary Thoughts', in Tarik Sabry (ed.), *Arab Cultural Studies: Mapping the Field* (London: I. B. Tauris, 2012), pp. 123–36.

McGann, Jerome, 'The Socialization of Texts', in *The Textual Condition* (Princeton, NJ: Princeton University Press, 1991), pp. 69–87.

Mehta, Brenda, 'Dissidence, Creativity, and Embargo Art in Nuha al-Radi's Baghdad Diaries', *Meridians: Feminism, Race, Transnationalism* 6(2) (2006): 220–35.

Mehta, Brinda, *Rituals of Memory in Contemporary Arab Women's Writing* (Syracuse, NY: Syracuse University Press, 2007).

Meininghaus, Esther, *Creating Consent in Baʿthist Syria: Women and Welfare in a Totalitarian State* (London: I. B. Tauris, 2016).

Mernissi, Fatima, *The Veil and the Male Elite: a Feminist Interpretation of Women's Rights in Islam* (New York: Basic Books, 1991).

Mikhail, Dunya, *Diary of a Wave Outside the Sea* (New York: New Directions, 2009).

Mikhail, Dunya, *The War Works Hard* (New York: New Directions, 2005).

Murphy, Ann V., 'Sexuality', in Hubert L. Dreyfus and Mark A. Wrathall (eds), *A Companion to Phenomenology and Existentialism* (Chichester: Blackwell, 2009), pp. 489–502.

Nehamas, Alexander, 'Writer, Text, Work, Author', in Anthony Cascardi (ed.),

Literature and the Question of Philosophy (Baltimore, MD: Johns Hopkins University Press, 1987), pp. 265–91.

O'Beebee, Thomas, *The Ideology of Genre: a Comparative Study of Generic Instability* (University Park, PA.: Pennsylvania State University Press, 1994).

O'Shaughnessy, Nicholas Jackson, *Politics and Propaganda: Weapons of Mass Seduction* (Manchester: Manchester University Press, 2004).

Osman, Khalil, *Sectarianism in Iraq: the Making of State and Nation since 1920* (New York: Oxford University Press, 2015).

Ouzgane, Lahoucine (ed.), *Islamic Masculinities* (London: Zed Books, 2006).

Pickthall, Mohammed Marmaduke (trans.), *The Meaning of the Glorious Quran* (New York: A. A. Knopf, 1930).

Podeh, Elie, 'From Indifference to Obsession: the Role of National State Celebrations in Iraq: 1921–2003', *British Journal of Middle Eastern Studies* 37 (2010): 179–206.

Rohde, Achim, 'Opportunities for Masculinity and Love: Cultural Production in Ba'thist Iraq during the 1980s', in Lahoucine Ouzgane (ed.), *Islamic Masculinities* (London: Zed Books, 2006), pp. 184–201.

Rohde, Achim, *State–Society Relations in Ba'thist Iraq: Facing Dictatorship* (London: Routledge, 2014).

Said, Edward, *Culture and Imperialism* (New York: Alfred A. Knopf, 1993).

Sartre, Jean Paul, *Qu'est-ce que la Littérature?* (Paris: Gallimard, 1948).

Selim, Samah, *The Novel and the Rural Imaginary in Egypt 1880–1985* (New York: RoutledgeCurzon, 2004).

Shabout, Nada, 'Images and Status: Visualising Iraqi Women', in Faegheh Shirazi (ed.), *Muslim Women in War and Crisis: Representation and Reality* (Austin, TX: University of Texas Press, 2010), pp. 149–64.

Shariati, Ali, *Man and Islam*, trans. Fatollah Marjani (Houston, TX: Free Islamic Literature, 1981).

Shirazi, Faegheh (ed.), *Muslim Women in War and Crisis: Representation and Reality* (Austin, TX: University of Texas Press, 2010).

Simons, Geoff, *Iraq: from Sumer to Saddam* (Basingstoke: Macmillan, 1996).

Sontag, Susan, *Regarding the Pain of Others* (London: Penguin, 2004).

Suleiman, Yasir, *Arabic in the Fray* (Edinburgh: Edinburgh University Press, 2013).

Suleiman, Yasir, *Arabic Self and Identity: a Study in Conflict and Displacement* (Oxford: Oxford University Press, 2011).

Suleiman, Yasir, *A War of Words: Language and Conflict in the Middle East* (Edinburgh: Edinburgh University Press, 2004).

Suleiman, Yasir, '*Bayān* as a Principle of Taxonomy: Linguistic Elements in Jāhiz's Thinking', *Journal of Semitic Studies* Supp. 14 (2002): *Studies on Arabia in Honour of G. Rex Smith*, John F. Healey and Venetia Porter (eds) (Oxford: Oxford University Press, 2002).

Suleiman, Yasir and Ibrahim Muhawi (eds), *Literature and Nation in the Middle East* (Edinburgh: Edinburgh University Press, 2006).

Taithe, Bertrand and Tim Thornton (eds), *Propaganda: Political Rhetoric and Identity 1300–2000*, 'Themes in History' (Stroud: Sutton, 1999).

Taylor, Philip, *Munitions of the Mind: a History of War Propaganda* (Manchester: Manchester University Press, 2003).

Thomas, Dominic, *Nation-Building, Propaganda, and Literature in Francophone Africa* (Bloomington. IN: Indiana University Press, 2002).

Tijani, Ishaq, *Male Domination, Female Revolt: Race, Class and Gender in Kuwaiti Women's Fiction* (Leiden: Brill, 2009).

Todorov, Tzvetan, *Genres in Discourse* (Cambridge: Cambridge University Press, 1995).

Tripp, Charles, *The Power and the People: Paths of Resistance in the Middle East* (New York: Cambridge University Press, 2013).

Venuti, Lawrence, *The Translator's Invisibility: a History of Translation* (London: Routledge, 1995).

Volkan, Vamik, *Bloodlines: From Ethnic Pride to Ethnic Terrorism* (New York: Farrar, Straus & Giroux, 1997).

Walther, Wiebke, 'Review of Women and the War Story, by Miriam Cooke . . .', *Die Welt des Islams* 40(3) (2000): 425–8.

Wedeen, Lisa, *Ambiguities of Domination: Politics, Rhetoric and Symbols in Contemporary Syria* (Chicago, IL: Chicago University Press, 1999).

White, Hayden, *The Content of the Form: Narrative Discourse and Historical Representation* (Baltimore, MD: Johns Hopkins University Press, 1987).

Wiley, Joyce, 'Alima Bint al-Huda, Women's Advocate', in Linda S. Walbridge (ed.), *The Most Learned of the Shia: the Institution of Marja Taqlid* (New York: Oxford University Press), pp. 149–60.

Ziadeh, Hanna, *Sectarianism and Intercommunal Nation-Building in Lebanon* (London: Hurst, 2006).

Yuval-Davis, Nira and Ruth Helm, *Gender and Nation* (London: Sage, 1997).

Zangana, Haifa, *Dreaming of Baghdad* (New York, Feminist Press: 2009)

Zim, Rivkah, *The Consolations of Writing: Literary Strategies of Resistance from Boethius to Primo Levi* (Princeton, NJ: Princeton University Press, 2014).

Index

‘Abbūd, Salām, 16, 37, 42, 48, 51, 77, 79, 86, 92–3, 205–7
‘Abd al-Amīr al-Mu‘alla
The Long Days, 84–7, 94
‘Ādil ‘Abd al-Jabbār
Dancing on the Shoulders of Death, 37, 46, 48–9, 52
Al-Ali, Nadje, 2, 42, 113, 172, 186, 192–3, 195
Al-Anṣārī, ‘Alyā’, 133, 145–6, 201, 213
A Travel Ticket, 133, 137–8, 140–2, 145
Al-Dawaf, Hiyām Nā’il, 8–9, 29, 172, 203
Al-Ḥusaynī, May, 17, 133, 145–6
And Darkness Dissipated, 133–5, 145
Al-Qazwīnī, Khawla, 17, 109, 111, 113, 125–30, 144–6
When a Man Thinks, 113, 125–33, 139
Al-Radi, Nuha, 18, 151–2, 166–77, 180, 187, 189, 194–5
Al-Raṣīf, Jāsim, 37, 41–3, 45, 47, 50, 54–5, 57
Red Line, 50–4, 57
The Third Troupe, 37, 41–3, 45, 47–50
Al-Ṣadr, Āmina, 17, 86, 111, 113–15, 118, 124, 145–6, 166, 195, 205, 208, 215
Anderson, 3–4, 31, 68, 96
Antoon, Sinan, 191, 194–5, 210–11
Arab nationalism, 43, 52, 71–2, 75, 83–4, 88, 92, 96, 110, 202, 211

Barthes, Roland, 14
Ba‘th (also ba‘thist), 1–12, 15–19, 25–32, 34, 39–40, 42–4, 47, 51, 53, 64–5, 68–9, 71–2, 74–5, 79, 81–3, 86–8, 91–3, 95, 97–8, 107–10, 112–14, 116, 123, 125, 135, 140, 142–3, 145–7, 151–3, 157, 160, 162–5, 168, 171–2, 177–8, 181–5, 187–8, 190–1, 193–5, 202–5, 207, 209, 212, 214–15
Bedouins, 78, 80, 158
Bint al-Hudā, 86, 111, 113–16, 118, 121, 124–7, 129, 131–2, 135, 140, 145, 205
Virtue Prevails, 113–15, 117–18, 120–1, 123–4, 129, 131; *see also* Āmina al-Ṣadr
bonds, 142, 145, 151, 174–5, 188, 195–6, 201
nationalist, 6–7, 15–16, 28, 34, 48, 55, 74, 76, 81, 95, 108
religious, 119, 123, 132, 142, 145, 147, 151, 174–5
book cover; 12–13, 73, 89, 92, 109, 145; *see also* preface

canon, 5, 11, 13, 15, 17, 25–6, 36, 111, 127, 202, 208
censorship, 6, 19, 33–5, 75, 113, 178, 182–3, 207–8
chastity, 17, 96–8, 108, 112, 117, 120, 176, 204
Cooke, Miriam, 32–3, 178
cultural production, 3, 5–8, 19, 26, 32, 79, 188, 191, 203

Da‘wa Party (Islamic), 69, 135
Davis, Eric, 30, 203

Foucault, Michel, 13–14, 19, 122, 207

General Federation of Iraqi Women (GFIW), 3, 16, 26–8, 107, 203, 205
Genette, Gérard, 5, 11–12, 15, 18, 86; *see also* paratexts

genre, 8, 15, 28, 32, 36–7, 46, 74, 78, 85, 96, 98, 108–11, 115–17, 126–7, 143, 146, 152, 154, 165, 168, 189–90, 192–4, 208, 211
Ghira, 82, 88–9
gold, 2, 27, 54, 112, 116, 130, 182

Hafez, Sabry, 110–11, 116, 140
Hijab, 109–13, 124–5, 139
history, 1–4, 8, 11, 13, 17, 26–9, 34, 40, 46–7, 68, 72, 80, 84, 98, 107, 109–10, 113, 124, 139, 143, 154–7, 162, 164–5, 168, 179–80, 188, 190, 192–3, 202–5, 207–10, 213
Hussein, Saddam, 1, 3, 7–9, 25, 27–30, 37, 40, 42–3, 49, 53, 145, 153, 160–2, 168, 171, 180, 191–2, 203, 205–6, 209–13
  novels, 10, 12, 14, 16–17, 42–4, 53, 64, 94–8, 113–15, 124, 166, 195, 204; *The Fortified Castle*, 50, 74–83; *Get Out, Damned One!*, 34, 70–4; *Men and a City*, 83–93, 70; *Zabiba and the King*, 65–70, 179, 202

ideology, ideological, 1–3, 5–8, 10–16, 26–8, 30, 32–3, 35, 38, 49, 52, 54, 68–9, 71–6, 83, 86, 92–6, 107–8, 111, 113–16, 120–1, 126–7, 130–1, 138–9, 144, 146, 152, 164, 175–6, 189, 194, 196, 204–5, 207–9
illiteracy, 2–3, 25; *see also* literacy
imperialism, 16, 71–2, 78, 109, 116–7, 125, 151, 162–3, 172, 174, 180, 188, 190
Iran–Iraq War, 1, 8, 16, 26, 29, 30, 39, 75, 79, 81, 86, 93, 97, 124, 140, 153, 160, 169, 203, 205–6, 213
  novels, 10, 12, 32, 34, 40–1, 43, 47–8, 66, 71, 138
  women, 7, 17, 28, 64, 134, 170, 176, 204, 216
Iraqi nationalism, 10, 30, 47, 50, 110, 205, 212; *see also* patriotism
Islam
  in Iraqi cultural production, 7, 12, 16, 43, 46, 66, 69–71, 74, 87, 96, 107–9, 111–12, 114–21, 123–4, 126–45, 174, 192, 194, 201
  and the state, 18, 57, 92, 110, 113, 125, 146–7, 204–5, 215, *see also* Islamic Da'wa Party

Kurd, 42–5, 75–6, 79–82, 95–7, 154, 156, 160–1, 174, 186, 192, 195

literacy, 25, 28, 202
literary criticism, 12, 27, 31, 33–6, 40, 64, 184, 190, 211

martyr, 37–42, 46–7, 49, 55, 75–6, 90, 129, 183, 206
martyrdom, 110, 114, 141
Mikhail, Dunya, 18, 151–2, 166, 177, 180, 187, 189–91, 194–5, 213
  Diary of a Wave Outside the Sea, 155, 166, 177, 179, 181–4, 186–7, 189
  Baghdad Diaries, 155, 164, 166–8, 170–1, 173–6, 181, 186, 189, 195
modesty, 3, 114, 121
  in dress, 109, 132, 135, 137, 204, 208, 215
  money, 53–4, 56, 133, 136, 184
  financial considerations, 9, 36, 54, 89, 121, 124–5, 135–7, 143, 170, 176; *see also* gold
mother, 2, 5, 107–8, 154, 156–60, 170, 195
  in the Iran–Iraq War novel, 44, 49–55
  in the Islamic novel, 118–19, 124–5, 127, 129–30, 133, 139, 142, 145
  in Saddam's novels, 69, 72–3, 76, 82, 87–9, 92–5, 97
Mukhīf, 'Alī 'Abd al-Ḥusayn, 38–40, 56, 79

Nāṣir, 'Abd al-Sattār, 37
national identity, 4, 6, 17, 50, 98, 133, 140, 151, 174, 181, 202, 204; *see also* Arab nationalism; Iraqi nationalism

paratexts, 11–13, 15, 86–7, 166, 194, 205, 207–8; *see also* book cover; peritext
patriotism, 30, 33, 44, 48–9, 52, 55, 75, 185, 208
peritext, 115, 162
poetry, 3, 9, 15–16, 37, 40, 74, 116, 166, 178, 182–4, 186–7, 189–91, 194, 210
power, 1–6, 10, 13–16, 19, 27, 30, 34, 39, 53, 64–6, 71, 74, 90, 94–5, 108–10, 112–13, 118, 120, 122, 136–8, 153, 162–6, 170, 180, 194–5, 201–3, 205–7, 214, 216
preface, 12, 35, 75, 84–8
propaganda, 1, 5–7, 9–10, 13–14, 15, 25–6, 29, 31, 33–6, 38–9, 42, 45, 47–9, 56–7, 66, 69, 73–6, 78–9, 83, 85, 87,

89, 93, 116, 124, 146, 152–3, 158, 165–6, 168, 172–3, 184, 187, 189, 192, 202, 206, 208, 210, 214
publishing, 7–10, 25–6, 29, 34, 36, 38, 64, 77, 145, 152, 160, 178, 182–3; *see also* readership

Qadisiya, 3, 11, 36, 41–3
Qur'an, 69, 71, 115, 118, 123, 135

rape, 45–6, 66–7, 77–8, 129
readership, 25, 107, 109
realism, 15, 27, 32, 36, 39, 42, 47, 65, 68, 79, 91, 93–4, 111, 116–17, 119, 123–4, 137, 166
religion, 2, 5, 15, 70, 90, 110, 116, 120, 130, 134–5, 141, 144, 146, 175, 185–6, 193, 204, 209; *see also* Islam; Shia
resistance, 4–6, 12–14, 16, 18–19, 32, 41, 73, 98, 112–13, 124, 140, 147, 152–3, 160, 162–3, 165, 170, 177, 179–80, 185–96, 205–8, 211, 213, 215
rurality (also pastoral), 17, 70, 76, 80–1, 90, 94–5, 98, 120, 155–6, 171, 180–1, 204; *see also* Bedouins

sanctions (American), 7, 32, 64, 144, 152–3, 166–8, 171–3, 176–8, 180, 182, 186, 189–91, 203
secularism, 7, 12, 16, 18, 33, 65, 88, 107–8, 110, 112, 115–16, 118, 121–2, 124–5, 130, 132, 135–6, 139–40, 142–3, 145–7, 152, 166, 171, 186, 196, 201–2, 204–5, 215
Shia, 5–6, 17, 56, 69, 76, 79–80, 86–7, 107, 109–11, 113–14, 116, 118–20, 124–5, 127–8, 131, 133–4, 140–1, 143–6, 166, 171, 174, 192, 194–5, 201, 208; *see also* Sunni
Sunni, 15, 76, 80, 82, 192, 195, 201, 215

Ṭālib, ʻUmar, 10, 36–7
tradition, 15, 70, 74, 87–91, 108, 174, 186, 193, 204
  literary, 3, 11, 66, 72, 111, 116, 126, 154, 186, 189, 191, 209–10
  Islamic, 110, 113, 118, 120, 127, 136, 140–1, 146
  and women, 5–6, 17, 26–7, 29, 40, 44, 48, 51, 53, 55, 57–8, 94, 107, 121, 130, 135, 147

Utopia, 4, 17–18, 28, 44, 50, 53, 67, 70, 80–3, 85, 87, 91, 93, 96, 112, 116–17, 144, 146, 155, 180, 196, 211–14; *see also* dystopia

Yuval-Davis, Nira, 5, 82

Zangana, Haifa, 18, 151–69, 171–2, 175, 180, 187, 189–90, 194–5, 213
  Dreaming of Baghdad, 153–4, 156, 158–9, 161–7, 172–3, 175, 190, 194

EU representative:
Easy Access System Europe
Mustamäe tee 50, 10621 Tallinn, Estonia
Gpsr.requests@easproject.com

www.ingramcontent.com/pod-product-compliance
Lightning Source LLC
Chambersburg PA
CBHW071831230426
43672CB00013B/2811
* 9 7 8 1 4 7 4 4 4 1 7 6 6 *